'This is an important and timely book. Tensions between religions are ever-present and yet, in the West, religion is increasingly seen as irrelevant. This book addresses both issues and shows not only the broad common ground religions share, its relevance and its importance but also how the obvious differences can be addressed. To quote but one line: "There is a desire amongst many young people to experience the divine, the mystery of the self and the joy of being. The young are put off by the exclusivist way of thinking and living, which is seen by them as divisive, not leading to a more fulfilled life." This book will be an invaluable resource for teachers and also religious leaders as they seek to show common ground shared by religions whilst not undermining the central claims of the different traditions. It also provides an excellent way of beginning to understand alternative perspectives other than one's own.

Each major tradition has contributions from two scholars and then a comment by the editors. Contributors and, of course, the editors show clear integrity and write accessibly but, above all, practically. Warmly recommended – an invaluable resource.'

*– Dr Peter Vardy was Vice-Principal of
Heythrop College, University of London*

'Those of any theological position will find this an excellent resource in thinking about and planning for worship or prayer involving people of different faiths. The contributors cover an unusually wide range of material, and the practical suggestions they offer are sensible, balanced and achievable.'

*– Michael Ipgrave, Bishop of Lichfield*

'Some theologians find good reasons to say why it is difficult to pray together. This book condenses some striking arguments why it is indispensable to do it anyway. A unique collection of interfaith perspectives to meet in love and face the divine.'

*– Rabbi Walter Homolka PhD PhD DHL, Professor of Modern
Jewish Thought and Interreligious Dialogue, School of Jewish
Theology at the University of Potsdam, Germany*

'A fascinating guide to the variety of approaches to worship, both within and between different faith traditions, as well as the possibilities and limitations of interfaith worship. What is clear is that the human need for inspiration and assurance from The Divine is universal.'

*Princess Badiya el Hassan, Princess of Jordan*

'This is a timely book which will serve as a handbook for those exploring the possibilities of interfaith worship. As the book's subtitle has it *we must pray together*, in other words coming together to pray in today's world is no longer an optional extra but a practical imperative. In the book representatives of twelve major world faith traditions give detailed, scholarly and personal explanations of how interfaith worship is understood and practised within their faith groups. *Interfaith Worship and Prayer* is an invaluable guide to those hoping to deepen their spiritual connection with people of other religions. It does not suggest that interfaith encounter is always easy, the writers and the reflective sections contributed by the editors highlight many of the difficulties encountered as we pray together. But taken altogether it is a clear sighted and open exploration of how followers of different religions can learn to worship together that deserves to find wide use across all faith communities.'

– *Rev Dr David Steers, Editor of* Faith and Freedom

'All who envision a peaceful future for the humanity with rich spiritual life must explore ways to build harmony among diverse faith communities that now encounter one another in all parts of our globalized world. Sadly, the encounters often turn into occasions for tensions. This timely collection of essays by scholars and followers from diverse faith traditions of the world invites readers to reflect creatively on the urgent need of our times to turn encounters into dialogs. With a focus on the most active manifestation of faith – worship – and with organizational principle of respect, the book opens windows to the worlds of many religious communities with whom the reader will feel inspired to pray, standing in their own place but being a part of a symphony. Pragmatic and accessible, the book offers an invaluable resource for teachers, students, and indeed all world citizens to cultivate understanding of perspectives other than their own. A highly recommended collection!'

– *Neelima Shukla-Bhatt, Associate Professor of South Asia Studies, Wellesley College, MA, author of* Narasinha Mehta of Gujarat, a Legacy of Bhakti in Songs and Stories *and co-author of* A Fire that Blazed in the Ocean: Gandhi and the Poetry of Satyagraha in South Africa 1907–1911; *worked as a research associate at the Pluralism Project, Harvard University for many years*

# INTERFAITH
# WORSHIP
# AND PRAYER

*of related interest*

**People of the Book**
An Interfaith Dialogue about How Jews, Christians and
Muslims Understand Their Sacred Scriptures
*Dan Cohn-Sherbok, George D. Chryssides and Usama Hasan*
*Foreword by Karen Armstrong*
ISBN 978 1 78592 104 9
eISBN 978 1 78450 366 6

**Towards Better Disagreement**
Religion and Atheism in Dialogue
*Paul Hedges*
ISBN 978 1 78592 057 8
eISBN 978 1 78450 316 1

**The Role of Religion in Peacebuilding**
Crossing the Boundaries of Prejudice and Distrust
*Edited by Pauline Kollontai, Sue Yore and Sebastian Kim*
ISBN 978 1 78592 336 4
eISBN 978 1 78450 657 5

**Learning to Live Well Together**
Case Studies in Interfaith Diversity
*Tom Wilson and Riaz Ravat*
ISBN 978 1 78592 194 0
eISBN 978 1 78450 467 0

**Multifaith Chaplaincy in the Workplace**
How Chaplains Can Support Organizations and their Employees
*Fiona Stewart-Darling*
ISBN 978 1 78592 029 5
eISBN 978 1 78450 279 9

# INTERFAITH WORSHIP AND PRAYER

## We Must Pray Together

EDITED BY **CHRISTOPHER LEWIS**
AND **DAN COHN-SHERBOK**

Foreword by His Holiness the 14th Dalai Lama

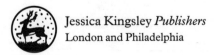
Jessica Kingsley *Publishers*
London and Philadelphia

All royalties for this book are being donated to
Médecins sans Frontières/Doctors without Borders

First published in 2019
by Jessica Kingsley Publishers
73 Collier Street
London N1 9BE, UK
and
400 Market Street, Suite 400
Philadelphia, PA 19106, USA

*www.jkp.com*

**Library of Congress Cataloging in Publication Data**
A CIP catalog record for this book is available from the Library of Congress

**British Library Cataloguing in Publication Data**
A CIP catalogue record for this book is available from the British Library

ISBN 978 1 78592 120 9
eISBN 978 1 78450 385 7

Printed and bound in Great Britain

# Contents

THE DALAI LAMA

# FOREWORD

Our world has become so closely interconnected that we can no longer remain insensitive to issues that threaten our neighbour.

One of the essential preconditions for genuine world peace is greater understanding and harmony between the world's religions. Although faith traditions may differ philosophically, the fundamental aim of all religions is to contribute to human wellbeing. As citizens of the world, it is essential that we each recognize the global nature of the problems facing us and that together we make the effort to confront our common problems.

*Interfaith Worship and Prayer*, edited by Christopher Lewis and Dan Cohn-Sherbok, aims to bring people from different religious faiths closer to one another. I welcome their contribution to a more peaceful and harmonious world and to the wellbeing of all humanity.

4 February 2019

Chapter 1

# INTRODUCTION

## Dan Cohn-Sherbok

In previous centuries religions generally stood apart from one another or were in direct conflict. In 1263, for example, the Jewish apostate Paulus (Pablo) Christiani proposed to King James I of Aragon that a formal disputation debating the fundamentals of faith should be held between him and Rabbi Moses ben Nahman (Nahmanides). Yet there were occasions when positive interfaith interaction took place. In the sixteenth century, for example, Emperor Akbar the Great encouraged tolerance in Mughal India, which included Muslims, Hindus, Sikhs and Christians.

In modern times positive interfaith encounter was initiated by the 1893 Parliament of World Religions. This congress, which took place in Chicago, Illinois, is regarded as a landmark in the development of the interfaith movement. The opening session included hymns and an invitation to all those present to join in the Lord's Prayer. At the beginning of the following century the International Association for Religious Freedom was founded with the purpose of advancing understanding and dialogue between religions. In 1914, just after World War I began, the Fellowship of Reconciliation was created in order to bring people of faith together to promote peace. Two decades later, in 1936, the World Congress of Faiths was formed in London to enrich people of faith in their understanding of their own religion and those of others.

Following the devastation of World War II, the Fellowship In Prayer was established in the belief that unified prayer would bridge theological differences between the world's faiths. From the academic side, the Centre for the Study of World Religions was founded at Harvard Divinity School in 1958 to promote the sympathetic study and understanding of the faiths. Two years later the Temple of Understanding was established to provide interfaith education in order to break down prejudicial boundaries. During Vatican II, in 1965, Pope Paul VI established a special secretariat for relationships between Christians and people of other faith traditions.

In 1970 the first World Conference of Religions for Peace was held in Kyoto, Japan. In the following decade the Minhaj-ul-Quran was founded in Pakistan as an international organisation working for peace, tolerance, interfaith harmony and education. In 1993, on the centennial of its first conference, the Council for the Parliament of the World's Religions hosted a conference in Chicago with 8000 participants from religions around the world. In the next year, the Interfaith Alliance was created to celebrate religious freedom and to challenge bigotry and hatred. In ensuing years a number of other interfaith organisations were established to promote enduring interfaith cooperation and to end religiously motivated violence.

A choir of children of many faiths sing 'There is one almighty... Our Family is One' at the Salt Lake Parliament of World Religions 2015
Credit: Helen Hobin

Interfaith encounter and dialogue have thus become a major concern amongst the world's religions, and interfaith prayer and worship have become key elements of these encounters. Today, public forms of interfaith worship take place throughout the world; in addition, there are private ceremonies involving adherents of different faiths.

As Marcus Braybrooke (2012), a president of the World Congress of Faiths, has noted, there are many different forms of interfaith worship and prayer. One of the main purposes of this book is to explore this variety within the context of a number of different faiths, reflecting on the manner in which actual practice is planned and carried through, along with a study of the ways interfaith prayer and worship are evaluated by representatives of particular faiths. For example, is it best to plan an event where each faith takes it in turns to pray or alternatively where all agree on a united service on a common theme?

Such activity serves as the framework for this theological exploration of the issues connected with interfaith worship and prayer across the globe. The book begins with an initial overview of this topic followed by 12 chapters organised approximately according to the historical origins of the religions: Hinduism, African Traditional Religion, Judaism, Jainism, Buddhism, Zoroastrianism, Shintoism, Christianity, Islam, Sikhism, Unitarianism and Bahá'í. We have sought out two contributions from each of these religions in order to discover their insights into interfaith prayer and worship, with three from the two most high profile and numerous: Islam and Christianity. At the end of each chapter the editors reflect on the central issues raised. The book ends with a concluding summary and evaluation of these various contributions.

As readers explore these chapters it will become clear, as indicated in the second chapter, that there is a key issue to consider regarding interfaith worship, which is dealt with in different ways by contributors to this volume. Throughout history many faithful have viewed their religious beliefs as absolute truths. Some faiths are monotheistic, some polytheistic, some nontheistic. In many cases believers appeal to divinely revealed texts as the bedrock of their convictions. Given the multifarious religious tenets across the world's religions (which inevitably differ widely), how is it possible for members of different traditions to pray together? For some, it is impossible. Those of a more rigid cast of mind frequently protest against such activity, regarding such worship as scandalous. Others of a more inclusive attitude feel differently. In their view, interfaith worship is imperative given the state of the world and its challenges. Only by gaining a sympathetic understanding of other faiths, they contend, will human beings be able to live in peace and harmony. But how is this to be done? What shift in religious consciousness must take place for Shintos, Jews, Buddhists, Hindus, Christians and others to be able to pray together? And what form should interfaith worship and prayer take, given such a dilemma?

Adopting various approaches, the authors of this volume wrestle with this and other issues, highlighting the ways that their respective faiths contribute to an understanding of the nature of interfaith worship. Recently there have been a number of scholarly publications which study this topic, such as *Understanding Interreligious Relations* (Oxford University Press, 2014), edited by David Cheetham, Douglas Pratt and David Thomas, and *Ritual Participation and Interreligous Dialogue* (Bloomsbury Academic, 2015), edited by Marianne Moyaert and Joris Geldhof. These are important collections of chapters. This book, however, seeks to break new ground by providing a framework for members of faith communities from around the globe to reflect on the nature of interfaith worship and prayer. The hope is that the material found here will stimulate others to perceive the necessity of praying and worshipping together in our troubled and wonderful world, and to help to untangle some of the complex issues connected with interfaith encounter.

## REFERENCE

Braybrooke, M. (2012) 'Should people of different faiths pray together?' *The Interfaith Observer*, February.

Chapter 2

# THE ARGUMENT FOR INTERFAITH PRAYER AND WORSHIP

## Christopher Lewis

The starting point for interfaith worship and prayer is respect. That is, both respect for fellow human beings who are sharing our ever more fragile-seeming world and also respect for (and courtesy to) the religious 'others' who are following a different path from our own, reaching out to the Divine. This attitude of respect is not, of course, reserved for interfaith relations; it is the basis for all ethical behaviour, even in its most elementary form: treat others as you yourself would wish to be treated (the colloquial version of the 'golden rule', 'do as you would be done by'). Here, however, the focus is more particular: the failure to honour the faiths of others is linked to a failure to honour them as human beings and fellow believers, central parts of God's creation.

From this start, consequences flow. The first is to tackle the question: how do we engage with people of another faith: the 'religious other'? Much work has been done in trying to give an answer in the general field of dialogue between faiths, but there has been less work when it comes to the special cases of worship and prayer.[1] The difference may be explained by the fact that the most prominent and often problematic aspect of religion tends to be the stated beliefs of

---

1   There is much worship and prayer material, but little examination of the issues involved in interfaith worship. An exception is a good collection of essays in Moyaert and Geldhof 2015. On interfaith matters in general, see Cheetham, Pratt and Thomas 2013.

religious groups or individuals, so it is reckoned that dialogue should major on those matters of belief. Other aspects of religion, however, are just as important. Religion is hard to define with precision, in part because it has a number of different dimensions, but what sets religion apart from other facets of human life is that it has as its aim to relate people consciously to a spiritual order of being (often named God, although not, for example, by many Buddhists and some Hindus) for the sake of good and the avoidance of harm. A 'sense of God' or, differently expressed, the transforming experience of spiritual reality, has been a feature of every society throughout recorded history; that is the basis of religion. So, perhaps that experience should be the prime focus for interfaith relations. Experience, of course, may mislead, yet experiences of the Divine may also be shared by many people (a cumulative process) so that the transcendent becomes part of a collective understanding, leading on to the fundamental religious activities of worshipping and praying together. Experience provides the common ground for prayer and worship. Worship is a natural response to the Divine. Prayer is the language of love for God and for the world. In prayer and worship, belief comes alive.

## ATTITUDES TO 'OTHER' RELIGIONS

How do believers see the 'other' with whom they come into contact? There is a spectrum of attitudes for which categories have been suggested (Race 2001), varying from absolutist/exclusivism at one end of the spectrum, through inclusivism, all the way to a pluralism which values the major religions as having rough parity regarding their efficacy and truth. All categories of this kind have limitations. In this case, they may 'fit' some situations (and religions) better than others and therefore must be handled with caution. The categories describe tendencies rather than 'defining' individuals or groups.

Thus, exclusivism is shorthand for the attitude of believers who see their religion as the only path to God. A principal reason for contact with those of other faiths is then to learn about them, an immediate or eventual aim possibly being to convert people from their current religion to what is perceived to be the true one. A particular impetus is given to this mission if it is believed that only the adherents to the true religion have been or will be 'saved', others being consigned to an uncertain future: separation from God in this life and some kind of limbo (or perhaps eternal damnation) after they die. The meaning of 'salvation' varies depending on the context, but it can be taken to mean liberation from a state of estrangement which separates people from fellow human beings and from the Divine, thus entering a state of flourishing with (unity with) God both now in this life and also beyond death.

It is stating the obvious to say that conservative forces in religion are strong. Almost all religions have extreme wings which exhibit, for example, fundamentalist attachment to a particular holy book or the marriage of nationalist or other political fervour to religious commitment. The first time that I (as a cathedral member of staff) as a target for such attitudes in an interfaith context was through involvement in a Festival of Faith and the Environment in and around Canterbury Cathedral (UK) in 1989. This event involved Bahá'ís, Buddhists, Christians, Hindus, Jews, Muslims and Sikhs and led to a torrent of vilification from groups of Christians on the grounds that seven different faiths were involved as equal participants on Christian ground. The fact that all were showing their concern for the world around us appeared to be of little significance. Cathedral staff members were accused of compromising the uniqueness of Christianity, endorsing blasphemy and dabbling in the occult.

There have been similar reactions to the Commonwealth Day Observances held each year since 1972 in Westminster Abbey in London and attended by the monarch. From the start, the event has used a series of contributions from the six different faiths of the British Commonwealth (Buddhist, Christian, Hindu, Jewish, Muslim, Sikh) and more recently has been based on five themes: care for the natural world; the dignity and worth of the human person; the need to establish justice and peace; the supremacy of love; service and sacrifice for the common good. Similar events based on the Observance have been held in other countries including Australia and Canada, in the latter the occasion in 1990 being described as more than an 'Observance': 'un service multi-religieux'. In 1991 there was a petition opposing the London event which attracted about 77,000 signatures and led to a characteristically misleading newspaper headline (in the *Daily Telegraph* of 12 March 1991): 'Royal approval for Koran at Abbey'. The Abbey authorities were told that they were hampering missionary activity, thus depriving members of other faiths of their chance of eternal life.[2] The Observances continue.

A counter point rarely made concerning exclusivist arguments is that serious contact with other faiths, far from leading to syncretism

---

2   Correspondence in the Westminster Abbey Archives, used with permission.

and confusion, may strengthen the faith of the believer. Two well-documented examples are of Roman Catholics who acknowledged their debt to Islam in bringing them to faith. For Charles de Foucauld, it was the piety of Moroccan Muslims that started him on the road back to Catholicism. The French theologian Louis Massignon met God through Islam and, on becoming a Christian, described himself as 'a Christian converted in a Muslim context' (Waardenburg 2005, pp.322–323). Many have had similar experiences as a consequence of interfaith activity; they have learned to appreciate and deepen their own faith through contact with that of others. The argument that a more pluralistic attitude flattens out variety and leads to indifferentism is rarely relevant; the opposite can be the case. Bede Griffiths' Christian faith changed radically through his contact with Hinduism but did not become less strong (Griffiths 1983).

Exclusivism generally leads to a rejection of interfaith worship and prayer; the belief that the truth has been revealed decisively results in the wish to persuade (and, at times, both past and present, to force) others to conform.[3]

Another point on the spectrum of possible attitudes is that of 'inclusivism', of which there are many versions. It starts from a firm belief in the creation of all things by God and holds that all who respond to the Divine in faith, hope and love are on a path to salvation. There is thus a respect for many routes to the Divine and a rejection of exclusivism. Yet at the same time inclusivism holds that one religion is the fulfilment of all that is best in other religions. Other religions are on a similar path and may indeed have insights which the true religion, as expressed in particular cultures, has missed. Inclusivism has an important role in that it has enabled many (distinguished theologians among them) to relate, often with enthusiasm, to religions other than their own. When it comes to interfaith worship and prayer, much can be done from an inclusivist position in sharing with others and learning from them. There remains, however, an implicit or explicit truth claim which may overshadow relations between faiths.

## MODERATE PLURALISM

Further along the spectrum is what is usually called 'pluralism' and my own position is that the best attitude to religions other than mine is pluralism in a moderate form. By pluralism is meant the recognition

---

3    For a reasoned discussion of worship from an Exclusivist perspective, see Bookless 1991.

of more than one ultimate principle, so in the case of religion there is recognition of God's work of salvation in the world religions, seeing them as part of God's creation. In other words, they are not 'mistakes'; they are of great value. I have complete confidence in the uniqueness and worth of my own faith; my experience of it is similar to falling in love. That attitude does not, however, prevent me from having a sincere wish to relate to another faith or to other faiths, motivated by neighbourliness or admiration/fascination or the wish for peace in the world. Then, also, the wish to have no motive for the 'other' to be converted; conversion does not mix well with true interfaith relations and dialogue, for it brings with it a hidden (or maybe open) agenda which compromises the occasion of friendship, worship and prayer. The pluralist attitude to other great religions is thus one of respect, supported by the belief that each is a valid path to the Divine, and that all may learn from each religion to their benefit, for the experience is likely to be both inspiring and challenging to the participants.

My position is that of a Christian who believes in God as Creator together with what is unique to Christianity, namely that God is revealed in the particular humanity and divinity of Jesus, through the power of the Holy Spirit. I am happy with this religious identity while at the same time being aware that I am an imperfect expression of what it is to be a Christian. What is more, I know that Christianity (like other religions) has been conditioned by all kinds of cultural and other factors, one consequence of which is that it has become too much identified with 'the West'. Having learned to know a loving Creator God, I believe that it is God's will that people should seek the Divine in a number of religions. Consequently, the plurality of religions is not an evil to be overcome; instead, it is a richness to be welcomed. What then are the consequences for mission and conversion? The answer is that there is a major missionary task within one's own religion and to the secular world.

That way of putting the task is reminiscent of the words of the theologian Edward Schillebeeckx: 'there is no salvation outside the world' (in contrast to the traditional 'no salvation outside the Church'), meaning that the religious aim is to work for human flourishing in God's creation (Schillebeeckx 2014, p.5). It follows that I understand the great religions as paths to salvation (or, in some traditions, to enlightenment). We now know, as earlier peoples did not, that there are untold millions who have followed the paths available to them through the ages and across continents. To believe that the vast majority of them have been or will be left in limbo or eternally damned is against ordinary justice and absolutely contrary to what may be believed of a loving deity. The biographer of Silouan, a Russian 'staretz' or holy man, tells the story of a conversation which Silouan had with a dour hermit who believed in eternal damnation. Silouan asked: 'Tell me, supposing you went to paradise, and there looked down and saw somebody burning in hell-fire – would you feel happy?' 'It can't be helped. It would be their own fault,' said the hermit. Silouan's reply was 'Love could not bear that. We must pray for all' (Wild 2015, p.82).

## LIMITS TO PLURALISM

There are vital limits to the pluralist position. The first is to recognise that religions are distinct and at times contradict each other. Respect for the 'other' does not mean ignoring differences or wishing to iron out real variety, both within and between religions. It is fruitless to try to 'rank' world religions, but nor does it help to call them 'equal', for they are different. World religions (and the numerous versions of them) have grown up from distinctive origins and in cultures that are often dissimilar. They certainly do not appear to be 'all going the same way' (as the saying goes) when it comes to their beliefs, rituals, prayers, ethical teaching, art, religious buildings and institutional structures. We can respect the great religions as special, much as we can respect individuals. Comparative religion shows that there are similar aims and themes in religions, but that does not mean that they can be bundled together. Even expressions such as 'religions of the book' are not necessarily helpful as a reference to the similarities of Judaism, Christianity and Islam. These religions do not make up an elite club, their books are dissimilar and are interpreted differently; what is more, the Guru Granth Sahib is the central scripture for Sikhs, and many other religions revere particular books.

It follows that pluralism needs to guard against relativism, which means that any path will do, that anything goes. What is more, there is no new religion called 'interfaith', even if some people appreciate the insights (and worship) of many religions. This is the second of the limits to the pluralist position: to focus on the great religions. For myself I draw a line after the well-tried religions of the world, which seek to reach out to the Divine and to work for the transformation of human beings. It is not exactly the subject of this book, but I consider that these religions offer valuable paths to travel, in a sense that many spiritual, sectarian and cultic groups do not. The great religions are deep rooted across time and across the world; whatever happened to Baal and Marduk?

The third limit to the pluralist position is that respect must not conceal or gloss over 'bad religion'. Again, the attitude is similar to that adopted to another person. Once you get to know them well, the relationship can have an element of challenge. There is a need to be able to distinguish between good and bad religion and work has been done on the criteria which may be of use, always being aware of the differences of cultural context that condition the manner in which a particular religion presents itself (Vardy 2010). For example, good religion is open to new insights, fosters human flourishing, gives a proper place to women, cares for the world in which we all live, works for justice and against violence, protects the poor, fights suffering. If those criteria sound very 'Western' and abstract, so be it; they are the best we can do at the moment towards some kind of 'global ethic'. The difficulties facing the people of the world are massive and the record of the great religions in addressing them is patchy. The different religions have often been the context of (or the rationalisation for) the horrors of discrimination, injustice, violence, oppression and nationalism, for they are enmeshed in the world. Yet they are not 'drowned' in the world, for the same religions are challenging those horrors and making their principles, which sound abstract, become concrete in particular places. There is an opportunity for interfaith worship and prayer to provide a means for mutual support and to be a real power-house for change. It is hard to argue that such a movement is not in line with God's will. A principal purpose of religions is to see the world in the light of the Divine and to lead to the transformation of people, individually and collectively.

## EXAMPLES OF WORSHIP AND PRAYER FROM THE PAST

The current enthusiasm for interfaith worship and prayer needs to be seen in the light of a fascinating past. Through the ages, religious people have been conscious to some degree of the significance of other religions although, with modern communications and with the movement of people, awareness has greatly increased. There was a time when the division was often on the basis of 'cuius regio, eius religio' (your religion depends on where you live) which signified some kind of co-existence and was an attempt to avoid religious rivalry and conflict. There are, however, many remarkable examples of interfaith worship activity, sometimes with the blessing of religious authorities and theologians, but frequently on the initiative of ordinary believers.

I have chosen examples mainly from the world of Judaism, Christianity and Islam because they are the religions which have a reputation for exclusivism. Eastern religions appear, at least on the surface, to be more accommodating of difference.

The synagogue of Doura Europos, Syria: a city of many faiths in the third century
Credit: Christopher Lewis

Tim Winter, who is a British Muslim, refers to evidence that, in the Prophet's city, Muslims and Jews were able to worship together: ritual forms and boundaries had some flexibility (Moyaert and Geldhof 2015, p.84). He goes on to give examples of more recent occasions when same/other models of religious practice have been questioned. There is evidence of multiple religious belonging in India with the devout engaging in both Muslim and Hindu practices, and a long tradition of similar patterns followed by Muslims and Christians. During Ottoman rule in the Balkans, Muslims regularly had their babies christened and many people went to the mosque on Fridays and to the church on Sundays. Both would celebrate the feast of St George, attaching different meanings to the occasion. No doubt such practice was sometimes for reasons of political pragmatism, but it appears that many genuinely had loyalty to both religions.

I visited the Greek Orthodox convent of Saidnaya in Syria in peaceful times, in 2009. It has a beautiful position and a history going back to Byzantine rule. Yet perhaps the most startling fact about it is that both Muslims and Christians have come here for centuries in great numbers to pray and to revere the Virgin Mary. Actually 'startling' is probably the wrong term, for Christianity is a Middle Eastern religion; Eastern Christians and Muslims have lived near each other for over a thousand years, and that has only been possible owing to mutual tolerance and some shared customs. William Dalrymple went to Saidnaya in 1994 and tells of the many Muslim visitors and also of three Muslim Syrian cosmonauts who came to pray at the convent for a safe (Russian) journey into space. After their adventure, the cosmonauts returned both to offer thanks for a safe return, and to give the nuns a picture of themselves and a present of a sheep (Dalrymple 1997).

Convent of Our Lady of Saidnaya: a pilgrimage site for Christians and Muslims

In early 2016 the Museum of Mediterranean and European Civilisations in Marseilles (MuCEM) arranged an exhibition to counter the popular narrative of interreligious conflict and the 'clash of civilisations'. It displayed details of numerous holy sites where people of different faiths come together. One of the sites covered by the exhibition is La Ghriba on the Tunisian island of Djerba, which has an ancient Jewish synagogue containing the tomb of a revered woman and a stone allegedly brought from Jerusalem 2600 years ago by Jewish immigrants. In spite of threats and an attack by Al Qaeda, Jews and Muslims gather for an annual pilgrimage in order to celebrate, eat, sing and pray together. Personal prayers are written on eggs and placed in the crypt; other prayers and songs are collective. It is an emotional and moving event, attended not only by visitors from many countries but also by some of the local population.

Annual pilgrimage of Jews and Muslims to the La Ghriba synagogue

Prayer at La Ghriba

Other examples could be given from all over the world and from different epochs, for example from twelfth-century Andalucia. The past is by no means the territory of exclusivism; current contact is

not a modern aberration. People of different religions have coop-
erated, shared rituals and indeed adopted forms of multiple religious
belonging. The mention of holy places and special festivals is
particularly significant, for here people can come together to worship
and pray, exploring boundaries which may be more open than had
been believed, and at times influencing each other. The fact that
the places 'belong' to another religion means that others can learn
something of its rites first hand and, if guests are truly welcome,
then the place takes on the character of 'common ground' where
participation is possible without feeling intrusive.

## TYPES OF WORSHIP AND PRAYER

Given these examples, it is apparent that interfaith worship is just
as much a case of the natural religious instincts of ordinary people
coming together to reach out both to each other and to the Divine,
as it is a matter of highly organised occasions arranged by religious
authorities according to carefully crafted rules.[4] There may be many
motives for contact, of which I have already mentioned four: the great
attraction to holy places which many feel, neighbourliness, gratitude
and political conformity. Neighbourliness may take on special
significance if one group wishes to show solidarity with another group
which is the victim of some atrocity or of persecution. For example,
people of another religion may keep Ramadan as a sign of love for
Muslims persecuted in Myanmar. To those motives should be added
the hunger for understanding of 'others' and the wish to be educated
in their ways. Hospitality, both given and received, is an essential for
all of these experiences of sharing, for otherwise the sense of common
ground is swept away and the reciprocal bond of host and guest is
replaced by awkwardness and a feeling of trespass. Lastly, there is the
particular motive which springs from interfaith marriage, where the
couple need to work out what kind of worship pattern they wish to
adopt and how it will affect their children.

It might be said that some of the examples just given are not
true interfaith worship for they can be mere observation: experiments
or cases of 'dipping in' for the sake of a passing experience. That
comment can be true at times, but the host-and-guest model is crucial
and should not be dismissed, for through it can come profound

---

4    There are now numerous resources, mainly on the internet, but also in
     book form. An example of the latter is Potter and Braybrooke 1997.
     It contains contributions from many faiths and chapters on interfaith
     worship and prayer. More specialist (for hospital and other chaplains) is
     Sanders 2015.

learning, a love of the ways of another community of faith, and a renewal of the faith of the guest. There is a lesson from the ancient Greeks for whom 'xenos' meant both host and guest: the two were united in a single word. We may receive an invitation from a friend to a Sikh gurdwara, or chance upon a holy place and be invited in. Or a group of people from different faiths may meet to meditate and pray together in silence on a common theme.

When it comes to arranged occasions, they are often of three kinds.[5] The first is a serial event such as the Commonwealth Observance discussed above, where different faiths take it in turns to read and to reflect, usually interspersed with songs and music, chosen as likely to be acceptable to all. A variation is for one religion to be the host and plan the occasion, with others contributing a reading, an address or prayers. In a serial event there is no assumption that all will agree with everything that is said or done, although there is usually consultation beforehand about the form that worship will take and about whether it has a theme such as 'mercy'.

The second model is that of the 1986 Day of Prayer for Peace held at Assisi at the invitation of Pope John Paul II, where the various religions each had their own place for prayer, as it were in parallel, with a shared introduction and conclusion together with a common focus. Many Christian organisations were represented, as were ten other religions: African and American indigenous religions, Bahá'í, Buddhism, Hinduism, Islam, Judaism, Shintoism, Sikhism and Zoroastrianism. Each group could pray as it wished and the occasion was therefore less open to accusations of syncretism or of seeking a lowest common denominator, although such criticisms were, of course, made. A reasonable question was posed at the time: which is the greater danger, the threats to peace or the possibility of seeing faiths as on a level?

Syncretism is also the charge often made of the third form of event: the attempt to have a genuinely united service following a particular theme. If each contribution is not to be reduced to banality, then the occasion requires a lot of joint work around the theme and a willingness to participate in an event which contains material specifically and obviously from particular religions, not hiding from real differences between them. Much more is thus demanded both of the organisers and of the worshippers. At different stages of the occasion, they may either be observers or participants.

---

5    For a thorough discussion of the different types of prayer and worship, see Pratt 2006.

Schools where more than one faith are represented present a particular challenge, although there is now much material available for the teachers. Some form of serial worship is often the most suitable, or perhaps a rota of events, each occasion stemming from a particular faith.

People differ on the question of the degree to which we can share in the religious experience of another faith through worship and prayer together. Some say that there will always be an element of the observer, whereas others disagree on the grounds that what we worship (God, the Divine, the Ultimate Reality, the Creator) is known by many names and is so loving, mysterious and great that we can never fully comprehend what this Being is like, and can thus fully join in worship and prayer with people of other faiths. This latter position is in part supported by knowledge of the inadequacy of religious language, which is often stretched beyond breaking point; we are mortals with our feet very much in the mud (or the sand!), while we reach for infinity. In other words, there is a Reality to which many of us are reaching out (knowing that the Creator has always been reaching out to us) and we can worship and pray together without compromising our distinctiveness, understanding that we will express ourselves differently. There are theological grounds for joining fully in worship, to which is added the urgency of the issues that surround us: the fragile state of our one world, the cry of the suffering, the longing for peace.

## SPECIAL RITUALS

As well as the collective events which I have mentioned, there are needs of a more personal and poignant kind. The different religions have often failed those who need joint occasions for 'rites of passage' such as births, marriages and deaths. Much depends on the religious officials in contact with the people concerned and one can only wonder at the stories of refusal or of the sudden invention of restrictive rules. There may be an argument for a ceremony to take place principally within a particular religious tradition in order to avoid confusion, but there is rarely a reason why representatives of another religion should not take part. For example, in a Christian baptism service from which no part is omitted, there will be Christian godparents, but there can also be Hindus present who read from a holy book and say prayers. The number of interfaith marriages is increasing all over the world; it follows that sensitive arrangements should be made for those involved (Macomb 2003). Prayer and worship often require hard work.

I like the story of the Vietnamese Buddhist priest Thich Nhat Hanh who was lecturing in the United States at the height of the Vietnam War and was questioned by a student who was 'into' fashionable techniques of meditation. The student asked: 'Could you tell us how you meditate in your monastery in Vietnam?' Thich Nhat Hanh replied: 'In our monastery no one is allowed to meditate until he has spent at least three years learning how to serve tea to the older monks' (Nicholl 1981).

Prayer, in all its forms, is not a matter of easy 'spirituality' or individual therapy and it is linked to action. It has been called 'the language of love' and it is of central importance. The human instinct in the presence of God is to worship and pray; whatever the way in which they are done, prayer and worship are basic to religion. Indeed, they have often been given primacy in another sense, namely as guiding belief rather than as following it. The expression 'lex orandi, lex credendi' is roughly translated as 'the law of prayer becomes the law of believing'. In other words, it says that religious beliefs are guided and conditioned by prayer and worship. That is an ancient principle and one that finds sympathy in many religions. What is done guides what is understood and believed, or at least the two should interact.

Global religious awareness has grown, stemming from the movement of people and the ease of communication. The situation can lead to rivalry and tension or to creative interaction. Interfaith relations become ever more crucial for the good of the world and for the good of believers. It follows that we must pray and worship together.

# REFERENCES

Bookless, D. (1991) *Interfaith Worship and Christian Truth*. Nottingham: Grove.

Cheetham, D., Pratt, D. and Thomas, D. (eds) (2013) *Understanding Interreligious Relations*. Oxford: Oxford University Press.

Dalrymple, W. (1997) *From the Holy Mountain*. London: HarperCollins.

Griffiths, B. (1983) *The Marriage of East and West*. London: Fount.

Macomb, S. (2003) *Joining Hands and Hearts*. New York: Atria.

Moyaert, M. and Geldhof, J. (eds) (2015) *Ritual Participation and Interreligious Dialogue.* London: Bloomsbury.

Nicholl, D. (1981) *Holiness.* London: Darton Longman & Todd.

Potter, J. and Braybrooke, M. (eds) (1997*) All in Good Faith – A Resource Book for Multi-Faith Prayer.* Oxford: World Congress of Faiths.

Pratt, D. (2006) 'Interreligious prayer: Prospects and parameters.' *Interreligious Insight 4*, 4, 54–63.

Race, A. (2001) *Interfaith Encounter.* London: SCM Press.

Sanders, M. (2015) *Interfaith Ministry Handbook.* Berkeley, CA: Apocryphile Press.

Schillebeeckx, E. (2014) *The Collected Works of Edward Schillebeeckx*, vol. 10. London: Bloomsbury.

Vardy, P. (2010) *Good and Bad Religion.* London: SCM Press.

Waardenburg, J. (2005) 'Louis Massignon.' *Die Welt des Islams 45*, 3, 312–342.

Wild, R. (2015) *A Catholic Reading Guide to Universalism.* Eugene, OR: Resource Publications.

# Chapter 3

# HINDUISM

## 1

## Divine Unity and Human Solidarity: A Hindu Perspective on Praying Together

Anantanand Rambachan

### THEOLOGICAL CONTROVERSY OVER HINDU PRAYER

On March 3, 2015, a Hindu was invited as a guest chaplain to offer a prayer in the Idaho State Senate before the commencement of its proceedings. Senate meetings begin with prayer, usually offered by a Christian chaplain, and this was the first time a Hindu was invited to pray. Three state senators refused to be present for the prayer and entered the room only after the prayer was over. One of the objecting senators, Sheryl Nuxoll, explained that the Hindu tradition is 'a false faith with false gods', and a Hindu prayer in the senate would give legitimacy to such beliefs. In addition, she explained, 'the United States is a Christian nation'. Senator Lori Den Hartog claimed that it would be disingenuous to her Christian faith to attend (News Minute 2015). On July 12, 2007, Christian protesters vocally disrupted the first Hindu prayer in the United Sates Senate. Ante Pavkovic, one of the protesters, shouted from the visitor gallery, 'Lord Jesus, forgive us father for allowing a prayer of the wicked, which is an abomination in your sight. Blessed is the nation whose God is the Lord. Thou shalt have no other gods before me. You are the One true living God.'

These recent examples are important for us since they reveal the attitude and objection of some Christians to Hindu prayer and to praying with Hindus. We see in these examples that, if a faith and its deity are regarded as 'false', then its prayer is also invalidated and to join in such prayer is sacrilegious. To be even within hearing distance of such prayer is regarded as legitimizing a false tradition and as betraying one's loyalty to one's own deity.

## RESOURCES FOR INTRA-RELIGIOUS PRAYER

Whenever such incidents occur in the United States, where I live and work, or in any other part of the world, I reflect on my attitudes as a Hindu to the prayer of another tradition and to the meaning of praying together with people of other religions. Although concerned not to represent my tradition in idealistic or irenic terms, I do not feel compelled by my tradition to denounce the God that others worship as false. My tradition does not exclude the possibility of praying with others and does not regard such prayer as an act of disloyalty. I venture to say also that most people in my tradition share this disposition. Thomas Thangaraj, a Christian theologian from South India, noted the willingness of his Hindu friend to pray in spaces that were not Hindu places of worship and asked, 'How can my Hindu friend worship God so easily in a Christian setting, while I have so much difficulty doing the same in a Hindu temple?' (Thangaraj 1997, p.7). Clearly the teachings and practices that shaped the Hindu's worldview were different from those that informed Thangaraj's Christian outlook on Hinduism.

With the risks of generalizing about a tradition as diverse as Hinduism, I wish to identify salient features that are relevant to the issue of praying together.

The Upanishads, which constitute the final or wisdom sections of the Vedas, speak of God as 'That from which all beings originate, by which they are sustained and to which they return' (Taittiriya Upanishad 3.1.1). Other Upanishads speak of God as the indivisible and uncreated One from which the many emerge. The Upanishads contest the existence of anything but the One Being before creation, and the emergence of the world from anything other than this One. The Bhagavadgita (9:17–18) describes God as father and mother of the universe, and as its nourisher, lord, goal, and friend. The God of the Hindu tradition is not the tribal deity of a particular religious, or ethnic community, but the source of all life and existence. God is not limited by our theological, cultural, or national boundaries and we should never assume that our community is favored or privileged by God above all others.

The Hindu tradition developed in the Indian subcontinent in a context of significant diversity, cultural, linguistic, and historical. Regional communities named differently that which they regarded as ultimate. Vaishnavas spoke of the ultimate as Vishnu, Shaivas as Shiva, and Shaktas (worshippers of the divine feminine) called Her Durga and Kali. As these communities interacted, understood better each other's claims, and were enriched by the influence of the other, there was a movement away from exclusive viewpoints which rejected the God of the other as false or which hierarchically subordinated the other's God to one's own.[1] Although such exclusive or hierarchical interpretations of diversity are not entirely absent from the Hindu tradition, the widely shared theological orientation is to see that the God of the other is not false, nonexistent, or subordinate to one's own, but a different way of naming and imagining the One. A different name for God does not mean that God is different. Even with different understandings among Hindu traditions, there are sufficient shared claims to recognize God as the same. In the vast sanctum space of the Maple Grove, Minnesota, temple where I worship, there are separate temples for all the major God representations on the Hindu tradition. I never think that we are worshipping a different God at each shrine and I am certain that the priests who move from shrine to shrine performing *puja* do not regard themselves as serving different Gods.

The earliest example of such an interpretation of religious diversity is the Rig Veda text (I.164.45–46):

Speech hath been measured out in four divisions.
The Wise who have understanding know them.
Three kept in close concealment cause no motion;
of speech men only speak the fourth division.

They call him Indra, Mitra, Varuna, Agni, and he is
the noble-winged Garutman.
The One Being (*ekam sat*) the wise speak of in many ways:
They call it Agni, Yama, Matarisvan.[2]

---

1    This is not to deny historical conflicts between Vaishnavas and Shaivas. See Klostermaier 2000.
2    Griffiths 1973. Translation modified.

In addition to highlighting the diversity of cultural and historical contexts, these verses also provide a commentary on the finitude and limits of all human language in relation to God. In trying to describe the One Being (*ekam sat*), language will be diverse, since this One exceeds all descriptions. Each word, each symbol, precious in its particularity, is inadequate and reflects the historical and cultural conditions under which it occurs. The consequence is an epistemological and philosophical humility expressing itself in a theology of diversity that can accommodate different understandings and names for God. The Rig Veda text reminds us that our discourse about God should not be made absolute and our symbols must not be confused with the reality to which these symbols point. We use many names (Indra, Mitra, Varuna, Agni, Yama, Matarisvan, Garutman) not because the gods are many, but because of the limits of human language and the diversity of experiences. One name will never be enough. In the Hindu tradition, God as Vishṇu has at least a thousand names and so does Shiva and the divine feminine, Durga. Each name and form is spoken of as an ishtadevata (chosen God), reminding us that there is also an element of cultural creation in our respective ideas about God.

Within the Hindu tradition, the implication of a theology of 'The One Being the wise speak of in many ways' is that Hindus do not think of Shiva, Vishnu, or Durga as separate deities, but as the single recipient of all prayer. A traditional verse conveys this well:

> May Hari, the ruler of the three worlds, worshipped by the Shaivites as Shiva, by the Vedantins as Brahman, by the Buddhists as Buddha, by the Naiyayikas, clever in the means of knowledge, as the Creator, by the Jainas as the liberated, by the ritualists as karma, may he grant our prayers.[3]

Maitri Upanishad (5.1) makes a similar point about divine unity:

---

3   *yam shaivah samupasate shiva iti brahmeti vedantinah*
    *bauddhah buddha iti pramanapatavah karteti naiyayikah*
    *arhanityatha jaina-shasana-ratah karmeti mimansakah*
    *so yam vo vidhadhatu vanchita phalam trailokyanatho harih.* Cited by Radhakrishnan 1976, p.34. Translation modified. The origin of the text is uncertain, but certainly as early as the fourteenth century. I recognize also that a verse like this may not be welcomed by some of the traditions listed and who may read it as a form of Hindu homogenization. It does, however, articulate the Hindu orientation to seeing ultimate reality as single, even with differences that ought not to be dismissed.

You are Brahma, you are Vishnu too:
You are Rudra, you are Prajapati,
You are Agni, Varuna, Vayu:
You are Indra, you are the Moon. (Roebuck 2003, p.362)

Even with significant theological differences existing among the diverse Hindu traditions, I have no hesitation joining with other Hindus in prayer. My fellow Hindus who honor God as Vishnu, Shiva, Durga, or Ganesha are not oriented to different divine beings but to the One True Being (*ekam sat*).

## RESOURCES FOR INTERRELIGIOUS PRAYER

Extended to other religious traditions, I may say that, even as the Rig Veda text (I.164.45–46) does not allow for the separate existence of ultimate divine beings such as Shiva, Vishnu, or Agni, it does not allow for a Jewish, Christian, Hindu, or Muslim God existing alongside but distinct from each other. Such a position, asserted literally, affirms a polytheistic universe, in addition to the contradiction of asserting multiple ultimate realities. Vaishnavas, Shaivas, Christians, Muslims, and Jews understand God to be the infinite source of all life. My Hindu tradition enables me to think of persons in other traditions, not as strangers with alien, false, or rival deities, but as fellow beings whose God is our God and with whom I can join in prayer. My neighbor of another tradition, who speaks a different religious language, and I are addressing and relating ourselves to One ultimate being. Through differences of name, symbols, cultures, and theologies, we comfortably clothe this One with an identity that is similar to our own and fail to recognize the One in other theological and linguistic dresses. Thinking of my Jewish, Christian, and Muslim friends as being oriented towards the same One Being enlarges my understanding of the boundaries of community that now includes all who understand themselves in relation to this One. It motivates me to build dialogical relationships with those whose lives are centered on this One Being and to pray together with them.

## PRAYING TOGETHER AND RESPECTING DIFFERENCE

Let me clarify and state unequivocally that my approach as a Hindu to the possibility of praying together with people of traditions does not imply the claim that all religions are the same or share the same soteriological goal. It does not imply that religious differences could be reducible to semantics or that all ways of speaking about the One are of equal worth. We are aware of ways of speaking in the name of the One that awaken hate and instigate violence towards others within and outside our traditions. Religious ways of speaking, even prayer, can legitimize injustice and oppression even as others can liberate and advocate for equality. It is naive and dangerous to grant equal validity or moral equivalency to all religious voices. The Rig Veda text attributes different ways of speaking to the wise and not to the ignorant. By acknowledging that wise people may speak differently about God, the text invites a respectful and inquiring response to religious diversity.

We must not hastily and arrogantly denounce the religious speech and prayer of the other as undeserving of sincere and serious contemplation. Wisdom must not be identified solely with our way of speaking or praying. We should not assume that wise persons always speak identically or that wisdom is manifested only in consensus. Being attentive to difference must deeply inform our relationships but should not a priori rule out the possibility of praying together. Our religious choices are not limited to the dualism of asserting the exclusive validity of our own traditions or an uncritical relativism.

## RELIGIOUS DIVERSITY AND GOD

My willingness to join people of other traditions in prayer is also informed by the teachings of Hindu sacred texts and especially by the Bhagavadgita. There are several teachings in this text affirming that religious diversity expressed in differing modes or prayer and worship has divine approval. In a well-known verse (4:11), Krishna, regarded by many Hindu traditions as God incarnate, teaches, 'In whatever ways people approach me, so do I accept them; for the paths people take from every side are Mine.'[4] The Divine responds appropriately to the longing in the human heart for God, wherever and in whatever forms such seeking may be expressed. Divine freedom implies the freedom to respond positively to religious diversity. Consequently, it will be improper of me as a Hindu to insist on one name and one form of worship, to regard all other ways as sacrilegious and to refuse to join a prayer different from my own. Jealousy is not an attribute of divinity in the Hindu tradition. We are not the gatekeepers of acceptable prayer to God.

---

4    Shri Bhagavadgita, Sargeant 1993. Translation modified.

## FORMS OF INTERFAITH PRAYER

In describing my willingness to join with people of other religions in prayer, it is very important that we clarify the multiple meanings and forms of such prayer. Thomas Thangaraj has suggested a number of possibilities (Thangaraj 1998). These include (1) visiting other places during worship; (2) using the resources of other traditions in prayer and worship; (3) offering of separate prayers from different traditions in a multifaith gathering; (4) offering of prayer from a single tradition to a multifaith gathering; (5) the sharing of words or rituals with people of other traditions acceptable to all participants. The third possibility is the most common practice in interreligious gatherings and underlines the concern to preserve the particularity of each tradition. I have participated in many such events and I do not regard my participation as a betrayal of my own religious commitments. The fifth possibility is perhaps the most challenging and requires thoughtful and diligent work to find the words and symbolic gestures that represent what participants can say and do together. I do not hesitate to join in such acts of praying together if the preparation is truly interreligious, the outcome consensual, and if no single tradition's mode of prayer or content is privileged.

I recognize also that every tradition has core claims that are expressed in distinctive ritual actions and theological affirmations. I express profound respect for such claims by understanding their uniqueness and the reasons why participation is meaningful only to members of the religious community. The Christian Eucharist or the Islamic *shahada* (there is no God but God and Muhammad is God's messenger) are examples of rituals and words that I am unable to take part in or recite if these form part of an event of praying together. An act of praying together must not require that I affirm claims that delegitimize and negate my own core commitments. In the same spirit of interfaith generosity, I must understand the reluctance of my friends of other traditions to join in Hindu prayer or ritual (*puja*) requiring the perception of a *murti* (icon) as a living divine embodiment. I do not interpret their abstention as disrespectful.

The act of praying together becomes more meaningful when, without overlooking our rich differences, we affirm our unity as human beings in relation to the One Being who is the source, support, and goal of our lives.

## CONCLUSION

My commitment as a Hindu does not permit me to think of persons of other religious traditions or those without religious commitment as wicked or existing outside of divine reality just because they do not share my faith. Their sacred worth is not contingent on their profession of my religious identity or any other identity or participation in a ritual that is unique to my community. I understand human dignity to flow from the fact that every being equally embodies the Divine. No human intermediary or ritual brings God to us. Every human encounter is an encounter with God who is already and always present in each one. To shun and regard another with disdain in speech or act is to be both ignorant and irreverent.

My ability to pray together with persons of other faiths is an affirmation of this truth that lies at the heart of my tradition. This truth also requires me to identify and to stand together with others in joy and in sorrow. In a world where our interconnectedness only grows deeper, where we increasingly rejoice and suffer together, praying together is an important expression of the divine unity that connects us all and of our solidarity with each other in community.

## REFERENCES

Griffiths, R.T.H. (trans.) (1973) *The Hymns of the Rigveda*. Delhi: Motilal Banarsidass.

Klostermaier, K. (2000) *A Survey of Hinduism*. Albany, NY: State University of New York Press.

News Minute (2015) *News Minute*, 9 March. Accessed on 6 December 2018 at https://www.news18.com/news/world/idaho-senate-opens-with-hindu-prayer-3-lawmakers-refuse-to-attend-it-971504.html.

Radhakrishnan, S. (1976) *The Hindu View of Life*. New York: Macmillan.

Roebuck, V.J. (trans. and ed.) (2003) *The Upanisads*. London: Penguin Books.

Sargeant, W. (trans.) (1993) *Shri Bhagavadgita*. Albany, NY: State University of New York Press.

Thangaraj, M.T. (1997) *Relating to People of Other Religions*. Nashville, TN: Abingdon Press.

Thangaraj, T. (1998) 'A theological reflection on the experience of interreligious prayer.' *Pro Dialogo* 98, 2, 186–196.

## 2

# Does God Understand Sanskrit? A Hindu View on Allowing God to Love

Shaunaka Rishi Das

### THE DEVIL IN HIS SKIRT

One fashionably grey Saturday afternoon in 1988 I led a chanting party past City Hall, Belfast. It was a *kirtan* party, *kirtan* being congregational chanting of God's names in the mood of prayer, asking, 'Please Lord, engage me in your service.' As the chant was in Sanskrit, and we were dressed in Indian attire of *dhoti*, *kurta*, and sari, and it was Belfast, the subtlety of this form of prayer was not immediately discerned.

Outside City Hall stood the Rev Ian Paisley with some of his congregation, preaching through his megaphone, as he did on most Saturdays. He was also engaged in the Lord's service, in his own glorification, his own *kirtan*. In recognition of his sincere efforts to serve God I bowed my head to him, to which he replied, by megaphone, 'There they go – the devils in their skirts.' He did have a sense of humour, although in this case he may have been trying to make a serious point.

It was admittedly a bit of a culture clash, and a photograph of the encounter could have gone viral if we had the technology of today, but I have wondered if it was more a clash of religious norms than a conflict of spirituality or intention.

To complicate matters I was born an Irish Catholic and had adopted the ways of worship of a Hindu. Dressed as I was and being something of a hybrid Southern Irish Catholic Hindu, I was a bit of a red rag to Rev Paisley. I was unacceptable on many levels. Although the situation was in retrospect funny, the tragedy was the gulf we created by investing our differences with energy – and by creating an altar on which a portion of our compassion was sacrificed to the circumstances of birth and tradition.

On that Saturday, in Belfast the added difficulty for Rev Paisley was in accepting the new reality that after hundreds of years spent advertising the need to convert the Hindus in India to Christianity, the Irishman before him seemed to have misread the memo. Since our encounter in the 1980s more and more people, Irish and Indians among them, are exploring their spirituality in nontraditional ways. Although my own life choices are a testament to this it is more empirically seen in the research of Linda Woodhead and others (Heelas *et al.* 2005).

I acknowledged the Rev Paisley with a nod of the head because I recognised that, although our appearance and approach could not have differed more, our intention to love and serve God was the same. Both of us were having our *kirtan* and shared a space for a brief minute. We might have been more loving and a better example of the teachings of our respective traditions on that Saturday. A mutual acknowledgment of our intention would have been a powerful message and could have excited the technology of the day – word of mouth – in an enthusiasm of comment. We both let an opportunity to serve God pass us by, an opportunity to pray together simply by offering mutual respect. 'Serve which God?' you may say – well, everyone tells me there is only one.

## IN A TEMPLE WITH THE ONE AND THE MANY

On a recent visit to the Parthasarathi temple, in Chennai, I alighted from my rickshaw at the temple gates to be met by a procession coming from within. It was preceded by musicians and up to seventy chanting priests, followed by a palanquin carrying the beautifully decorated temple Deities, all followed by another twenty chanting priests.

The sonorous mantras of the priests represented a formal form of Hindu prayer, *vandana*, offering respect and glorification. Although these particular prayers were in Sanskrit we find this form of prayer in every religion and culture.

I should explain here two aspects of Indian thought, arising from Vedic literature – literature given the status of scripture which has had a major influence on the philosophies and religions of India. The first is the idea of *rita* – cosmic order. It is the simple observation that we are born into a world that is highly organised and we have a part to play, as servants of the greater whole.

The second is unique to Hindu cultures, the idea of *atma*. It speaks of the physical, mental, intellectual, and spiritual energies that go to make up who we are – and asks which of these aspects of who we are is most substantial – which endures the most. In short it is concluded that our identity is made up of two primary energies, material and spiritual, respectively temporary and eternal. In this understanding it is accepted that our real identity is the spiritual and eternal aspect. The eternal endures the most.

In considering both of these ideas we can begin to appreciate the origins of the pluralism of Indian and Hindu thought. With *rita* we see that each individual is a small cog in the big cosmic machine, each charged with finding the part they must play on the cosmic stage. Each responsible for their own part, each part an individual contribution to the whole. Thus we appreciate and interpret the world and its truth from the perspective of our small role in the cosmos, meaning that there are as many perspectives, religions, and prayers in the world as there are people.

With *atma* – and I continue here with the interpretation of the *bhakti* schools of thought, the schools of devotional service to God – we are eternal individuals who realise our perfection in relationship with the Supreme. This interpretation says we should not be bound by temporary identities of gender, race, caste, nation, or religion, nor should we bind others to such temporary identities. The Supreme alone has the bandwidth to comprehend the bigger picture and to understand reality as it is. We can understand truth in part, from our limited vantage point, and that by the grace of the Supreme. Thus none of us can claim a monopoly on truth, individually or collectively. Our devotion and prayers, and the love we share, are unique and individual offerings.

Observing the Deity in the procession, which of the many Hindu deities were the priests glorifying? I actually didn't recognise the form as it journeyed past. I am from a similar Vaishnava denomination as these priests, yet their particular prayers and culture of worship were very different.

From consideration of *rita* and *atma* I appreciated that these were sincere people trying to offer their service to God in their own way and using the language and culture God had given them. They, like me, considered that there is one Supreme Lord, although able to manifest in many ways, in many forms, with many names, and accessible to all. A Hindu monotheism – with a pluralist twist.

I entered the temple and in the queue for the main altar I was shoulder to shoulder with fellow worshippers from all backgrounds, each individually a different religion from me, and each other, some possibly as different from me as the Rev Paisley. But on this occasion we all meandered around the granite columns together in prayer, developing our individual relationship with the Lord.

Our need was very personal but our appeal for shelter and meaning – unashamedly reaching beyond ourselves – was communal, and there was great comfort in that. Such a congregation of different faiths, philosophies, and perspectives in prayer together in that temple, that microcosm, was an inspiration.

As soon as we stood at the temple gate, ready to leave, and putting our shoes back on, it was as if we were putting our egos back on – the identities that are necessary to negotiate the world, but which can also serve to separate us.

It is a pious hope to think that in everyday life we will abandon all ego save that of being God's eternal servant. That identity is very personal, but maybe we can expect to be able to be that together for a day, a weekend, even an hour.

How do we find the tolerance, humility, and kindness needed to stand beside someone who is praying to God knows who, for God knows what? We already experience this in our respective places of worship as only God knows the heart and intention of the person praying beside us. I can only account for my intention, which is full of holes, and a person of another faith (which is every person) can account for theirs, yet we can pray together.

## NOT ONE OF US

During an illness my late wife Keshava used to read online message boards for inspiration. On one such site, run by a faith other than her own and dedicated to sharing and discussing prayer, she became so enthused by the mood of kindness and affection among the members that she uploaded a medieval Bengali prayer, one close to her heart.

It was a prayer of yearning, called *prarthana*, a petitionary prayer. This type of prayer is often devotional, reflecting the desire of the composer to find their love for God, although burdened by mundane desire. They are prayers spoken in the moment out of deep spiritual emotion and realization, directly inspired by the Lord. These prayers are sometimes sung as *bhajan*, a hymn set to music – in itself a form of prayer. The prayer she offered was:

One should chant the holy name of the Lord in a humble state of mind, thinking oneself lower than the straw in the street; one should be more tolerant than a tree, devoid of all sense of false prestige, and should be ready to offer all respect to others, expecting none for oneself. In such a state of mind may I pray to the Lord constantly. (Bhaktivedanta Swami 1975a, 17–31)

The message board went crazy. Everyone loved this prayer and wanted to know where it came from, chapter and verse. Realising, a little too late, that this could be awkward, Keshava took the risk of revealing that this prayer, although devotional, was not from a source they might recognise. She added that maybe it could still be considered a meaningful prayer, based on how members found themselves and their Lord in it. She was bemused to see the reaction to her proposal swing from serious consideration to serious rejection.

She quietly withdrew, disappointed that her enthusiasm disappointed others and that she was now deprived of a daily prayer fix. I was sad too because she depended on these sources of grace during a long illness. She loved the prayers and thoughtful reflections but was excluded because her prayer was foreign. It was an immigrant prayer which wandered across the border of tolerance. The message board community rejected a neighbour in need. Setting aside our religion in order to share our affection for God with another can be difficult, but maybe prayer should be a special area where difference is ignored – *prière sans frontières*.

## DOES GOD UNDERSTAND THE DIFFICULTY?

Another form of Hindu prayer is *smarana*, contemplative prayer without words, but one which remembers the presence of God.

In 1998 I attended a meeting to organise the first interfaith conference in Northern Ireland. Invited by the Northern Ireland Interfaith Forum, representatives from all of the province's religious communities attended – a feat in itself. Having dealt well with all the logistics we tentatively proposed an act of collective prayer and worship as a sign of solidarity and brotherhood. Each and every proposal as to how we could pray together was vetoed, until we got to the idea of a simple collective silence.

Everyone seemed to brighten at that idea, relieved that maybe we could agree on something, until the representative of one of the Christian denominations sighed, saying it wouldn't work. 'There will surely be someone in our community who will object,' he said, 'because we won't know who you are thinking about.' An audible groan arose. We all understood the conundrum but it was a pity that the argument was won by fear.

Bhaktivinode Thakura (1836–1914) was one of the Hindu intellectuals of the Bhadraloka,[5] who responded to their encounter with Christianity and the enlightenment. He says of another's way and place of worship:

> If you go to someone else's place of worship, you should think: 'The people here are worshipping my Lord, but in a different way. Because of my different training, I cannot comprehend this system of worship. However, through this experience, I can deepen my appreciation for my own system of worship. The Lord is only one, not two. I offer respect to the form I see here and pray to the Lord in this new form that He increase my love for the Lord in His accustomed form.'
>
> However, consider the following point. Although it is worthless to criticize a mere difference in a religious system, if people see a real fault, they should not simply accept it. (Bhaktivinode Thakura 1886)

Bhaktivinode wants to be trusting, and yet to make informed choices. A real fault in this context would include actions against norms of decent behaviour and the law. In his mind it is perfectly possible for us to be together in silence or in prayer without fear of losing God's love for us.

In the Bhakti traditions, and in my reading of Christianity, fear cannot be the deciding factor in any spiritual disputation or negotiation. Surely love would be a better motivation. God, being omniscient as he is, can certainly discern sincerity for himself. We can also imagine that he can hear the heart yearning for a relationship, for help, for service, for affection, in any language and from any place of worship, from any country, from any caste, gender, or race. Maybe the Lord does not need our interpretation of religion to advise him as to who is acceptable association, nor our understanding of the quality of another's prayer for him to see it more clearly.

---

5    A cultured and prosperous class that arose in Bengal between 1757 and 1947. Possibly the greatest factors that led to the rise of the Bhadraloka were the fortunes made from trading with the East India Company and the introduction of Western education.

## CONCLUDING WORDS

In a beautiful Tuscan Hindu temple, outside Florence, my friend Mahaprabhu and I stood in prayer before the shrine. Mahaprabhu comes from a Jewish family and, like me, chose Vaishnava spirituality as his practice. He was wearing a tweed cap and I playfully took it from his head and told him to have more respect in the house of God. He smiled and said that as an Irish Catholic I would say that, but as a Jew he would respectfully wear his cap and, as he returned it to his head, added that he was sure Krishna didn't really mind either way.

Neither of us thought for a minute that this was not the case, nor did we pause to take either the cap or our cultural heritage, or indeed our different visions of the Lord seriously. To sustain our friendship, we trusted our intention. I don't know what people are thinking when they pray, whether it's a petition for a bigger car or for love of God, and frankly it's none of my business. It's between my brother and the Lord. At least we have come before the Lord and that is a start, and that we can trust.

Without establishing confidence that we can pray together, those from traditions with faith in God risk sitting idly by, silently watching the rapid growth of a Godless and impersonal civilisation. We can do business with anyone from any faith, we can play sports with them, we can break bread with them, we should also serve God with them, and pray with them, and the world will be a better place for it.

A prayer offered among friends:

May the entire universe be blessed with peace and hope. May everyone driven by envy and enmity become pacified and reconciled. May all living beings develop abiding concern for the welfare of others. May our own hearts and minds be filled with purity and serenity. May all these blessings flow naturally from this supreme benediction: May our attention become spontaneously absorbed in the pure love of the transcendent Lord. (Bhagavata Purana 5.18.9; Bhaktivedanta Swami 1975b)

## REFERENCES

Bhaktivedanta Swami, A.C. (1975a) *Sri Chaitanya Charitamrita: Antya-lila.* Los Angeles, CA: Bhaktivedanta Book Trust.

Bhaktivedanta Swami, A.C. (1975b) *Srimad Bhagavatam: Canto-five*. Los Angeles, CA: Bhaktivedanta Book Trust.

Bhaktivinode Thakura (1886) *Chaitanya Shikshamrta*. Calcutta.

Heelas, P., Woodhead, L., Seel, B., Tusting, K. and Szerszynski, B. (2005) *The Spiritual Revolution: Why Religion is Giving Way to Spirituality*. Oxford: Blackwell.

## FURTHER READING

Satsvarupa dasa Goswami (1989) *Entering the Life of Prayer*. Pennsylvania, PA: GN Press.

Satsvarupa dasa Goswami (1992) *Vandanam*. Pennsylvania, PA: GN Press.

Shaunaka Rishi Das (1999) 'ISKCON in relation to people of faith in God.' *ISKCON Communications Journal 7*, 1, 30–41.

# Reflection

## The Editors

Interfaith worship and prayer face a question. How is it possible for believers from a wide variety of faiths – all of whom embrace the truth claims of their various traditions – to worship together? This is the dilemma that Anantanand Rambachan confronts at the beginning of his contribution. He describes the reaction of several US state senators when a Hindu was invited to offer a prayer at the Idaho State Senate. One said that the Hindu tradition is a false faith with false gods; another claimed it would be disingenuous to her Christian faith to attend. On another occasion protestors disrupted the first Hindu prayer in the United States Senate, and asked God for forgiveness for allowing such an event to take place.

Confronting such objections, Rambachan draws on his understanding of Hinduism to provide a framework for interfaith activity. Hinduism, he argues, does not impel Hindu worshippers to exclude the possibility of praying with others. On the contrary, the Upanishads describe God as the indivisible and uncreated One from which the many emerge. It is a mistake, he contends, to view the God of the Hindu tradition as a tribal deity. Rather he is the source of all existence. God is not limited by theological, cultural or national boundaries.

How then should Hindus regard other faiths? According to Rambachan, God in other traditions should not be viewed as false, nonexistent or subordinate. Rather, the varied religious traditions should be perceived as different, culturally conditioned, ways of perceiving the Divine. In this context, he cites the Rig Veda's interpretation of religious diversity. These verses, he stresses, highlight cultural and historical variety, and also provide a commentary on the limits of human language. Inevitably, human beings utilise concepts from their own traditions. The Rig Veda reminds us that discourse about God is not absolute. Vishnu, he points out, has at least a thousand names, as does Shiva and the divine feminine Durga.

In this context Rambachan asserts that the Hindu tradition does not think of persons in other faiths as strangers with false beliefs, but rather as fellow beings with whom the Hindu can join in prayer. Though speaking different languages and holding multifarious religious convictions, they are relating themselves to one ultimate being. This does not mean, however, that all religions are the same or share the same soteriological goal.

Nor does it imply that religious differences are of no significance. Yet, such differences should not prevent the common activity of interfaith worship.

In this context, Rambachan outlines a range of common worshipful activities: visiting other places of worship; using the resources of other traditions in prayer; offering separate prayers from different traditions in interfaith gatherings; and sharing words and rituals with people of different traditions. Such activity, he contends, is not in any way a betrayal of one's religious commitments as a Hindu.

In a similar vein Shaunaka Rishi Das stresses the importance of Hindu interfaith activities. Each person, he states, is a small cog in the cosmic machine. Each is responsible for his or her part and can contribute to the whole. In this context, we should see ourselves as individuals who relativise our perfection in relationship with the Supreme. Hence, we should not be bound by temporary identities of gender, race, caste, nation or religion. The Supreme alone has the capacity to comprehend ultimate reality. None of us can claim a monopoly on truth.

In an interfaith context, we should perceive that worshippers in different traditions seek to offer their services to God in their own fashion, using their own language and culture. There is one Supreme Lord able to manifest himself in numerous ways with many names. Hence, when entering someone else's place of worship, Das advises that one should recognise that God – being omniscient – can hear the heart yearning for relationship, for help, for service, for affection, in any language and from any place of worship, from any caste, gender or race.

These Hindu contributors provide an understanding of religious diversity which they believe should enable members of other faiths to join together in prayer. Both stress that there is one Supreme Lord who manifests himself in myriad ways and is conceived differently in the various faith traditions. No doubt there are many Hindu believers who share such a view. Yet at the same time there are other Hindus who view the Hindu gods as separate deities rather than manifestations of the One Eternal Reality. Inevitably this group poses a challenge to members of more monotheistic traditions. Nonetheless both Rambachan and Das provide an interpretation of Hinduism that offers a valuable route to interfaith prayer.

# Chapter 4

# AFRICAN TRADITIONAL RELIGION

## 1

## Indigenous Forms of Prayer: Unity, Identity, Development and Respect in a Diverse Society

Nokuzola Mndende

### INTRODUCTION

While considering African Traditional Religion (ATR) and interfaith prayer and worship, it is important to give a brief historical background of our country, South Africa. With the advent of apartheid in 1948, South Africa was declared to be a monoreligious country, so interfaith prayer was seen as irrelevant. The indigenous religion was sent into underground exile, as it was practised only among the community members in their sacred places, while Christianity was regarded as real religion or true spirituality. South Africa was called a Christian country.

After the country's liberation in 1994, South Africa was transformed from being a monoreligious state to being a secular state of many religions. This transformation led to the inclusion and recognition of other faiths like Judaism, Islam, Bahá'í, Hinduism and ATR, in addition to Christianity. These other religions were easier to include than ATR (in its own place of birth!) because they already had a documented literature and recorded customs which could be imported from their countries of birth. Moreover, Judaism and Islam, as 'Abrahamic faiths' like Christianity, found rapid recognition as among the religions which are 'nearest' to God.

Although ATR was accepted in principle in the Bill of Rights in the country's constitution (Constitution of the Republic of South Africa 1996), in reality the religion had first to fight for its practical recognition and for inclusion in interfaith programmes. It had to make sure that it first rejected the definitions imposed on it by people of other faiths, as they constantly defined ATR from a colonial perspective. Colonialism always saw ATR as an outdated and exclusively African cultural feature, or as a form of indigenous healing. Some Christians classified ATR as a section of the African Initiated Churches, which are themselves indigenous forms of Christianity. Alongside these distortions or misinterpretations, another demeaning feature brought by the opponents of the religion was to associate ATR with those self-acclaimed 'traditional healers' who use '*muthi*', a term that refers in a derogatory manner to herbal medicines applied to other human beings for evil purposes like witchcraft, or to scams to rob people of their money.

So ATR has often been seen as primitive and culture-bound: a secular spirituality (Du Toit 2006). The other reason for the exclusion of ATR from interfaith programmes is the lack of trained clergy in the field. ATR was never regarded as an independent religion in the theological institutions and was written about and taught by people who were not practitioners of the faith. The Icamagu Institute is up to now the only institution that has trained a few students to be ATR clergy (*iiNjoli*) so that they can, from an informed perspective and without fear, participate in interfaith prayers and other government programmes.

Politics plays a crucial role in further distortions of ATR because those in parliament, law-makers or government leaders, are only paying lip-service to the independence of this religion. They are abusing their power by silencing the legitimate representatives of ATR and are still defining the religion either as diviners or as African Initiated Churches. Unfortunately some of these opponents are lawyers who have no theological background and yet have power as members of the ruling party, putting the practitioners of ATR back on the periphery. If defined as a cultural and secular phenomenon, ATR can be seen as a 'preparatio evengelica': its practitioners may merely be viewed as potential converts to Abrahamic faiths.

All the above is merely to give a picture of the challenges faced by the practitioners, but they are not deterred, as spirituality is from within each individual. Using the Constitution, ATR practitioners pave their way into all spheres, to be part of the interfaith programmes whether in public prayers or in literature produced for schools.

## PRAYER

Before we can discuss interfaith prayer in general, including ATR prayer, it is fair for the benefit of those who are not familiar with this religion to briefly explain the significance or understanding of the term 'prayer' from this religion's perspective. Since this may appear to be a 'new' field of study, it is also important to explain the definition of the religion, as ATR is one of the indigenous religions of the world. One must remember that the study of our religion as an academic subject was first explored by scholars who did not belong to the religion and who interpreted ATR from the perspective of their own faiths and doctrines. The religious beliefs and practices of the indigenous African peoples were in an oral and practical form, passed on from generation to generation, in other words, acted out and not documented. These scholars were also writing not in indigenous languages but mostly in English. Their interpretation of people's practices and beliefs in foreign language/s resulted in many mistranslations, misinterpretations and distortions.

Some scholars, when referring to ATR, always speak of it in the past tense, an indication that they do not believe that many Africans are still practising it today. In South Africa, most Africans are nominal Christians, practising ATR at home as 'culture' while on paper they profess to be Christians because they attend different denominations on Saturdays and Sundays. These people of dual allegiance will not classify their ATR spiritual communication as prayer because to them prayer only refers to the Christian form of communicating with the triune God. If prayer is seen exclusively in this way, it excludes the prayers of ATR practitioners because they only pray in one way, namely by communicating with the Creator through their ancestors.

Today the practitioners of ATR are part of interfaith prayers at different levels of government structures and organisations. ATR practitioners bring distinctive beliefs in the Creator, in ancestors and in a communal way of life through rituals performed by the family and witnessed by community members.

Although I am not going to dwell much on the definitions of this religion, it will be important to highlight features for the benefit of those who are reading about ATR for the first time. Idowu Bolaji (1973, p.104) defines African Traditional Religion as 'The indigenous religion of the Africans south of the Sahara. It is the religion that has been handed down from generation to generation by the forebears of the present generation of Africans.' Dopamu agrees with Idowu and explains it as follows:

> When we speak of African Traditional Religion we mean the indigenous religion of the Africans. It is the religion that has been handed down from generation to generation by the forebears of the present generation of Africans. It is not a fossil religion (a thing of the past) but a religion that Africans today have made theirs by living it and practicing it. (Dopamu 1991, p.21)

One other important aspect in the religious practices of this religion is the fact that it believes in the communal way of life: each individual is part of the whole, part of creation. The basic beliefs are in the Creator (God), in ancestors and in ritual practices, communally acting out the beliefs in order to seal the relationship between the living and the spiritual world. ATR practitioners believe in a creator who is named according to his attributes, so different linguistic groups use different names like the following:

| Linguistic Group | Name of Creator | Meaning |
|---|---|---|
| isiXhosa | Mdali | Creator of the universe |
| isiZulu | Mvelingqangi/ Mvelatanci | These names suggest that the Creator existed before the creation |
| isiNdebele | Zimu | The greatest of all |
| chiShona | Mwari | The name associated with greatness, kindness and power |
| Setswana/ seSotho | Modimo | The name associated with greatness and power |
| isiXhosa | Qamata | Personal name of the Creator |

The reason for emphasising the above is that the understanding of prayer or prayers may differ from that of other faiths, although there are many similarities. In ATR an individual's prayer may differ from the prayers of others who are present, but all are communicated to the spiritual world. During most occasions for prayer, there are responses from the people around to confirm that they are also part of the communication.

## DIFFERENT FORMS OF PRAYERS

In ATR prayer as a communication between individual/s and the spiritual world or the Divine may take many different forms. It may be by way of invoking, or in the form of singing, or it may be silent prayer. Different prayers are used in different rites of passage, or during drought or at a time of thanksgiving, but prayers are always inclusive of the individual and those around him/her because no one lives as an island. Prayer begins from within an individual and may involve those who are close to the individual, like near relatives or associates; it then broadens to other members of the community. This interaction trains an individual not to think about personal interests only but to consider how the subjects of prayer affect others around him/her. It celebrates similarities and also signifies that differences between people or communities or beliefs should be acknowledged and respected and should not be a means of suppressing or demeaning the other. As a form of respect for differences between religions, ATR does not evangelise or convert other groups but, rather, it learns more about diversity for a common cause.

How then does ATR manage to participate as one religion among others in interfaith prayers? In compliance to the Constitution, government departments had to change their policies and be inclusive of all faiths. For example, I have participated in the amendment of many government laws and policies in order to open space for the inclusion of ATR. Although it was not easy, at least there was a change in the following areas:

- policy on religion in schools

- religious broadcasting by the South African Broadcasting Corporation

- Department of Defence and Military Veterans

- correctional services

- South African Police services

- arts and culture

- Home Affairs, and many other areas.

Ever since liberation ATR has participated in almost all interfaith prayers including government activities, moral regeneration movements, climate change ceremonies, prayers against the abuse of women and children and many more. Praying during the activities mentioned is not new to ATR communities, the only difference being that they were done in local sacred places. They are now inclusive of other faiths which, in the past, distanced themselves. Some activities are new, like the inauguration of the president of the country; ATR was represented there (see below). Praying for rain during drought, for instance, is something that is organised by the traditional leadership in communities that are always made up of different groups, which are either clans or ethnic groups but are invariably inclusive. Promotion of morality is a part of each activity, whether it is a clan ritual performance or a societal ritual.

There are now several other occasions when interfaith prayers play a crucial role. These may be fixed yearly events which are political in origin, like celebrations for Freedom Day (April), Youth Day (June), Women's Month (August), and Heritage Month (September). In all these politically related celebrations, all faiths are invited.

There are also special prayers organised mostly by government in response to certain crises, like drought, the need for moral regeneration or the abuse of women and children. Although ATR is invited to these activities, it sometimes feels as if the invitation is only so that the public can see the occasion as inclusive. ATR will be given just a few minutes while other religions such as Christianity are given much more time.

As one of the tenets of ATR is a communal way of life and it is believed that no one lives alone, we say, '*Umntu ngumntu ngabantu*': an individual is an individual because of other people. This belief means that ATR practitioners are at ease in working with other people irrespective of their places of origin. Praying together does not imply that an individual must affirm other faiths' doctrines that may appear to demean or negate one's own core commitments, but rather it indicates that there is one humanity and also shows that diversity is respected. Although ATR believes that each prayer must always first thank the Divine, it is expected that prayer must also address other issues that may affect Creation, such as peace and harmony, a communal way of life and respect for life. Below are prayers offered together with those of other faiths during the inauguration of former president Thabo Mbeki on 27 May 2004 at the Union Buildings in Pretoria. The country was also celebrating ten years of democracy.

## PRAYERS

- Today every individual in South Africa is celebrating freedom equally, all races and religions without discrimination. Camagu! This is my prayer.

- With the will and power of our Creator, Qamata, we believe that you have sent the ancestors to ensure that this freedom is witnessed and forever written in the history books of the world; the chains that were binding African Traditional Religion have been broken, the religion of our forebears, the religion that we are still practising today, the same religion that was discriminated against by the oppressive governments of the past, today its dignity has returned. Now we can truly say that the darkness has subsided and the light has come forth. That is an example of true freedom.

- We ask you, Qamata, to protect the president and those around him, give them the strength to free this nation and not to break their oaths. Give them the strength to motivate those who are still struggling to succeed, take them out of poverty so that they can make something fruitful of their lives. I am invoking and praying and I say let there be peace and happiness!

- We also call on all those ancestors who bled and lost their lives for this freedom that we are now celebrating. We say let their 'bones' shake and revolve and fix all that needs to be fixed, we know all those heroes are here in spirit celebrating with us today. (Mndende 2006, p.57)

- Extract from the prayer to end the abuse of women and children:

  - Camagwini! We plead with you, Qamata, to help with destroying this scaring escalation, to help with this new battle which is women and children's abuse. All these cowards, those who attack and rape women and children should be removed.

- They are cowards because they attack innocent lives of those who cannot defend themselves.

- We also ask you Qamata, our Creator, to touch and change the hearts of the evil men who have abducted hundreds of girls; they must think of the consequences and what they will do when they stand in front of you and their ancestors.

- They must be reminded of the way they have embarrassed the ancestors of the Black Nation and how they have angered the Creator.

- We say to them, go back to your roots and your identity. (Mndende 2006)

To conclude, interfaith prayers from an ATR perspective do not only concern the specific faith but also the needs of all humanity, for we believe that we are created by one God, the differences are the variety of ways to that Being.

## REFERENCES

Bolaji, I. (1973) *African Traditional Religion: A Definition.* London: Orbis Books.

Constitution of the Republic of South Africa (1996) Pretoria.

Dopamu, P.A. (1991) 'Towards understanding African Traditional Religion.' In E. Uka (ed.), *Readings in African Traditional Religion.* New York: Peter Lung.

Du Toit, C. (2006) 'Secular spirituality versus secular dualism: Towards post-secular holism as model for a natural theology.' In C. Du Toit and C. Mayson (ed.), *Secular Spirituality as a Contextual Critique of Religion.* University of South Africa, Pretoria: Research Institute for Theology and Religion.

Mndende, N. (2006) *Umthonyama.* Dutywa: Icamagu Institute.

# 2

# Joint Worship Ceremonies of Africanists and Christians in the Kingdom of Swaziland

Hebron L. Ndlovu

## INTRODUCTION

This chapter focuses on four national ceremonies in the Kingdom of Swaziland in which many adherents of African Religion and of Christianity – led by the Swazi sacred monarchy (*iNgwenyama* or the Lion and *iNdlovukazi* or the She Elephant) – worship God together. The four ceremonies are: (1) *Ncwala* or first fruits ceremony and kingship ritual, (2) *Buganu* or Marula Wine Festival, (3) *IGudi* or Good Friday Ceremony, and (4) Beginning of Year and End of Year Christian services.

I contend that the active involvement in these ceremonies of *iNgwenyama*, *iNdlovukazi* and of many Swazi people demonstrates their simultaneous commitment to the African Religion and the Christian faith. I also argue that praying and worshipping together by adherents of African Religion and Christianity signifies the emergence of a new pattern of interfaith relations between Christianity and African Religion wherein adherents of the two distinct religious traditions strive for mutual convergence and partnership, instead of confrontation and hostility as has been the case in yesteryears.

## PERSPECTIVE AND CONCEPTUAL FRAMEWORK

I am a bona fide Swazi national and an ecumenical theologian. I follow the pluralist paradigm of interfaith relations that posits the view that 'no one [religious] tradition can comprehend the fullness of ultimate truth' (Race, Kenney and Rao 2005, p.14), and hence that followers of the different religions of the world need to talk to one another, so as to share their differing but complementary visions of transcendent truth with one another. In agreement with this way of thinking, I welcome the pattern of joint worshipping of God through ceremonies of African Religion and Christianity in Swaziland. This pattern challenges Africanists and Christians to liberate themselves from what Alan Race calls 'the religious temptation to idolatry, that is, treating our thought-forms as though they somehow captured the lasting truth about the divine' (2014, p.7).

In addition, I follow the pluralist model of interfaith religions because it is consistent with the indigenous African social teaching of *Buntfu/Ubuntu/Botho* or humanness, which holds the view that the ideal person is one who relates well with others and embodies virtues and values such as kindness, fairness, mutual respect and harmonious living with other people, regardless of their status, race, ethnicity or religious affiliation (Teffo 1995).

## CO-EXISTENCE AND RELATIONS BETWEEN AFRICAN RELIGION AND CHRISTIANITY IN SUB-SAHARAN AFRICA

Many analysts of contemporary Africa observe that, in much of sub-Saharan Africa, (1) the Christian religion co-exists with indigenous African Religion; and (2) most Africans identify themselves as Christian while they also uphold fundamental doctrines and practices of African Religion (Maluleke 2010; Ndlovu 2014b; Olupona 2014). This reality is somewhat inevitable because African Religion is typically a lived religious tradition that is intertwined with the dynamic cultures, history and politics of African peoples.

Over the years, relations between Christianity and African Religion in contemporary African society have been complicated. Whereas adherents of African Religion have generally welcomed followers of diverse Christian denominations, attitudes of African Christians towards African Religion have been inconsistent. These attitudes have assumed three typical forms. First, most Christians belonging to African Indigenous Churches tend to affirm indigenous African beliefs and practices such as ancestral veneration and the reality of witchcraft, unashamedly. Second, most Christians belonging to former mission churches of the ecumenical type tend to recognize the validity of African Religion while privileging the Christian faith as superior to it. Third, most Christians belonging to conservative evangelical and Pentecostal churches tend to belittle and defame African Religion while they appropriate its metaphors and worldview with regard to the primacy of the invisible spirit world and life-affirmation.

In the Kingdom of Swaziland, however, the most notable relationship between Christianity and African Religion at public level is that of accommodation and complementarity. Let me now give brief descriptions of Christian and indigenous African ceremonies that reflect this pattern of complementarity and mutual understanding between Christians and Africanists in Swaziland. I preface this with an outline of the historical and cultural context of Swazi society.

## THE KINGDOM OF SWAZILAND: HISTORICAL, CULTURAL AND RELIGIOUS LANDSCAPE

Swaziland is the only country in sub-Saharan Africa that is ruled by a sacred monarchy that wields real power. With an estimated population of 1.3 million, the country is ruled by the *Ngwenyama* and the *Ndlovukazi* who are regarded by the nation as the undisputed symbols and custodians of Swazi culture. The Constitution of the Kingdom of Swaziland (Swaziland Government 2005, p.15) declares that the Swazi people believe that 'it is necessary to blend the good institutions of traditional law and custom with those of an open and democratic society so as to promote transparency and the social and cultural development of our nation'.

Some of the indigenous institutions that have been retained and blended with modernity in Swaziland include Swazi Religion and its dominant rituals, such as the *Ncwala,* or ritual of sacred kingship, and *Umhlanga*, or Reed Dance. In recent times two extra indigenous rituals have been revitalized and retained, namely the *Butimba* or the Hunting Festival, and *Buganu* or Marula Wine Festival (Ndlovu 2014a).

Despite their attachment to African culture and religion, the Swazi dual monarchs welcomed European and American missionaries into the country and permitted them to evangelize freely among the Swazi during the colonial era (1903–1968) and in post-independence Swaziland. Today, with an estimated following of 66 per cent, Christianity is the traditional faith for the majority of Swazi belonging to all social classes and groups. But while they commended Christianity to the Swazi, most of whom converted, the *Ngwenyama* and *Ndlovukazi* resisted formal conversion. They have retained the roles of high priest and priestess of the Swazi Religion.

Apart from Christianity and Swazi Religion, the Kingdom of Swaziland is home to a small number of Muslims and members of the Bahá'í faith (Ndlovu 2014b).

## NATIONAL CEREMONIES THAT CELEBRATE CONVERGENCE OF AFRICAN TRADITIONAL RELIGION AND CHRISTIANITY

### Ncwala ceremony

The *Ncwala* is held in November/December to celebrate the first fruits of summer harvest and sacred kingship.[1] During the *Ncwala* the nation requests God – through the national ancestors – to bless the *Ngwenyama* and the nation. All Swazi are expected to participate in the ceremony, wearing their indigenous *Ncwala* attire. Nonparticipation in the *Ncwala* without a valid reason is seen as some form of civil disobedience and denunciation of fundamental Swazi values and beliefs (Ndlovu 2011).

But, until the post-independence period, Christians belonging to mission churches had been forbidden to participate in the *Ncwala*. Today, more and more Christians are seen participating in the ceremony. At the end of the 2015 *Ncwala* ceremony, the *Ngwenyama* (King Mwati III), in his address to the nation, commended all the participants at the ceremony, including the *Lutsango* (or Women's Regiment), *iNgabisa* (or Maiden's Regiment) and *Libutfo Labokhololo* (or Pastor's Regiment), for participating in the ceremony. He concluded his speech by beseeching the ancestors and God to bless the participants and the entire Swazi nation.

---

1   The word *iNcwala* is a proper name for the first fruit/kingship ceremony. The singular phoneme 'i' means 'the'. Hence one cannot write 'the *iNcwala*' since that sounds tautological. Instead one has to drop the 'i' and say 'the *Ncwala*'.

The same rule applies to the other proper nouns such as *iNgwenyama* (the king) and *iNdlovukazi* (the queen mother). One can write of the *Ngwenyama* and the *Ndlovukazi*. But one cannot write of the *iNgwenyama* and the *iNdlovukazi*.

## *Buganu* festival

The *Buganu* ceremony is a national marula wine festival that is held in February/March in honour of the *Ndlovukazi* at her rural residences situated at Buhleni and Hlane, in the north-east of Swaziland. The ceremony celebrates motherhood and the gift of life through the marula fruit harvest. During the festival, *Lutsango* (the regiment of all adult Swazi mothers) brings along large quantities (at least twenty litres each) of fresh wine made from wild marula fruit. There are three main standardized activities and performances of the *Buganu* festival, namely: (1) feasting and drinking, (2) song and dance, (3) brief speeches by the *Ndlovukazi* and the *Ngwenyama*.

The speeches by the dual monarchs typically begin with the *Ndlovukazi*'s address. The *Ndlovukazi* normally enjoins women to continue serving the nation as pillars of Swazi families. She also encourages women to embark on commercial enterprises, and to address developmental critical issues affecting women such as the HIV pandemic, marriage counselling, innovations in horticulture and commercial ventures. The *Ngwenyama*'s address at the *Buganu* festival is normally light-hearted and simple. He usually begins by thanking *Mvelinchanti* (God) and the ancestors for good rains and a bountiful fruit harvest. He also enjoins the Swazi nation to take pride in its cultural traditions and encourages women to address developmental issues.

## *IGudi* or Good Friday ceremony

*IGudi* or Good Friday ceremony is a national ceremony in which Christians celebrate Easter with the *Ngwenyama*, the *Ndlovukazi*, *Emakhosikati* (the queens), royalty, politicians and the nation at large. The ceremony takes place at three main venues, namely: (1) on Easter Friday at the National Church, situated next to the residence of the *Ndlovukazi*, (2) on Easter Saturday at Lozitha Palace, the official residence of the *Ngwenyama*, (3) on Easter Sunday at Somhlolo National Stadium. On Saturday the *Ngwenyama* hosts the church leaders. On Sunday, the main day, the *Ngwenyama* hosts the Christians (Ndlovu 2007).

Her Majesty *iNdlovukazi* at the Swazi National Church on Good Friday 2016

The King of Swaziland on Easter Sunday 2011

In 2015 the *Ngwenyama* said, in part:

> I greet you in the name of Jesus. Brethren I am delighted that
> we are gathered here to celebrate the death and resurrection
> of our Lord Jesus Christ. Jesus died so that you and I should
> be cleansed from our sins; so that the whole world can be
> cleansed from its own sins. (Ndlovu 2015)

In a similar vein the *Ndlovukazi*, who is culturally the custodian of all national ceremonies, declared 'We are a monarchy that loves Jesus' (Ndlovu 2015).

The *Ngwenyama* and the *Ndlovukazi* have not renounced African Religion and are unlikely to do so. On the contrary, both monarchs always attend the ceremony dressed in the full traditional regalia of sacred kingship, which includes its sacred symbols such as the mystical rod of kingship that can only be carried by the *Ngwenyama* and the mystical crown of queen motherhood worn only by the *Ndlovukazi*.

## Beginning of Year/End of Year Christian services

These are new standardized annual ceremonies that are held in January/February and November/December at Lozitha Palace. Held immediately after the annual *Ncwala* ceremony, the Beginning of Year Christian service is a petitioning-cum-thanksgiving ceremony hosted by the *Ngwenyama* in which selected church leaders are invited to proclaim the Gospel of Jesus Christ to the sacred monarchy, royalty, political leaders and Christians from various Christian denominations. The selected clergy preach from the Bible guided by the given theme of the day. The theme of this year's ceremony (2017) was 'God supplies all our needs according to his riches'. The stated objective of the ceremony, however, is to invoke God's guidance and blessings in the beginning of the year.

The End of Year Christian service is normally held in November/December before the beginning of the annual *Ncwala* ceremony. As in the case of the Beginning of Year Christian service, during this thanksgiving service selected church leaders are invited to preach from the Bible to the sacred monarchy, royalty, political leaders and Christians from various Christian denominations.

Significantly, the climax of both Christian ceremonies is sermons given by the *Ndlovukazi* and the *Ngwenyama*, who normally preach after all the selected clergy have preached. The regal sermons are culturally crucial because both the *Ngwenyama* and the *Ndlovukazi* are recognised as moral and spiritual leaders of the nation. In January 2017, for example, the *Ngwenyama* thanked all church leaders, musicians, visitors and special guests for gracing the ceremony with their attendance. Among other things, the *Ngwenyama* further urged the nation to strive to live by Christian faith under Jesus's guidance. He said:

It is gratifying that Swazi have not departed from the instruction of King Somhlolo that the Swazi must take the scroll [Bible] and avoid the coin.

We must hunger for Jesus in the same way that we hunger for food. We are here to ask Jesus to walk with us. If God is on our side we shall prosper. We must follow after God. (Ndlovu 2017)

## CONTINUING CONTROVERSY

It might be tempting to dismiss the foregoing accounts of interfaith relations between African Religion and Christianity in the Kingdom of Swaziland as a classic example of civil religion or the politicization of African culture and religion by unscrupulous political elites. Indeed, in the Kingdom of Swaziland, one of the most controversial subjects among Swazi Christians is the relationship between Christianity and certain aspects of Swazi culture and religion that are seen as radically opposed to Christian faith and practice. For example, most, if not all, evangelical churches see indigenous African beliefs and practices such as ancestral veneration, consultation of diviners and herbalists, participation in national royal rituals, polygyny and mourning customs and taboos as problematic and un-Christian.

In the most recent times, for example, one vocal Swazi clergyman belonging to a popular charismatic church has openly denounced the Swazi annual *Ncwala* ceremony as evil. This unprovoked act elicited different reactions from the Christian fraternity, with a few clergy from charismatic churches endorsing it, while leaders of African Initiated Churches and Swazi Religion condemned it in no uncertain terms.

However, while this controversy continues, and while it may take various directions, the fact that African Religion is a social reality in African society and in African Christian spirituality cannot be denied. Here in Swaziland is a home-grown model for integrating African Religion and Christianity in contemporary African society and for praying and worshipping together. It must be recalled that in the daily lives of many Africans, which include health and wellbeing, birth rites, puberty and marriage ceremonies, death and burial rites, the integration of African Religion and Christianity goes on unabated, albeit with tensions here and there.

## REFERENCES

Maluleke, T. (2010) 'Of Africanised bees and Africanised churches: Ten theses on African Christianity.' *Missionalia 3*, 369–380.

Ndlovu, H. (2007) 'The dual Swazi monarchy: Its religio-cultural genius.' *BOLESWA Journal of Theology, Religion and Philosophy 1*, 3, 116–134.

Ndlovu, H. (2011) 'Swazi religion and the environment: The case of Incwala.' *BOLESWA Journal of Theology, Religion and Philosophy 3*, 3, 83–99.

Ndlovu, H. (2014a) 'Christian identity amid African religion: *Buganu* ceremony and the construction of multiple religious identities in Swaziland.' In H. Kroesbergen (ed.) *Christian Identity and Justice in a Globalized World from a Southern African Perspective.* Wellington, South Africa: Christian Literature Fund.

Ndlovu, H. (2014b) 'Swaziland.' In T. Riggs (ed.) *Worldmark Encyclopedia of Religious Practices*, 2nd edn, vol. 4. Farmington, MI: Gale.

Ndlovu, H.L. (2015) Speech given at Somhlolo National Stadium, Swaziland on Easter Sunday 5 April.

Ndlovu, H.L. (2017) Speech given at Lozitha Palace, Swaziland on Saturday 28 January.

Olupona, J.K. (2014) 'African Traditional Religion.' In T. Riggs (ed.) *Worldmark Encyclopedia of Religious Practices*, 2nd edn, vol. 1. Farmington, MI: Gale.

Race, A. (2014) 'Editors' page: Need for critical thinking.' *Interreligious Insight 12*, 1, 6–7.

Race, A., Kenney, J. and Rao, S. (2005) 'Interreligious Insight paradigm: An invitation.' *Interreligious Insight 3*, 1, 8–19.

Swaziland Government (2005) *The Constitution of the Kingdom of Swaziland.* Swaziland: Mbabane.

Teffo, L. (1995) 'The other in African experience.' Inaugural Address: University of the North, South Africa.

# Reflection

## The Editors

The previous chapter was on Hinduism; now we encounter another ancient religion, yet one which has developed in a very different context. It shares with Hinduism a history of difficulties when existing alongside some other religions and yet has reached a position where it can appreciate – and indeed contribute to – interfaith worship and prayer.

As with any religion, there is a degree to which it is improper to comment, as an outsider, on African Traditional Religion (ATR). Yet this is especially true here, because ATR (in common with some other indigenous religions such as Shinto) is so varied, so embedded in the culture – in this case of sub-Saharan Africa – and so oral in its transmission, that it stands out as especially impervious to the kind of academic and other generalisations which are often made about religion. As our task is to look in particular at the subject of interfaith worship and prayer, perhaps we may escape at least some of the pitfalls.

The first comment concerns anger as expressed in Nokuzola Mndende's contribution. Religions often have tragically painful pasts in their relations with each other; here resentment is recent and deeply felt. ATR has been dismissed as primitive and as mere culture by missionaries who have brought in another religion (usually Christianity or Islam), often unaware of their own imported cultural assumptions. Those assumptions involve particular ways of perceiving the Divine and the world, conditioned by home social contexts from which, of course, no religion can escape. The feelings of resentment can, however, be harnessed to prayer and worship and their frank expression can both protect participants from the banality which is such a common danger in religion and lead to closer understanding and love between religions. Honesty about the past must be a benefit, so long as it does not dominate creative relations between religions. South African religious history, like that of many other countries, is complex and made the more so by the fact that the origin of apartheid and its eventual abolition were both bound up with the activities of particular Christian religious groups. In other words, arrogance and exclusivism have been a part of that history, although it is right also to recognise that some Christians were prominent in opposition to apartheid.

The matter of dual allegiance is raised favourably by Hebron L. Ndlovu, somewhat in the manner in which it is referred to by Shinto contributors in Chapter 9 and indeed (in relation to religious history) in Chapter 2. It is a theme of numerous writers on African Religion both today and in the past, a lively and splendidly nonacademic example being Graham Greene's account of his travels in Liberia in the 1930s: *Journey without Maps* (2006 [1936]). What is seen as impossible by exclusivists is practised happily by many, bringing new and unexpected life to worship and prayer. Where would African Religion be without dance? Much prayer and worship could benefit from dance!

Nobody is an island. Everybody is immersed in a spirit/spiritual world that involves an intimate relationship with nature, with the seasons, with rites of passage and with other family ties. This last link, in the form of ancestors, provides a route to the Divine and also a consciousness of solidarity both with the past and with the future. Forebears and descendants are integral to the significance of religious practice. This collectivism can provide valuable insights to worship and prayer, both of which can suffer from individual fragmentation and often do.

All the themes mentioned in the previous paragraph may contribute to an enhanced understanding of God as Creator. The creation in all its different senses provides common ground for worship and prayer, for it not only sees the world as having divine origins, but also respects the natural world and believes that care for that world is the duty of all. That belief has political consequences, for many secular forces and some religious ones (where religion is exclusivist and individualistic) do not have a care for nature and somehow manage to see the greed of the present as having precedence over the needs of future generations. A religion which gives such significance to forebears and descendants, and which is so immersed in its rituals in the natural world with its seasons and its crops, is going to be acutely conscious of the cavalier manner in which many treat the environment. If that brings religion onto a collision course with political policy, it is the policy which must alter.

Both contributors put emphasis on collective state occasions. Institutional exclusion was resented and civic and other inclusion is greatly valued. That view can again be linked to the fact that ATR is seen as a collective matter, something which is engrained in the culture and therefore not a matter of personal chance and choice. Of course public events can be used in order to manipulate people or to consolidate power, but there is nevertheless an important part that religion can play in expressing common values in a form to which different religions bring their own special insights.

## REFERENCE

Greene, G. (2006 [1936]) *Journey without Maps*. London: Vintage.

Chapter 5

# JUDAISM

## 1

## But Where Should We Pray?

Aaron Rosen

I had an unusual photographer at my bar mitzvah ceremony. My Jewish relatives from Chicago and Washington, DC, who had flown to Bangor, Maine, were surprised to see Sister Mary Norberta, clad in her habit, documenting the most formative moment in my life as a Jew. Sister Mary was actually in the majority. For many attendees, this was the one and only time they would observe a Jewish worship service. The space itself also represented a comingling of traditions. At the time, Congregation Beth El, a recently formed Reform community, worshipped in a Unitarian Universalist building, periodically transforming it into a synagogue. All liturgical furnishings were set on wheels, ready to be pushed into position. Years later, reading George Steiner's description of diasporic life – 'Like a snail… the Jew has carried the house of the text on his back' (Steiner 1998, p.309) – I would think back to this rolling *aron kodesh*. My concept of Jewish space has thus always been adaptable. Even before I was able to formulate the insight theologically, I intuitively sensed that Jewishness could be performed anywhere, alongside anyone, without compromising its authenticity. A space need not be exclusively Jewish to be genuinely Jewish.

While other chapters in this volume focus upon *when* or *how* people of different faiths might pray together, I am particularly interested in exploring *where* we might pray. Rather than treating the space in which ecumenical prayer occurs as incidental or supplemental to the experience of worshippers, I believe that it is a formative, even primary factor for participants. No space, after all, is ever neutral, especially when it comes to religion. Indeed, even the most inoffensive airport chapels – however enveloped in ecru – still frame worship in specific ways. Building upon my own experiences as a Reform Jew, in this chapter I want to explore how it is that three different settings – private, public, and sacred – can shape different possibilities for Jews and non-Jews to pray together.

## PRIVATE SPACE

Much as synagogue observances punctuate and enrich Jewish life, it is the home which anchors Jewish existence. But can a home be fully Jewish when it is shared by a Jew and non-Jew? I think so. My wife Carolyn is a priest in the Episcopal Diocese of Montana, and trained previously in the Church of England at Cambridge. From Cambridge to Billings, we have always wagered on the chimeric capacity of our home to be as Jewish and as Christian as it needs to be for each of us through our different liturgical years.

At no time of the year do we expect more theological flexibility from our home, and our own religious imaginations, than during Passover, especially when it coincides with Holy Week. When we celebrate seder in our home, we consider it to be a Jewish house, both for ourselves and for our guests, who are always a mix of Jews and non-Jews. During the seder, we recite the words of *HaLachma Anya* over the *matzot*:

> This is the bread of affliction that our ancestors ate in the land of Egypt. Let all who are hungry come and eat. Let all who are in need come and celebrate Passover. This year we are here. Next year in the land of Israel. Now we are slaves. Next year may we be free.

While this message of liberation, charity, and equality is fundamentally and fittingly universal, the meal remains a Passover feast, expressing a hope for redemption inflected by centuries of identifiably Jewish dreams and experiences. Judaism is thus entitled to the first word on this evening, though not necessarily the last.

Non-Jews celebrating seder with us are doubly guests, welcomed both into a home and into a religion; a position of honor but also responsibility. This sense of responsibility is important, especially at a time when seder celebrations are increasingly popular among Christians. On the positive side, this passion for Passover carries significant potential for interfaith dialogue. However, there are reasons to be cautious. For some Christians, the primary attraction of the seder lies in discovering what the Last Supper was 'really like.' There is profound paschal imagery in the Eucharist, to be sure, but this is anachronistic since the haggadah only developed many centuries after Jesus's death. Even more worrying, when Judaism is valued principally for the light it sheds on Christianity, supersessionism reigns.

So if non-Jews cannot learn as much about their own religion from Passover as they might hope, what *can* they learn? They can learn about Judaism: real, living, changing, contemporary Jewish life. There is a tendency in interfaith relations to assume that religious groups are monolithic. It is important to remember that there are many ways of celebrating Passover. In our home, for instance, we place Miriam's cup alongside Elijah's to symbolize women's contributions to the faith, and include an orange on the seder plate to honor the struggle for inclusion by LGBTQ individuals. Above all, the seder presents non-Jews with an opportunity to ask questions. A good guest at Passover questions, laughs, and perhaps even argues. We are often told that it is bad manners to talk religion or politics over dinner. But debating during Pesach is not disrespectful to Jewish tradition, it *is* Jewish tradition. Open, honest discussion leads to liberation. In celebrating Passover, Jews and non-Jews alike can talk our hopes for humanity into reality: 'Now we are slaves. Next year may we be free.'

## PUBLIC SPACE

We have looked at an example of ecumenism in the home. But what happens when we open the door? The great nineteenth-century poet Yehudah Leib Gordon famously enjoined his Eastern European countrymen: 'Be a man in the streets and a Jew at home.'[1] In the twenty-first century, not only have Jews grown accustomed to displaying and exploring their identities in public, so too have other minorities. What might it mean for Jews, Muslims, and others to pray together 'in the streets'? Over the past several years, I have been

---

1    Yehudah Leib Gordon (1863) *'Hakitsah 'ami'* (Awake My People!).

exploring this and related questions through a public arts project called Stations of the Cross, held during Lent in London in 2016, Washington, DC in 2017, and New York in 2018, with Amsterdam and Detroit exhibitions scheduled for future years.[2]

During Lent many Christians follow a devotional practice in which they retrace the final 14 episodes (Stations) of Jesus's final journey through Jerusalem, from condemnation to crucifixion and entombment. According to Catholic tradition, by praying in front of the Stations – usually arranged around the aisles of a church – worshippers in effect walk the *via dolorosa* in Jerusalem, accruing the same spiritual rewards as if they were processing through the holy city itself. Thus, by their very nature, the Stations of the Cross constitute a sort of virtual pilgrimage. In the Stations project, my collaborators and I set out to utilize twenty-first-century technology to accentuate this virtual experience in ways that were innovative yet also traditional. Using a custom-built smartphone app, *Alight: Art and the Sacred*, we charted our own *via dolorosa* through the streets of London, allowing visitors to trace their route via GPS while listening to podcasts from artists, clergy, and academics. Rather than imposing a spiritual topography on the city, we used technology to render visible the religious significance that the metropolis already possessed.

While Christian tradition provided the framework for the exhibition, we aimed to tell a story that resonated across and between faiths. To visualize London as a 'new Jerusalem' for the twenty-first century offered an opportunity to imagine both London *and* Jerusalem as the best versions of themselves, places in which people from different faiths could pray together peacefully. This vision came together poignantly in two works dedicated to the plight of Syrian refugees. In *Sea of Colour* (2016), commemorating the tenth station, when Jesus is stripped of his garments, the Turkish artist Güler Ates worked with volunteers to weave a tapestry of children's clothes which she hung in the Salvation Army International Headquarters. At St. Stephen Walbrook Church, Michael Takeo Magruder created *Lamentation for the Forsaken* (2016) for the thirteenth station, in which Jesus is taken down from the cross. In Magruder's digital sculpture, images of refugees gradually emerge and fade from the

2    For more information on the Stations exhibit in London, see www.artstations.org.

surface of a tomb-like structure, trading places (or indeed faces) with the figure of Christ from the Shroud of Turin.

Güler Ates, *Sea of Colour*, 2016 (Salvation Army International Headquarters, London)
Photograph credit: Mazur/CCN/Catholic Bishops' Conference England & Wales.
Art: copyright Güler Ates

The Stations exhibition culminated during Holy Week with a pilgrimage, in which participants from various faiths stopped at both Ates's and Magruder's pieces. I offered reflections at each location, followed by prayers from Cardinal Vincent Nichols and the Bishop of London, Richard Chartres. As a Jew, I was acutely aware that my role in the pilgrimage (not to mention the exhibition at large) could be easily misread, whether as a disavowal of Jewish tradition, a capitulation to Christian claims of universalism, or an appropriation of tragedies unfolding in the Muslim world. I tried to keep in mind something akin to what I expect from my seder guests. Even as I hosted this exhibition, I viewed myself as a guest, participating in a religious tradition that was not my own, praying for victims whose experiences I could barely fathom. Rather than diluting or obscuring my sense of Jewish identity, curating the Stations of the Cross sharpened and strengthened my Judaism. In a way that would have been inconceivable to my ancestors, I found it possible not only to be a Jew 'in the streets' but to walk the *via dolorosa*.

## SACRED SPACE

I began this chapter by sharing my experiences growing up, attending a synagogue which met inside a Unitarian Universalist building. When Congregation Beth El finally raised enough funds to acquire its own building, it settled upon a structure that had previously been a Baptist church. Beth El's journey is not unique. When seeking a sacred space, many Jewish congregations – especially in America – have looked to existing religious structures, usually churches. The process has also worked in the other direction. As American Jews left urban centers for the suburbs in the latter half of the twentieth century, for example, many former synagogues in cities like Detroit and Chicago became homes for predominantly African American congregations. Tracing the intersecting destinies of congregations, especially among minority communities, has the potential to uncover powerful resonances, which might be tapped by ecumenical worship. But what about building such interconnections into sacred spaces from the start? I want to look briefly at two projects currently in development – one in Germany, the other in England – which are taking innovative approaches to multifaith worship, and which could provide trajectories for the future.

In Berlin, the House of One is currently raising funds for construction of a building on Museum Island in the city center. After an international competition, the commission was awarded to the German firm Kuehn Malvezzi in 2012 for a building which will house a fully functional church, synagogue, and mosque. As the architect Wilfried Kuehn explains, each of these sanctuaries connect to a 'space with a dome and a centralized plan, higher than the three surrounding houses of prayer...acting as a threshold to the sacred spaces' (Kuehn 2015, p.236). The commission arose from a redevelopment plan for St. Petri's Church, which was severely damaged during World War II, and then subsequently razed by East German authorities. In the early twenty-first century, when archaeological excavations revealed remnants of the medieval church, a committee was formed to resurrect the church. When concerns arose about the ability to sustain a sizeable Protestant community in this area, the remit for the site began to evolve into a multifaith space. Complicating the narrative of Christian tolerance, whereby churches lend facilities to other faiths as a gesture of benevolence – implicitly signifying their hegemony – in this instance diversity represented a strategy for survival and growth. For the local Jewish community, meanwhile, the project has offered a welcome opportunity to participate in the shaping of a Jewish presence in the city, alongside the absence signified by Daniel Libeskind's Berlin Jewish Museum and Peter Eisenman's Memorial to the Murdered Jews of Europe.

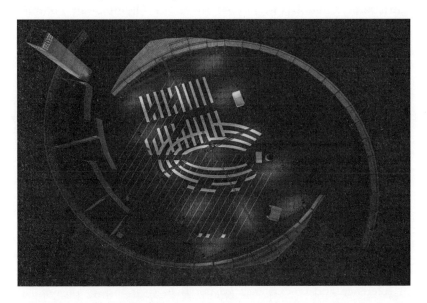

Dan Leon, Matthew Lloyd, and Shahed Saleem, Friday–Saturday–Sunday, visualization of ongoing project

Design: copyright the architects: Dan Leon, Matthew Lloyd, and Shahed Saleem

In contrast to the Berlin team, British architects Dan Leon, Matthew Lloyd, and Shahed Saleem drafted their own brief. Each runs their own firm in London, and they have all worked on commissions for religious communities in their respective faiths: Judaism, Christianity, and Islam. During the 2012 Olympics in London, when prayer spaces were being constructed in the athletes' village, they recognized a need for flexible spaces that could be easily adaptable to the needs of diverse communities like those of East London. Unlike the House of One, which allows for simultaneous worship at connected but separate sanctuaries, Friday–Saturday–Sunday operates on a model of shared space utilized in different ways at different times. It is designed to function as a mosque on Fridays, a synagogue on Saturdays, and a church on Sundays, while constituting a communal space during the weekdays.

For the London architects, unity exists less in any single feature of the space than the hospitality involved in cyclically receiving and returning the space to others. 'The underlying idea of our project,' the architects write, 'is not that differences should be disregarded, or that all faiths are or should be one. It is rather that these three faiths have an entwined and symbiotic series of relationships, and a history of tolerance and co-existence greater than their history of conflict' (Rosen 2015, p.235). While the Berlin project responds to the needs of an existing community, Friday–Saturday–Sunday endeavors to generate – or discover – communities drawn to its vision of exchange and adaptability. From a Jewish perspective, it will be especially interesting to see how intra-faith relations determine possibilities for interfaith exchange. While Leon comes from an Orthodox community, for instance, it may be that the vision of ecumenism embodied by this project will appeal more to progressive Jews. As a member of the project's steering committee, I am as intrigued by the differing responses to the project *within* communities as between them.

## CONCLUSION

Revealingly, the Berlin and London projects have already succeeded in generating dialogue, demonstrating a growing thirst for thinking about how people of different faiths might pray together. To me, this suggests an important lesson: ecumenism thrives on imagination. Whether in domestic, public, or sacred spaces, interfaith worship demands – as I have observed in this chapter – a creative capacity to make room for others. Within Jewish tradition, we might call to mind the concept of *tzimtzum*, by which God contracted his presence in order to provide space for creation to unfold. When we speak about interfaith prayer we usually begin by talking about what we must generate and develop, whether liturgically, theologically, or politically. Before anything else, however, we must create *space*.

## REFERENCES

Kuehn, W. (2015) 'Meditations on religion, art, and the city.' In A. Rosen (ed.) *Religion and Art in the Heart of Modern Manhattan: St. Peter's Church and the Louise Nevelson Chapel*. Farnham: Ashgate.

Rosen, A. (2015) *Art and Religion in the 21st Century*. London: Thames & Hudson.

Steiner, G. (1998) *No Passion Spent: Essays 1978–1995*. New Haven, CT: Yale University Press.

## FURTHER READING

Britton, K.C. (ed.) (2010) *Constructing the Ineffable: Contemporary Sacred Architecture*. New Haven, CT: Yale University Press.

Promey, S. (ed.) (2014) *Sensational Religion: Sensory Cultures in Material Practice*. New Haven, CT: Yale University Press.

Quash, B., Reddaway, C. and Rosen, A. (eds) (2016) *Visualising a Sacred City: London, Art and Religion*. London: I.B. Tauris.

Rosen, A. (2011) 'Emmanuel Levinas and the Hospitality of Images.' *Literature and Theology 25*, 4, 364–378.

Rosen, A. (ed.) (2015) *Religion and Art in the Heart of Modern Manhattan: St. Peter's Church and the Louise Nevelson Chapel*. Farnham: Ashgate.

## 2

# Balancing the Universal and the Particular

Alan Brill

Rabbi Menachem Fruman of Tekoa, who recently passed away, often proclaimed: 'I think that all of theology, all religions, and all words spoken in the world about God spring forth only from the need to explain the simple instinctual human activity called prayer' (Fruman 2015, p.179). All religious people pray. Nevertheless, from my Jewish perspective, prayer has two distinct aspects: a universal activity and a specific required *mitzvah* of reciting the liturgy. From the perspective of traditional practice, therefore, personal prayer does not replace *davening* ('praying' in colloquial Yiddish inflected language) and *davening* does not preclude personal prayer.

## PRACTICE

When I entered the world of interfaith encounter, I entered right from the start at the formal international and institutional level. As a junior participant to those who had been active since the 1960s, I did not have specific views on how to proceed and I tended to follow the example of my senior colleagues. I asked questions and learned the Orthodox denominational guidelines.

My mentor, Rabbi Walter Wurzburger, consistently advised me throughout on procedure. When discussing the guidelines for interfaith prayer, he stated that Rabbi Joseph Soloveitchik told him to recite psalms, because we share them as a means to call to God. Yet, they maintain our distinctiveness since psalms do not count as formal Jewish prayer. For Rabbi Wurzburger, the important element was the preservation of the distinct uniqueness of Jewish liturgy from being compromised theologically. Rabbi Wurzburger (1994) insisted that joint celebrations of either Jewish or Christian liturgies were off limits.

I have seen this in practice in diverse contexts in that the opening prayers of conferences or at special events were either a psalm or a universal prayer. In fact, during a recent visit to a local Catholic seminary, our hosts asked if we wanted to join them for prayer. They quickly added that they were not conducting Mass or reciting any official Catholic prayers, rather, they would be praying with verses from the Hebrew Bible set to music. Our hosts were familiar with the distinction between formal prayers that fulfill our specific distinct religious obligations from universal acts of prayer.

Truly interfaith prayer preserves the distinction between formal prayer and universal acts of prayer, so any Christian–Jewish liturgy should be explicitly supplemental and should never be an attempt at fulfilling either community's obligations to statutory prayer. As Judaism and Christianity remain distinct religions, participation in a joint service is not intended by either side to fulfill the obligation for statutory prayer. For example, a Catholic's participation in a joint service does not fulfill her obligation to attend Mass. It would be inappropriate for a church to have a joint service instead of Sunday Mass or for a synagogue to have a joint service instead of its regular Shabbat service.

However, even when following these guidelines, the actual practice of interfaith prayer is diverse and creates an opening to the other faith. For example, I have witnessed a room of Haredi (Israeli ultra-Orthodox) rabbis, whose parents came from Arabic-speaking lands, sing songs of praise to God in Arabic. They spontaneously broke out into singing Hebrew *baqashot* and Arabic Sufi praises of God, facilitated by the common borrowing of popular Arabic melodies by Sephardi cantors.

I have also seen joint Jewish–Evangelical prayer services performed at Israeli holy sites led by Orthodox rabbis, whose maintenance of the Jewish integrity of the Jewish service was above question. Those concerned with the implications have worked out for themselves an explanation: 'Since the service was led by Jews, in an authentic worship style of Judaism, reciting a series of psalms that include the mandate where the nations are obligated to praise God for what He has done for us' (Wolicki 2015).[3]

In general, interfaith events regularly acknowledge the universal quest for prayer, but avoid specific liturgies. Interfaith participants can ask for God's blessing and help, can praise God in song and celebration, can meditate on God's presence, and, in general, can seek strength to make the world a better place.

---

3    For two other articles from Jews writing in Charismatic Evangelical sources offering perspectives of joint Evangelical–Orthodox prayers, see Berkowitz 2015; Nekrutman 2015.

## A COMMON LIFE OF FAITH AND TOLERANCE

In the United States rabbis are included in political prayer breakfasts. In these cases, the rabbis invoke God and recite psalms, but they do not participate in any of the formal prayers during the service. After the September 11 attack, for example, there were frequent interfaith events attended by clergy of many religions and denominations, including Orthodox rabbis. These interfaith prayers in times of public tragedy are now common. Before elections, rabbis publicly offer various formulations of the traditional prayer to give the government wisdom and good council.

I have also observed the activity of leaving the doors open when each religion engages in formal prayer so that one group can watch and observe the rhythm of another faith's prayer, a form of 'show-and-tell' approach to interfaith encounter. At a large interfaith event sponsored by King Abdullah of Saudi Arabia, some of the Jewish contingent proceeded to use the formal Jewish afternoon prayer in a large prayer quorum in the lobby, to show everyone Jewish prayer. In a different, much smaller interfaith venue, the Jewish, Christian, and Muslim participants prayed at different times to allow members of the other faiths to watch and listen.

I have also attended events where members of other religions participate in Jewish life including that of prayer and blessing. For example, I have been to Shabbat meals on college campuses when the Catholic or Muslim students joined the Orthodox community for the kosher Shabbat meal complete with Kiddush, *zemirot*, and grace after the meal.

Recently, I have begun making the same distinctions between participating in universal prayer and preserving Jewish formal prayer's distinct uniqueness in my work on Jewish–Hindu encounter. I have come to appreciate a chance to meditate or sing together with Hindus while avoiding participating in formal *puja*, the worship of an *Ishwara* (personal representation of a deity). Most public lectures and symposia in a Hindu setting open with universal invocation to wisdom, knowledge, and for our eyes to be illumined.

Finally, one case of interfaith prayer that I have found difficult to navigate is that of the local administrative monsignor at my university; when he performs the grace before meals at public functions, he usually uses an English translation of the first paragraph of the Jewish grace after meals. Clearly, the priest is both sincerely and affirmatively reclaiming the Jewish roots of Christianity and demonstrating openness to the Jewish presence on campus. On the one hand, I am glad that it is a universal prayer that I can affirm because it does not mention Christian theological words or concepts. On the other hand, the use of a blessing that I say every day in a different context makes me feel awkward.

I also witness greater uses of Judaic practices in American Christianity, both Catholic and Evangelical. I have observed the Christian use of the Tallit, Passover seder, and Shofar. I believe that the issue of this coming decade will be to articulate boundaries for Christian appropriations that do not violate the integrity of each faith.

## THEORY

I entered interfaith work after I studied the phenomena of religion, which led to a doctorate in religion and theology. When I read William James, Rudolph Otto, or Émile Durkheim, I had no trouble seeing their portrayal of religion as having deep resonance with the practice of Judaism. There is a universal phenomenon of religion, which includes common practices such as prayer, adoration, ritual, and rites of passage.

Further, when I read the Christian classics that were so dear, at the time, to modern Orthodox Jewish thinkers, the sentiment they described was also reflected in current Jewish thought and practice. The wisdom contained in these works did not need justification. Other religions and their theologies did not appear to be an incomprehensible realm. Judaism assumes that there is wisdom among the gentiles.

While many frame the debate about engaging in interfaith as a zero-sum game, I have never seen it as a binary choice to engage in interfaith prayer or to refrain from it. One does not have to face a false dichotomy of syncretic mixing of traditions or a ban on praying together as a violation of one's tradition. There is both a universal phenomenon of prayer and a particular liturgy for my group. In the Book of Jonah, the protagonist had to be reminded by the prayers of the sailors of this universalism concerning both prayer and moral concern.

To paraphrase Rabbi Soloveitchik, the Jew faces a double confrontation of the universal and the particular. I am not going to blur the lines of my particular commitment with the theology of another faith, but I can share the universal elements of the human phenomena of prayer. Our destinies as faith communities may be divided, but our commonality as humans – soulful humans who pray – is connected.

Alternately, Rabbi Abraham Joshua Heschel wrote that the prerequisite for interfaith is faith. The religious phenomena of faith and prayer are universal, but more importantly, one starts from one's own practice. To continue with Rabbi Heschel's thought, one starts with the teachings of one's own tradition and with a desire for having one's own faith confront others with different commitments. I am not dealing with the broader general meaning of religious destiny and covenant. Instead, we encounter the other and respond.

Observing the diversity of religious life, similar to and different from one's own, teaches us about the broader issues of religious life. In the end, God transforms the self. As the Jewish pietist Bahye ibn Pakuda (eleventh century) wrote in his work, *Duties of the Heart*, in seeking wisdom, we see ourselves anew.

Understanding demands a sense of humility that Judaism endorses in principle, an openness to the wisdom of others. The investigation needs to note both differences and similarities between Judaism and other religions. Only in this way can there be a mutual respect and enrichment for both religions. Faith does not compel us to affirm other traditions, but it does not require us to think that what we already have is all we can know. The encounter produces a more intelligent faith and the diversity may itself be providential.

When we look at another religion, we have to understand that we are not all the same and that we have to respect differences. The quest for common features does not mean that all religions are the same, rather that differences will persist and may emerge in a sharper, more interesting way. Yet at the same time we are not all different from each other and share many commonalities. Even when we look at the commonalities, we have to understand that nothing is identical, so we keep differences large and small in mind.

## WHAT IS THE STARTING POINT FOR ENCOUNTERING OTHER RELIGIONS?

We engage in interreligious encounters not only to clear up misconceptions on both sides, but also to show our sincere and committed endeavor to work with others. To sanctify God's name, we present ourselves to a wider world in a dignified and respectful manner. Interfaith encounter simultaneously cultivates better religious self-understanding and aids in the bettering of relationships with other faiths.

Hospitality, a term stressed by the Jewish thinker Emmanuel Levinas, is openness to new perspectives through leaving one's safe precinct. An important element in approaching other faiths is the need to travel out of one's comfort zone. One actually needs to meet someone of another faith, placing oneself in a situation where one may be confronting new perspectives. One needs to see, meet, talk, and enter the realm of the other.

When looking to another religion, we should not start with an assumption that we are opposites or unable to communicate, in a zero-sum duality, like Elijah's choice on Mount Carmel. We should not assume irreducible differences, rather potential commonality. The preferred method is to let us first know each other and to see the commonalities as well as the universal human elements. Then, and only then, can we grapple with the irreconcilable differences. Even after grappling with the dissimilarities, differences of liturgy can be used to create binary opposites, or drive a wedge, or they can be seen as two alternative paths. We encounter the other as both same and different. Nothing is entirely dissimilar so there is implicit comparison. Opportunities for clarification and distinction abound once we engage the other faiths.

I generally assume that Judaism is a system, as are most religions, in that each works by its own rules. Even when I see a commonality between two religions, I understand the common practice as belonging to two different structures. I can recognize similar practices to my own Judaism and at the same time other practices that are quite different.

Hence, I am deeply uncomfortable with the framing by Rabbi James Diamond (1990), who once wrote an article for the interfaith journal *Cross Currents*, titled 'Liturgical chastity'. He wrote that one should 'understand the act of worship in terms phenomenologically similar to those in which we understand the act of sex…both are private. They flow from the deepest regions of the self. They are connected to how we live out and express as individuals our most fundamental identities' (p.19). If this is so, Diamond writes, then interfaith worship has the character of group sex. Though at first it may seem 'innovative and even exciting' at the end of the day it is 'trivial and inauthentic' (p.19).

The distinction between universal and particular prayer also allows one to preserve group identity, while simultaneously seeking broad inclusion. Prayer often creates and defines a group, and prayer expresses the identity and desire of the community. This is why participation in interfaith or even ecumenical services is uncomfortable for those seeking to adhere to strict particularity in doctrinal interpretations. Interfaith services create broader boundaries of inclusion than these groups are generally comfortable with acknowledging. The retention of the particularity, however, allows one to operate on two planes, similar to distinguishing between Torah and secular studies as two planes of knowledge.

## TRADITIONAL PROBLEMS

What of the traditional Jewish hindrances to such encounter? Is interfaith prayer idolatrous and forbidden? From all the examples of actual practice given at the start of the chapter, it is obviously not completely forbidden. This is why I opened with the actual current practice, then afterwards offered my understanding of the tension of the universal and particular in religion and only now conclude with broadest questions.

Contemporary Orthodox Jews who are engaged in interfaith encounter consider Muslims and Christians to be monotheists to whom traditional prohibitions against idolatry do not apply. The halakhic and theological mechanisms are diverse and complex, but, in practice, observant Jews consider contemporary gentiles as nonidolatrous. Most ultra-Orthodox and Haredi Jews, however, do still view the other faiths as idolatrous and almost never put themselves in situations of interfaith encounter. On the other hand, observant Jews will still not use, look at or offer prayers in a room with Christian iconography; they also will not generally enter churches.

King Solomon asked in his dedication prayer of the completion of the Temple for God to listen to the prayers of everyone who comes to the Temple so that 'all the peoples of the earth may know Thy name, to fear Thee' (I Kings 43). This remains a model for balancing universalism with particularism.

## REFERENCES

Berkowitz, A. (2015) 'Rabbi Shlomo Riskin: Interfaith prayer "bringing us closer" to messianic age.' *Breaking Israel News*, 14 October.

Diamond, J. (1990) 'A response to Lawrence Hoffman: Liturgical chastity.' *CrossCurrents 40*, Spring, 18–21.

Fruman, M. (2015) *My Hasidim Will Laugh from This*. Jerusalem: Amtat Hai Shalom Publishing.

Nekrutman, D. (2015) 'A day to praise: Join Israel in thanking God for his continuous protection.' *Charisma News*, 23 March.

Wolicki, P. (2015) 'When interfaith prayer is NOT a "foreign fire."' *Times of Israel*, 13 September. Accessed on 13 November 2018 at https://blogs.timesofisrael.com/when-interfaith-prayer-is-not-a-foreign-fire.

Wurzburger, W. (1994) 'Scripture and hermeneutics: A Jewish view.' *Immanuel 26–27*, 42–48.

## FURTHER READING

Brill, A. (2010) *Judaism and Other Religions: Models of Understanding.* New York: Palgrave Macmillan.

Brill, A. (2012) *Judaism and World Religions: Christianity, Islam, and Eastern Religions.* New York: Palgrave Macmillan.

Brill, A. (forthcoming) *Rabbi on the Ganges: A Jewish-Hindu Encounter.* Lanham, MD: Lexington Books.

Hoffman, L. (1990) 'Jewish-Christian services: Babel or mixed multitude?' *CrossCurrents 40*, Spring, 5–17, 21.

Resnicoff, A.E. (1987) 'Prayers that hurt: Public prayer in interfaith settings.' *Military Chaplain's Review*; expanded and reprinted in (2009) *Curtana: A Journal for the Study of the Military Chaplaincy 1*, 1, 30–40.

# Reflection

## The Editors

In his contribution to this chapter, Alan Brill discusses the legitimacy of interfaith prayer within the Jewish world from an Orthodox Jewish perspective. Is interfaith prayer idolatrous and forbidden? The answer is no. Yet, in his view, there are limits to the sorts of activities that can legitimately take place. His mentor Rabbi Walter Wurzburger advised him that it is vital that Jewish distinctiveness be constantly maintained. Hence, joint celebrations of either Jewish or Christian liturgies are off limits. How then should participants in joint worship services proceed? Brill provides various examples based on personal experience.

Frequently, he states, special events and conferences are opened with a psalm or a universal prayer. At a recent visit to a Catholic seminary, for example, the hosts asked Jewish participants if they wished to join them for prayer. They stressed that they were not conducting Mass or reciting any official prayers. Instead they planned to use verses from the Hebrew Bible set to music. This is a striking example of the way in which religious distinctions can be maintained while engaging in interfaith activity. According to Brill, interfaith prayer must preserve the distinction between formal prayer which is peculiar to each religious tradition and universal acts of prayer. Hence, he maintains that any form of Christian–Jewish liturgy should be supplemental and never aim to fulfil a religious community's statutory prayer.

Another example relates to political prayer breakfasts. On such occasions rabbis frequently invoke God and recite psalms. Yet they do not participate in any of the formal prayers during the service. Brill also refers to occasions when a religious group conducts a worship service and leaves a door open so that members of other faiths can watch and listen. He also cites events where members of other religions participate in Jewish life, such as meals on college campuses when Christian and Muslim students join the Orthodox community for a kosher Shabbat meal complete with Jewish prayer. Finally, Brill records occasions when he has meditated or sung together with Hindus while avoiding participating in formal Muslim worship. In all these cases the distinctiveness of Judaism was maintained while providing an opportunity for interfaith worship.

By contrast, Aaron Rosen stresses that within Reform Judaism – as opposed to Orthodoxy – there is scope for religious openness when worshipping with members of other faiths. Instead of focusing on the need to preserve the distinctiveness of Judaism, Rosen argues that private, public and sacred settings offer possibilities for Jewish and non-Jewish participants to pray together. In the private sphere, he cites the example of Passover: at the Passover seder, Christian participants can learn about Judaism as a living faith and join in the recitation of the haggadah.

Turning to public spaces, Rosen points out that as a Jew he has been active in creating a Stations of the Cross project in which participants use modern technology to chart their own personal *via dolorosa* through the streets of London. Unlike Brill, Rosen sought in this project to create a space in which Jews and Christians could find common ground in a shared religious quest. As he explains, the Christian tradition provided a framework for telling a story that resonated between both faiths. Together with an Anglican bishop and a Catholic cardinal, Rosen offered reflections at locations on this spiritual pilgrimage. He stresses that such participation could be seen as a disavowal of Jewish tradition, but this would be a mistake. Instead – like a Passover seder shared with non-Jewish guests – the exhibition strengthened his commitment to the Jewish tradition.

Regarding sacred space, Rosen points out that in recent years many American Jewish congregations have purchased disused churches as a place of Jewish worship. Similarly, as American Jews moved out of urban centres to the suburbs, they have sold synagogues to African American congregations. Such a cross-over, he writes, has the potential to uncover powerful resonances which can be tapped by ecumenical worship. In Germany and England there are recent examples of such shared places of worship. In Berlin, the House of One is designed to include a fully functional church, synagogue and mosque. A parallel example of multifaith worship took place during the 2012 Olympics where prayer spaces were constructed in the athletes' villages which were designed to function as a mosque on Fridays, a synagogue on Saturdays and a church on Sundays while constituting a communal space during the week. According to Rosen, such projects generate dialogue and demonstrate how people of different faiths might pray together.

These two contributions illustrate the tensions within the Jewish world between those who are anxious to preserve the distinctive features of Judaism and those who seek to explore the ways in which other faiths amplify their understanding of the Jewish heritage. In other chapters this tension often emerges in explorations of interfaith worship within a particular religious tradition. Those of a more orthodox outlook are cautious about such activity and anxious to preserve the integrity of their tradition. However, the more liberal members of the same religious community view interfaith worship as a means of gaining a greater understanding of Judaism as well as the faith of others. This clash of views poses a dilemma for those seeking to devise an interfaith worship service inclusive of all.

Chapter 6

# JAINISM

## 1

## Praying Together in an Atmosphere of Interfaith Harmony

Vinod Kapashi

### THOSE WERE THE DAYS

I remember the days of my childhood when we used to see a Muslim procession in my village in India during the holy days of *Muharram*. Some devout Muslim youngsters were chanting loudly 'Ya Hussain, Ya Hussain...' and beating themselves with a chain. One or two youth would chant violently and pierce their cheeks. We all observed that with great curiosity and knew that it must have been very painful, but that is the way of life for them and we took it as a 'normal' thing. I also remember the days when we used to go to *Navratri* (Hindu nine days festival) and sing and pray to mother Ambika with our Hindu brothers. But that is not all; I had observed that Muslims, Hindus and people from other religious backgrounds would join in a Jain procession during our religious festival of *Paryushan* and joyfully greet everyone. Again, all this was considered normal. This was all taken for granted by us and we always thought that we were just brothers and sisters, each one following his/her own rituals. Perhaps these days are gone and everyone thinks that he (she) is a guardian of his religion and his duty is to remain 100 per cent immersed in his own tradition only.

But ever since my childhood I have asked the question, what makes us come together and enjoy in an atmosphere of friendship? What is the common thread? Is there a universal prayer too? What is an interfaith mode of worship? I have heard too many times that 'All religions are equal and there is just one God.' But then I found that, for some people, this was merely an excuse for not going to one's own place of worship and praying.

Although the idea that all religions are equal and that there is only one God helps one, to some extent, in developing feelings of brotherhood and living at peace with one and other this wishy-washy approach does not lead one anywhere. It does not make you understand what other religions are, nor does it promote interfaith harmony.

## THE JAIN BELIEF

When a Jain person joins a group of interfaith worshippers and recites the common prayers, it reminds him, at some of the meetings, that the prayers uttered are not universal and do not conform to the belief he holds. Worshipping almighty creator God and his creation, and praising Him for what He has given to us is not in strict conformity with Jain (and Buddhist) beliefs.

The Jains, like Buddhists, were against the idea of God as the creator. According to the Jain belief the universe has no beginning and no end. Matter and energy exist and will always exist in one form or the other. There is no creator, no divine superbeing who governs this mechanism.

The Jains sought the Divine in man and found essential divinity in all living beings. Every soul is divine in its essence. It is involved in the wheel of *Samsara* (worldly existence) due to encrustation of karma. Karma particles are the results of your good or bad deeds, created by your mind or speech or action. No one can take your karmas. No God or any spirit helps us in doing that. You are your best friend and your worst enemy. Jain 'gods' (*tirthankaras*) are the enlightened beings. They were humans but achieved enlightenment and freed themselves from the shackles of karma-bondage. This freedom from karma is called *moksha* or nirvana.

The Jains worship the *tirthankaras* not because they are gods, not because they are powerful in any other way, but because they possess the highest and divine virtues. The spark of divinity exists in all creatures, but the enlightened ones have shown the path to mankind.

The worship of the *tirthankaras* is to remind us that they are to be kept as ideals before us in our journey to self-realisation and/or nirvana. No favours are to be sought by means of worship nor are they there to grant favours to the devotees. The main motive of worship is to learn from the examples of the perfect being and to remind us that the way to perfection lies in the way they have shown us (Kalghatgi 1988). The Jain religion is one of renunciation where strict ascetic life prevails. Jain *tirthankaras* are not said to have any attachments and are not said to take any interest or interfere with mortal beings. Hence, for a Jain to pray for things such as a long life or prosperity would be fruitless according to Jain philosophy (Kapashi 2003).

## 'GOD' AS THE ROLE MODEL

In one of the Jain prayers, the poet Umaswatiji says in the prologue of the book the *Tattvartha Sutra*:

> We pray to those
> who have led the path to salvation,
> who have destroyed the mountains of karma, and
> who know the reality of the universe.
> We pray to them to acquire their attributes. (Desai Mohanlal
>     Dalichand 1933)

It would be totally wrong to say that prayers have no place in Jain philosophy. Jains do not consider prayers as a means of seeking favours from 'gods'. True Jain prayers are nothing but the appreciation and adoration of the virtues possessed by the enlightened beings and the expression of ardent desire to achieve these virtues in one's own actual life.

The Hindu religion made a great impact in the lives of Jains in India. In a famous verse of the Bhagavadgita, the Hindu holy book, Lord Krishna says to His disciple Arjuna: 'But those who worship me, surrendering all their actions to me...I become their saviour and liberate them from the ocean of death-bound existence...' (Duneja 2006, 12: 6–7).

Due to this influence over the period of two thousand years, Jain monks have composed quite a few prayers and songs in which devotees ask for all sorts of favours from the God or gods. But then these elders were merely voicing the concerns of laymen's feelings. People want remedies for their ailments, they want divine help in their troubled times and they seek solace in their grief. Many Jain *acharyas* (senior monks) and scholars maintained that there is no harm in asking for a favour even from the *tirthankaras*.

In a famous Jain prayer, which is in veneration of the 23rd *tirthankara* Parshvanath, the composer of the hymn *The Uvasaggaharam Stotra*, Acharya Bhadrabahu says: 'If people can hold this sacred mantra forever on their neck/throat, bad omens (effect of bad planets), disease, plague, fevers, etc, will subside' (Kapashi 2003, p.32).

Here one can see that a famous scholar and much revered *acharya* like Bhadrabahu talks about removing diseases and so on by worshipping the *tirthankaras*! But the very idea of divinity in all human beings and rejection of a creator God raises few difficulties in multifaith worship. I remember taking part in a multifaith prayer meeting a few years back when we mentioned creation and all that exists for the use of mankind. However, these days are gone and now the prayers reflect the multiplicity of viewpoints of other faiths.

## INTERFAITH PRAYERS

In some of the gatherings of the Harrow Interfaith Council, we used to sing beautiful verses which can be described as the universal prayer. In the following verse a devotee asks from the Lord and wishes for peace and love:

> Lord, make me an instrument of your peace.
> Where there is hatred, let me bring love...

The above prayer, sometimes referred to as the 'Prayer of St Francis', conveys the message of peace, love and forgiveness but may not be regarded as wholly in conformity with all that Jains believe. These very ideals, one can say, are generated from the main principle of Jainism: *ahimsa*. One cannot practise *ahimsa* or nonviolence if there is any hatred towards any living being in one's mind. Jain philosophy, code of conduct and everything they preach come from this single cardinal principle. That is why after the annual festival of forgiveness (*Paryushan*) Jains beg forgiveness like this: 'I forgive all living beings. May all living beings forgive me. I have friendship with all living beings and enmity towards none.' Perhaps this idea of love towards all living beings and the principle of acceptance of a multiplicity of viewpoints (*anekantvada*) makes a Jain a very tolerant and understanding person. Over the centuries Jains lived peacefully in India. There were, of course, hostilities from other ideologies but Jains, although dwindling in numbers in many states of India, managed to keep their ideology alive and in fact flourished in some parts of India.

The fundamental and basic Jain prayer tends to venerate the enlightened beings and other monks and nuns of high calibre. It begins with the sentence '*Namo Arihantanam*', meaning 'I bow down to the enlightened beings' (those who have destroyed their inner passions). No name of any religion or God has been mentioned here. Just veneration to the super-virtuous beings. The prayer is called *Namaskara Mantra* and it goes like this:

> I bow down to the enlightened ones, to those who have attained *moksha*, to religious leaders, to religious teachers and to all monks in the world. This fivefold obeisance which destroys all sin is the first and foremost and is the most auspicious of all auspicious things.

Jains say that this basic and first prayer comes to be synonymous with acceptance of the Jain values and it is with this prayer on his lips that the pious layman should wake each morning.

In his daily worship ritual, a devout Jain would systematically do the prayer ritual called *Chaitya Vandan* in which he would beg forgiveness for causing harm to any living beings. He would also accept the fact that he may have done something wrong, knowingly or unknowingly, whilst doing his normal day-to-day work. The prayer goes like this:

> O Venerable one!, Grant me permission that I may seek forgiveness for the wrong doing related to movements that I have committed until now...having gained your approval, my wish is to be relieved from the sins that may have arisen from any pain inflicted upon creatures during my movements... If I have crushed any creature [including seeds] or harmed... any living beings from one to five senses...I am asking for repentance [and forgiveness] for this wrong doing. I might have kicked them [small creatures], rolled them, covered them, assembled them, touched them, separated them from their own kinds, or killed them. In connection of all these things; may my sins or faults be forgiven [destroyed]. (Kapashi 1999, p.40)

Now, of course, the interfaith meetings and form of prayers have been changed. In a meeting held by the worshipful Mayor of Harrow, we proclaimed:

> We commit ourselves, as people of many beliefs
> To work together for the common good,
> Uniting to build a better society,
> Grounded in values and ideals that we share. (Harrow Council 2017)

Jains usually recite the following, which has a universal message and is widely accepted by the representatives of all faiths:

> Let the whole universe be blessed,
> Let all beings be engaged in one another's well-being,
> Let all weaknesses, sickness and faults be diminished,
> Let everyone, everywhere be happy [and at peace].[1]

Gary Zukav beautifully (perhaps not knowing about the Jain philosophy) mentions the Jain way of thinking: 'The purpose of our journey on this precious earth is now to align our personalities with our souls. It is to create harmony, cooperation, sharing, and reverence for life. It is to grow spiritually. This is our new evolutionary pathway' (quoted by Abdul Kalam 2015).

Albert Einstein writes about the philosophy of *ahimsa* in his own way:

> A human being is a part of the whole called by us universe, a part limited in time and space. He experiences himself, his thoughts and feeling as something separated from the rest, a kind of optical delusion of his consciousness. The delusion is a kind of prison for us, restricting us to our personal desires and to affection for a few persons nearest to us. Our task must be to free ourselves from this prison by widening our circle of compassion to embrace all living creatures and the whole of nature in its beauty.[2]

---

1    Original text of *Pratikraman Sutra* (a traditional prayer book).
2    Originally written by Einstein to Dr Marcus on 12th February 1950. This is also printed in Usher 2013.

## PRAYING TOGETHER, STAYING TOGETHER

There are other minor issues, too, in interfaith prayer meetings. Jains would not usually want to have such a meeting in a temple, where the consecrated statues and idols are installed. The main reason is that the consumption of any food or drink in the temple precinct is strictly forbidden in the Jain religion. Therefore, holding any meeting where food is to be served later in the same area of the temple would be unacceptable. However, there is nothing wrong in holding prayer meetings in other rooms or halls and serving food there. In Hindu or Sikh temples, or perhaps in any other place of worship, there are no such restrictions in force.

In spite of all these reservations over the centuries, Jains have tried to accommodate many beliefs and many ideologies. How an eleventh-century Jain *acharya*, Hemchandracharya, explained this phenomenon is worth noting. He was an ardent follower of the Jain philosophy, but whilst visiting a Hindu temple, he proclaimed: 'I bow down to him – He may be Brahma, Vishnu or Shiva [three main Gods of the Hindu religion] – who has destroyed attachment and aversion which are the causes of the cycle of birth and rebirth' (Kapashi 2000, p.25).

In conclusion, the Jain theory of many-fold aspects or accepting viewpoints of all paths and all ideologies (*anekantvada*), makes one very tolerant and broadminded. Jains have learned as well as taught that it does not matter how you pray as long as your belief in reverence for all life remains steadfast.

## REFERENCES

Abdul Kalam, A.P.J. (2015) *Transcendence*. Delhi: HarperCollins.

Desai Mohanlal Dalichand (1933) *Jain Sahitya*. Mumbai: Jain Shvetambar Conference.

Duneja, P. (2006) *The Holy Geeta* (translation), 4th edn. Pleasanton, CA: Geeta Society.

Harrow Council (2017) *Act of Committment*. Leaflet. Harrow: Harrow Council.

Kalghatgi, T.G. (1988) *Study of Jainism*. Jaipur: Prakrit Bharati Academy.

Kapashi, V. (1999) *In Search of the Ultimate*. London: Mahavir Foundation.

Kapashi, V. (2000) *Hem-Siddhi*. London: Zaveri Foundation.

Kapashi, V. (2003) *Nine Sacred Recitations of Jainism*. Mumbai: Hindi Granth Karyalaya.

Usher, S. (ed.) (2013) *Letters of Note*. London: Canongate.

## FURTHER READING

Baya, D.S. (2006) *Jainism, the Creed for All Times*. Jaipur: Prakrit Bharati Academy.

Kung, H. and Kuschel, K.-J. (1993) *A Global Ethic*. London: SCM Press.

Van Glasenapp, H. (1999) *Jainism, An Indian Religion of Salvation*. New Delhi: Motilal Banarassidas.

# 2

# Interfaith Involvement of Jains

## Natubhai Shah

Jains attend international, national and local interfaith services in London, different parts of the UK and the world, but hardly ever organise such services in Jain temples. I have been invited to attend national services at Westminster Abbey and St Paul's Cathedral for more than 15 years. The last service I attended was the service of Hope at Westminster Abbey on 5 April 2017 following the terror attack by a misguided person at the heart of London near the parliament building. Relatives of killed and injured persons prayed for justice, mercy, peace, hope, and harmony of the diverse communities from 270 countries and 300 spoken languages settled in the UK, in the presence of practically all world faiths, the royal family, government ministers, the mayor, police, armed forces and other dignitaries. The congregation in this service prayed together for solidarity, forgiveness and peace for all. There are different prayers and themes for each national or interfaith service, but the message given in these services includes that of nonviolence, love, compassion, forgiveness, equality, equanimity, education, health and vitality, environmental concerns, community cohesion, welfare and happiness for all, empowerment of women and young persons and peace around the world. I also attended the prayers at Lambeth Palace to celebrate the diamond jubilee of Her Majesty the Queen and presented a few pages from the Jain treasures. We were delighted to learn that these services included the message found in the Jain teachings and values of the *Art of Love* to all living beings, the *Art of Living* with humanity, progress for the physical as well as spiritual welfare of an individual, family and the community, and the *Art of Leaving* the material possessions and the passions that cloud the soul to keep it in the cycle of transmigration.

Leaders of different faiths meeting to pray together

## PRAYERS

Prayer can be a form of religious practice; it may be individual or together with the family members or in the congregation. It may involve the use of words, song or complete silence and may include music. When language is used, prayer may take the form of a hymn, incantation or a brief sermon. It may take place in public or private, and may be used in one's own home. There are different forms of prayer, such as petitionary prayer, prayers for praises of God, gurus or saints, thanksgiving, condolence, confessing transgressions (sins) or to express one's thoughts and emotions. People pray for many reasons, such as for personal benefit, asking for divine grace, spiritual connection and progress, for repentance, for the welfare of an individual, family, community or the country. When we analyse the Jain prayers they are found to be universal and are performed individually or together with the devotees. They include the hymns, devotional lyrics and praises of the *tirthankara* (founder of the path for spiritual liberation), expressions of obeisance and repentance, forgiveness and friendship, prayers for self-purification, for the recovery of the sick and for the peace of departed souls, for an individual, family, community, country or the world. Jains welcome members from other faiths and communities to join them in prayers.

## JAIN PHILOSOPHY AND VALUES

Jainism is an Indian religion (perhaps the oldest one in the world), revived by Mahavira, the 24th and last *tirthankara* of this cosmic cycle. It is followed by several million people in India and by a sizeable Jain diaspora in the UK, USA and other overseas countries. Its values are based on nonviolence and reverence for all life (*ahimsa*), non-attachment to the material world (*aparigraha*) and pluralism (*anekantavad*), introspection, calmness of self and spiritual liberation by self-effort. It believes in friendship to all and malice to none, improvement of the physical and spiritual quality of life for all, compassion, equality, animal welfare, environment enhancement and peace. It advocates that the true meaning of life is attainment of self-realisation, self-conquest and spiritual liberation: a state of permanent happiness and bliss, free from the cycle of transmigration. It can be attained by shedding karma attached to the soul with the observance and practice of Right Faith, Right Knowledge and Right Conduct together.

The principle of *anekantavada* teaches Jains tolerance, co-existence and respect for others. It frees one from spurious thinking that his or her faith is nearer to the truth than that of others. It respects the thoughts of others and urges people to study different religions, opinions and schools of thoughts which can help an individual to sound thinking to understand the truth. It tells its followers that there are many paths for the spiritual liberation and that progress can be achieved from any path that leads one to the ultimate goal of human life – spiritual liberation.

## PRAYING TOGETHER

There are many examples of praying together: in school assemblies, festivals and on special occasions pupils pray together on the relevant theme; at the start of each interfaith meeting participants pray together in silence; in churches, synagogues, mosques and temples people pray together with the prayers acceptable to their faiths; but we hardly find regular interfaith prayers in these places. The diversity of faiths, culture and communities is a fact in modern Britain; we cannot ignore it. Whether it is a state school, private school or faith school, it is expected to have some teaching about the cultural and religious differences and similarities of the communities that have settled in Britain. For the benefit of common good and community cohesion pupils should be encouraged to pray together. We have found praying together and understanding the meaning of prayers and beliefs of others makes people respectful and tolerant of each other.

## JAIN CENTRE LONDON

I am the founder of the Jain Samaj Europe and the Jain Network. As a practitioner of *anekantavada*, I am very keen on interfaith understanding and multifaith activities. I am involved in the Jain Network's project of development of the exciting 30,000-square-foot Jain Centre London, which will have community facilities on the ground floor; library, multifaith centre, multipurpose rooms, large hall and four residential rooms on the first floor; and the place of worship and study for all major Jain traditions on the second floor. The ground and first floor will be available to all communities to use. It is expected that the concept of the multifaith centre will encourage people from different backgrounds to pray together to improve interfaith relations. The present Jain Centre has provided office space for the Council of Dharmic Faiths and Barnet Hindu Council. In addition to the observance of Jain festivals and rituals, the Jain Centre celebrates interfaith week, Christmas and other national occasions and allows use of the hall by other faiths, where people from diverse faiths pray together. The Jain Centre also organises yoga sessions, where people from different communities benefit from yogic practices and pray together.

## JAIN PRAYERS

Over the years, since the revival of Jainism by Mahavira 2600 years ago, Jainism has developed four major Jain traditions: Swetambara, Digambara, Sthanakvasi and Terapanthi. They all believe in the same teachings and philosophy but have some minor differences in rituals, practices and historical beliefs. They have developed a series of prayers and rituals to be observed at different times: daily, fortnightly, four-monthly and annually. The prayers/rituals among the image-worshipper Swetambara and Digambara communities are colourful and varied compared to the devotional practices of non-image-worshipping Jains (Sthanakvasi or Terapanthi). The rituals and prayers may also vary at different local places. The consecrated images of *tirthankaras* serve as a focus for prayer and devotion. The lives of the *tirthankaras* represented by the images are the example which the worshipper seeks, through prayer, meditation and conduct, to emulate. Jainism has four orders of community: monks, nuns, laymen and laywomen. As monks and nuns cannot come to the Western world because of their vow of total nonviolence (they walk on feet to minimise violence to other living beings and do not use any vehicle to travel), we will discuss prayers from the laity's perspective.

Jains recite prayers at different parts of the day: some in the early morning after waking up, some at midmorning, some in the evening and some at night. They may pray individually or together in the congregation. It is believed that in the initial stages of the spiritual journey praying and observance of the rituals together has much more benefit to a layperson, as it motivates him/her to concentrate and learn the meaning of the prayer/ritual, and the prayer may become part of his/her lifestyle.

The Jain prayers are meaningful and often very beautiful. They evoke devotional feelings in worshippers. The Prakrit (and occasionally Sanskrit) language of prayers adds melody and dignity to the ancient prayers and has the additional advantage of uniting all devotees, whatever their daily language is. Prayers/rituals, undertaken with proper understanding, help the faithful to develop the right attitude towards their spiritual progress; they may take the form of austerities, visits to the temple, worship and observance of six essential duties.

The daily prayers envisage the solitary worshipper performing devotions whether in the temple or before the image of the *tirthankara* in the home; prayers are also performed together by several devotees. Community worship takes the form of the singing of hymns, interspersed by the chanting of prayers. The celebration of festivals may involve the whole community; it may open with the *Navakara Mantra*, continue with hymns, devotional singing and dancing, celebrating events in the life of a *tirthankara*, and end with the lamp-waving ritual of lights (*aarati*). A celebration of this nature will incorporate ritual elements, but is supplementary to the formal prayers, which constitute the recommended daily or periodic religious exercises of a pious Jain. It is observed that women, as well as men, perform the rituals and pray together in the home or in the temple.

The daily life of a pious Jain is interwoven with the ritual acts of the six essential duties. Every Jain learns the *Navakara Mantra* from childhood. The *Navakara Mantra* is a universal formula of veneration, meditation on the virtues and surrender, not a petition, to the five 'supreme beings' (*pancha parmesthis*: spiritual victors, liberated souls, spiritual leaders, spiritual teachers and saints). The rolling sounds of the ancient Prakrit language used in this *mantra* echo at every Jain religious gathering, chanted in unison by the congregation. The meditative, silent recitation of this *mantra* may be performed at any time, in any place and by anyone; it has spiritual as well as physical benefit.

## ESSENTIAL DUTIES OF JAINS

The six essential duties Jains are expected to perform, which include prayers, yoga, meditation and austerities necessary for spiritual progress, are:

*samayika*: sitting in one place for 48 minutes to practise equanimity

*chaturvisanti stava*: praying and appreciating the qualities of the 24 *tirthankaras* to attain Right perception

*vandana*: veneration of ascetics to attain humility and subdue passions

*pratikramana*: penitential retreat to confess and repent for the transgressions to others as well as to one's soul. It helps to shed karmas attracted by daily activities

*kaayotsarga*: meditation with bodily detachment to attain a detached attitude

*pratyakhyaana*: vow to renunciate items for a specified period such as food, indulgences, activities; the minimum renunciation undertaken by most laypersons is *navakaarsi*, the vow to take food 48 minutes after sunrise

## SPECIAL PRAYERS

Jains perform special prayers/rituals, penance and austerity on the 2nd, 5th, 8th, 11th and 14th or 15th day of each half of a lunar month, and on the five auspicious anniversaries of the *tirthankaras*: conception, birth, renunciation, attaining omniscience and spiritual liberation. They pray together with community members for elaborate penitential retreats on the 14th day of each lunar month, three times a year on the 14th day of the fourth month (*chaumaasi chaudasa*), and annually on *samvatsari*, the holiest day in the Jain calendar (late August or early September). They make special prayers during *paryusana*: an eight-day sacred period of forgiveness and austerities observed by Swetambaras and ten-day sacred period (*dasa laxani parva*) observed by Digambaras.

## TYPICAL DAILY PRAYERS

Typical daily prayers recited by Jains individually or together are:

**Prayer for Obeisance (*Navakar mantra*)**
*namo arihantänarm | namo siddhänam*
*namo äyariyänam | namo uvajjhäyänam*
*namo loe savvasähünam*
*eso pancha namukkäro | savvapävappanäsano*
*mangalänam cha savvesim | padhamam havai mangalam*

Obeisance to the spiritual victors, Obeisance to the liberated souls,
Obeisance to the spiritual leaders, Obeisance to the spiritual teachers,
Obeisance to all saints in the world, who practise nonviolence and reverence for all life,
This fivefold Obeisance removes all sins and is the most auspicious of all benedictions.

**Prayer for Forgiveness (*khämemi savvajive, savve jivä khamantu me*)**
*mitti me savva bhuesu, veram majjha na kenai*

I forgive all living beings; may all living beings forgive me
All living beings are my friends; I have malice towards none

**Prayer of Bliss for All**
*shivamastu sarvajagatah, parahitaniratä bhavantu bhütaganäh*
*dosäh prayäntu näsham, sarvatra sukhibhavatu lokah*

May the entire universe be blissful;
May all beings be engaged in each other's well-being.
May all weakness, sickness and faults vanish;
May everyone be healthy, peaceful, and blissful everywhere.

**Prayer for Peace**
Peace and universal love is the teaching of Mahavira.
The Lord has preached, equanimity is the dharma
Forgive do I creatures all, and let all creatures forgive me.
Unto all have I amity, and unto none enmity.

'Do not injure any living being.'
It is the eternal way of spiritual life.
Violence causes all miseries in the world,
and it keeps the soul in spiritual bondage

A weapon, howsoever powerful it may be,
Can always be superseded by a superior one,
No weapon can conquer the passions and the self
Conquering self is the meaning of life,
A path to bliss and peace.

## CONCLUSION

In conclusion, although Jains take part in interfaith activities and prayers, locally as well as nationally, they believe these prayers are for respect to others; they have no benefit for one's spiritual progress. Every faith has prayers relevant to its belief and tradition. A devotee will normally follow the same for his/her spiritual progress. Interfaith prayers are not a substitute for the prayers made by a devotee at the church, synagogue, mosque or temple; they only help to create understanding and respect for other faiths as taught by the Jain principle of *anekantavada* (pluralism); of course, they help to produce external peace. But one should remember that there will never be external peace without internal peace, which can only be achieved by understanding the philosophy relevant to each faith and carrying out the practices prescribed by it. There are different paths for spiritual liberation; one should follow the path of which one is convinced.

## FURTHER READING

Dundas, P. (2002) *The Jains.* London: Routledge.

Jain, J. and Fischer, E. (1978) *Jain Iconography, the Tirthankaras and Objects of Meditation* (2 vols). Leiden: Brill.

Jaini, P. (1979) *The Jaina Path of Purification.* Berkeley, CA: University of California Press.

Shah, N. (1998) *Jainism: The World of Conquerors* (2 vols). Brighton: Sussex Academic Press.

# Reflection

## The Editors

We have seen in previous chapters that interfaith prayer and worship can be challenging for participants due to divergent religious viewpoints. Some Hindus, including monotheistic Hindus, are seen to pray to a variety of deities. Jews, who believe in one Supreme Lord, regard this as polytheism, and thus misguided. The challenge is even greater when theists join nontheists in acts of religious piety. In his contribution Natubhai Shah directly confronts this dilemma. First, however, he stresses that Jain worship has universal implications. In his view Jain prayers are meaningful and beautiful, evoking devotional feelings in worshippers. Whatever their daily language, the Prakrit and Sanskrit language of such prayers unites all devotees regardless of their language. Such rituals help the faithful to develop the right attitude toward their spiritual progress.

According to Shah, the Jain religion is based on the values of nonviolence and reverence for all life, non-attachment to the material world, introspection, calmness of self and spiritual liberation through individual effort. Jainism embraces friendship to all and malice to none, improvement of physical and spiritual wellbeing, compassion, equality, animal welfare, environmental enhancement and peace. Further, it advocates that the true meaning of life is attainment of self-reliance, self-conquest and spiritual liberation. What is sought is a state of permanent happiness and bliss, free from the cycle of transmigration.

Such principles have universal application, yet Shah is aware that the religious tenets of Jainism are not all acceptable to members of other faith traditions. The diversity of faiths, he states, cannot be ignored. Every faith has prayers relevant to its beliefs and traditions. Hence, interfaith prayer services must recognise these differences.

In his contribution Vinod Kapashi wrestles with a similar problem. He remembers going to the nine days festival of Hindus and praying with them. In addition, he observed that Muslims, Hindus and people from other religious backgrounds joined in a Jain procession during the religious festival of *Paryushan*. He was pleased that all this was considered normal; it was taken for granted and the participants viewed each other as brothers and sisters.

Yet since his childhood he has been puzzled by the question whether there is a common thread that unites members of different faiths. Is there a universal prayer that binds them? Or is there an interfaith mode of worship? He stresses that he has frequently heard the view that all religions are equal and there is one God. Such a belief encourages a feeling of brotherhood and fosters a spirit of peace. But, in his opinion, it does not lead to a greater understanding of other religions; nor does it foster interfaith harmony.

When a Jain joins an interfaith group and worships with others, he or she is inevitably struck by the fact that the prayers uttered are not in fact universal nor do they conform to their religious beliefs. Worshipping a creator God and praising him for his creation is not in conformity with Jain belief. Jains – like Buddhists – do not accept the idea of a creator God. According to Jain philosophy, the universe has no beginning or end. Matter and energy exist and will always exist. There is no creator, nor divine super-being who governs the universe. Instead, Jains seek the divine in human beings and find divinity in all living things.

Kapashi goes on to explain that each soul is involved in the wheel of *Samsara* (worldly existence) due to the encrustations of karma. These karma particles are the results of good or bad deeds. No God or spirit can remove karma. For Jains 'gods' are the enlightened beings; they are human beings who have reached a state of enlightenment and freed themselves from the shackles of karma bondage. This freedom is called *moksha* or nirvana. Jains worship such individuals not because they are gods, nor because they are powerful in any other way. They are viewed with awe because they possess the highest virtues. The spark of divinity exists in all, but the enlightened ones have walked the true path. The aim of worship is to learn from these examples of perfect being – the Jain religion is one of renunciation where the strict ascetic life prevails.

Kapashi's explanation of the Jain understanding of prayer is thus far removed from worship in some other religious traditions where God is at the centre. Kapashi stresses that, although prayer has a critical role in Jain philosophy, Jains do not regard it as a means of seeking favours. True Jain prayers are the appreciation and adoration of virtues possessed by enlightened beings and the expression of the desire to attain them in one's own life. Nonetheless, despite the theological differences between Jains and members of theistic traditions, Kapashi and Shah are united in the belief that interfaith worship is both possible and necessary. The universal themes of Jainism unite all people and provide, in Shah's words, a basis for love, compassion, forgiveness, equality, equanimity, education, community cohesion, welfare, happiness and peace around the world.

Chapter 7

# BUDDHISM

## 1

## Buddhism and Prayer

### Bogoda Seelawimala

At first sight this might seem to be an unusual juxtaposition of these two subjects. Buddhism does not acknowledge the existence of a supreme being or god, an all-powerful creator who is concerned with the lives of all that he has created and who can be the recipient of prayer. In that case, who can Buddhists pray to? Certainly not the Buddha! He was a man, not a god, and he said, 'You yourselves must make the effort. Buddhas do but show the way' (Dhammapada (Dhp.) 276). This does not mean that there are no occasions when some (misguided) Buddhists do offer prayers to the Buddha in the hope of obtaining guidance or assistance. However, it is our actions in the past which determine what we experience today, and our actions in the present which determine what we shall experience in the future. This is the law of *kamma* and *vipaka*, cause and effect; good actions produce good results and bad actions produce bad results. This is an impersonal law and its operation cannot be influenced by prayer, worship or any external agency.

> Mind is the forerunner of (all evil) states. Mind is chief; mind-made are they. If one speaks or acts with wicked mind, because of that, suffering follows one, even as the wheel follows the hoof of draught-ox.

Mind is the forerunner of (all good) states. Mind is chief; mind-made are they. If one speaks or acts with pure mind, because of that, happiness follows one, even as one's shadow that never leaves. (Dhp. 1, 2)

## HUMAN RESPONSIBILITY

Buddhism gives full responsibility to human beings. It makes each person his or her own master. We create our own heavens and our own hells. Buddhism teaches us how to purify our minds of negative qualities such as greed, hatred and delusion, and how to generate wholesome qualities such as generosity, love and wisdom. The cause of suffering is rooted in our minds and the cure also lies within our minds. Praying to gods or performing complex rituals have no place in this teaching. The beginning of the path is the deluded mind and the ending of the path is the enlightened mind.

The Buddha taught that each of us has to take responsibility for our own actions. It is our own unwholesome qualities, especially ignorance, which prevent us from realising our full potential. 'Purity and impurity depend on oneself. No one can purify another' (Dhp. 165). Also, the Buddha said,

There are, O householder, five desirable, pleasant and agreeable things which are rare in the world. What are those five? They are long life, beauty, happiness, fame and (rebirth in) the heavens. But of these five things, O householder, I do not teach that they are to be obtained by prayer or by vows. If one could obtain them by prayer or vows, who would not do it? For a noble disciple who wishes to have long life, it is not befitting that he should pray for long life or take delight in so doing. He should rather follow a path of life that is conducive to longevity. (Anguttara Nikaya V, 43)

He goes on to recommend the same course of action in respect of the other four desirable things. The importance of self-reliance was emphasised again in one of the Buddha's last pronouncements: 'Dwell making yourselves your island (support), making yourselves, not anyone else your refuge; making the Dhamma your island (support), the Dhamma your refuge, nothing else your refuge' (Digha Nikaya (DN) 16 2.26).

According to Buddhism, no higher being sits in judgement over our affairs and destiny. Nature and the world are impartial; they cannot be cajoled or persuaded by prayers. There are no special favours which can be granted on request.

> Regarding the use of prayers for attaining the final goal, the Buddha once made an analogy of a man who wants to cross a river. If he sits down and prays imploring that the far bank of the river will come to him and carry him across, then his prayer will not be answered. If he really wants to cross the river, he must make some effort; he must find some logs and build a raft or look for a bridge or construct a boat or perhaps swim. Somehow, he must work to get across the river. Likewise, if he wants to cross the river of Samsara, prayers alone are not enough. He must work hard by living a religious life, by controlling his passions, calming his mind, and by getting rid of all the impurities and defilements in his mind. Only then can he reach the final goal. Prayer alone will never take him to the final goal. ('The Meaning of Prayer' in Sri Dhammananda 1987, pp.199–200)

## MEDITATION

This does not, however, mean that the word 'prayer' cannot be used in a Buddhist context. It depends upon how you define 'prayer'. Buddhists practise meditation, usually in silence, which has the objective of bringing about a change in one's state of mind. During the practice of meditation, the meditator may use a variety of techniques first to weaken and eventually to eliminate unwholesome qualities such as greed, hatred and delusion, and second to develop wholesome states of mind. This practice impacts every aspect of our lives in thought, word and deed. Qualities such as faith and devotion can have a powerful and beneficial psychological effect.

Another and very popular practice involves a monk or monks chanting various texts in a particular, formalised style. This is known as chanting *paritta* (in Pali). The words themselves, chanted according to the traditional manner, are believed to bring powerful benefits, such as protection from harmful forces. This practice helps the audience to develop calm, devotion and confidence in the teachings. Monks are often invited to visit a dying man and chant *paritta* in order to engender wholesome thoughts in his mind which will help to condition the new life in a happy situation.

Buddhists are often seen performing prostrations before an image of the Buddha, and this prompts the question: are they worshipping or praying to the Buddha? This may appear to be the case, but in fact Buddhists know that this image is used simply as a focus for them to generate in their own minds thoughts of respect and veneration for the Buddha, the wisdom that he developed and the human qualities which he perfected. This is coupled with a sense of gratitude for the teaching which he gave, and a strong determination to follow this path to reach the supreme bliss of Enlightenment. The act of prostration is also an act of humility and a counterweight to spiritual pride. To do this, it is by no means necessary to have an image of the Buddha. In fact, for approximately three hundred years after the death of the Buddha, no images of him were made. The creation of statues and sculptures owes much to Greek culture and their portrayal of their own gods.

There is a related meditation practice called 'Recollection of the Buddha' (*Buddhanussati* in Pali). This involves calling to mind the special qualities of the Buddha and making a determination to develop the same qualities in ourselves through our own efforts.

Giving is a most important practice because it helps to overcome the qualities of greed and attachment, which lie at the heart of so many of our problems. The act of giving generates what is called merit and it is possible to transfer this merit to the benefit of another person or, indeed, all living beings.

## SPIRITUAL POWER

There are different schools of Buddhism. In Mahayana Buddhism, a great teacher called Shantideva, who lived in the eighth century, wrote a book in Sanskrit called Bodhichariavatara (in English it means A Guide to the Bodhisattva's Way of Life). He composed many poems which resemble prayers or hymns. I would like to quote:

> May I be a protector to the helpless, a guide to those travelling the path, a boat to those wishing to cross over; or a bridge or a raft. May I be land for those requiring it, a lamp for those in darkness, may I be a home for the homeless, and a servant for the world.

He was very devoted to the Bodhisattva Avalokiteshvara, believing that he is in heaven looking with great compassion at those who are suffering.

Prayer wheels are used primarily by the Buddhists of Tibet and Nepal, where hand-held prayer wheels are carried by pilgrims and other devotees, who turn them during devotional activities. As the practitioner turns the wheel, it is best to focus the mind and repeat the *Om Mani Padme Hum* mantra. The mantra *Om Mani Padme Hum* invokes the spiritual power and blessings of Chenrezig (Bodhisattva Avalokitheswara), the embodiment of compassion. His Holiness the Dalai Lama says of the mantra *Om Mani Padme Hum*: 'it is a prayer which means the body, mind and speech are transformed from an impure level to a pure level through the practice of altruism leading to wisdom' (Dalai Lama 2017).

There are some prayers in popular Buddhism in Sri Lanka, for example in Bodhipuja. *Bodhi* means Enlightenment. *Puja* means offering. But here *Bodhipuja* is an offering to the bodhi tree. As Professor Lily De Silva (1978) pointed out, in Hinduism the bodhi tree is identical to the god Vishnu and worshipping the bodhi tree can lead to blessings from the god Vishnu. This view has influenced the Buddhist people in Sri Lanka and many Buddhists perform the Bodhipuja to get rid of the evil effects of the planetary influences (*grahadosa*) through the power of gods. As Professor Gombrich and Gananath Obeysekara have mentioned (1988), *Bodhipuja* is a bridge between deities and Buddhism. Many Sri Lankan Buddhist people perform *Bodhipuja* with prayers to deities for blessings in order to get good health and protection. But the real purpose of the bodhi tree is to remind us of the Buddha's Enlightenment.

## SHARING LOVING-KINDNESS

There is one particular kind of meditation which could be regarded as a form of prayer. This is meditation on loving-kindness (*metta bhavana* in Pali). *Metta* is unconditional goodwill towards all beings, wishing them to be happy and free from suffering. Starting with oneself, one radiates pure thoughts in an ever-widening circle so that all beings are embraced without exception or limitation. This practice is normally done by repeating simple phrases, such as 'May I be free from anger and ill-will, may I be free from fear and anxiety, may I be free from pain and suffering, may I be free from ignorance and desire, may I be happy and peaceful, may I be harmonious, may I be free from greed, hatred and delusion, may I attain the supreme bliss of Nibbana.' These words are then repeated in a variety of ways, replacing the word 'I' with 'beings in this room', 'beings in this town', 'beings in this country', 'beings in the world', 'beings in the universe' etc. I quote:

> May all beings be happy and secure, may their hearts be wholesome!
>
> Whatever living being there be – those mentally feeble or strong, physically long, stout or medium, short, small or large, those seen or unseen, dwelling far or near, those who are born and those who are to be born – may all beings, without exception, be happy minded! Let none deceive another nor despise any person whatsoever in any place, in anger or ill-will let one not wish any harm to another.
>
> Just as a mother would protect her only child at the risk of her own life, even so, cultivate a boundless heart towards all beings.
>
> Let thoughts of infinite love pervade the whole world – above, below and around – without any obstruction, without any hatred, without any enmity.
>
> Whether standing, walking, sitting or lying down, as long as one is awake, this mindfulness should be developed, this the wise say is the highest conduct here. (Metta Sutta, Suttanipata)

This sending of loving-kindness in every direction to all beings without exception can be regarded as a form of prayer, but there is no outside power or agent involved. The practitioner is generating potent forces within him- or herself which purify his or her mind of negative qualities such as anger, ill-will and resentment. 'The purpose of Buddhist prayer is to awaken our innate inner capacities of strength, courage and wisdom rather than to petition external forces' (Prayer in Buddhism).

## MEETING OTHER FAITHS

I have attended many interfaith services, held in many different places. In almost every service we have been given a period to keep silence, and we all observe silence, sometimes with gentle music playing. After a little while we start to experience very deep calm and peacefulness. Although we are a big crowd, with many different robes or different colours of skin, we can see the oneness of humanity. We breathe the same air, experience the same peace and a feeling of breaking down of barriers, regardless of our different religious beliefs. As a Buddhist I feel this to be a radiation of loving-kindness. Doubtless, followers of other faiths will interpret this experience in the light of their own religious beliefs. I think the important thing is to meet together in this silence. It is only when matters of doctrine come up that we become aware of differences and disagreements. There are many different instruments which make up an orchestra. However, when they play together in harmony, the results give pleasure to an audience comprising people from many different backgrounds. Likewise, people together sing hymns like waves of the ocean, the vibrations rise up and down and the vibrations affect our mind and enhance a feeling of harmony. We feel like we are floating in the air, going up and down.

I have experience of meditating together with people of other faiths. For example, at the London Olympics in 2012 there was a section of the village set aside for religion and I was the Buddhist chaplain. I remember Buddhists, Christians, Jews, Hindus and Muslims came together on a daily basis. There were shrine rooms for each major faith, which were interconnected. I worked there for 21 days, and we all had common meetings in the morning, and we moved from room to room. I remember that they came to my room, which the Olympic authorities had designed to be helpful for meditation. In my room there was a Buddha statue. I guided them in the practice of mindfulness of breathing. In meditation I ask my friends to visualise that we are like the lotus buds in a pond. In the process of blooming, from moment to moment we develop awareness in the present moment and this is a practice of transpersonal experience. There is no feeling of self, me and mine. We are like the buds in the pond in the process of blooming as part of nature, waiting to receive the morning sunshine. In this selfless feeling I hope we experience a very relaxed, fresh and enthusiastic state of mind. I remember a poem which goes like this: 'Happiness is not doing what we want to do, it is enjoying what we are doing. Patience is the greatest of all spiritual practices. There is no way to happiness. Happiness is the way.' I saw when they opened their eyes at the end of the meditation practice very calm and relaxed faces. For some people it was the first time they had come across this practice. Breathing is an object which all of us can understand. When we focus our mind on the process of breathing, closing our eyes and relaxing the body, it is possible to develop a stress-free mind in a busy environment.

I would like to quote:

> Let not a person revive the past
> Or on the future build his hopes:
> For the past has been left behind
> And the future has not been reached.
> Instead with the insight let him see
> Each presently arisen state,
> Let him know that and be sure of it,
> Invincibly, unshakably.
> Today the effort must be made:
> Tomorrow death may come, who knows?
> No bargain with mortality
> Can keep him and his hordes away,
> But one who dwells thus ardently,
> Relentlessly, by day, by night –
> It is he, the peaceful Sage had said
> Who has one fortunate attachment. (Bhaddekaratta Sutta, Majjhima Nikaya, 131)

As Buddhism does not believe in a creator or god, there are no such prayers as in theistic religions. As we have pointed out, Enlightenment depends upon one's understanding and effort, but thoughts like *metta* can be practised, wishing well being and happiness to all sentient beings and the environment. Likewise, 'May you be well'.

## REFERENCES

Batchelor, S. (1992) (trans.) *Bodhicaryavatara of Shantideva: A Guide to the Bodhisattva's Way of Life*. Ithaca, NY: Snow Lion Publications.

Dalai Lama (2017) 'The mantra Om Mani Padme Hum.' Accessed on 7 December 2018 at https://buddhismnow.com/2017/01/21/the-mantra-om-mani-padme-hum-by-the-dalai-lama.

De Silva, L. (1978) *The Cult of Bodhi Tree, Its Antiquity and Evolution*. Kyoto: International Association of Buddhist Culture.

Gombrich, R. and Obeysekara, G. (1988) *Buddism Transformed: Religious Change in Sri Lanka*. Princeton, NJ: Princeton Univesity Press.

Nanamoli, B. and Bodhi, B. (1995) (trans.) *The Middle Length Discourses of the Buddha Translation of Majjhima Nikaya Teachings of the Buddha.* Somerville, MA: Wisdom Publications.

Saddhatissa, V.H. (1985) (trans.) *The Sutta-Nipata.* London: Curzon Press.

Sri Dhammananda, K. (1987) *What Buddhists Believe.* Kuala Lumpur: Buddhist Missionary Society.

Thera, N. (1978) (trans.) *The Dhammapada.* Kuala Lumpur: Buddhist Missionary Society.

Walshe, M. (1996) (trans.) *Long Discourses of the Buddha: Translation of the 'Digha-Nikaya' (Teachings of the Buddha).* Somerville, MA: Wisdom Publications.

Woodward, F.L. (1986) (trans.) *Gradual Sayings of the Buddha (Anguttara Nikaya), Vol. V.* Oxford: Pali Text Society.

# 2

# Issues for Buddhists in Interfaith Settings

## Vishvapani Blomfield

Buddhists have long been active in interfaith activities in the UK. Internationally, Buddhist leaders such as Thich Nhat Hanh and Daisaku Ikeda have been prominent participants in interfaith meetings and advocates of interfaith understanding, while the Dalai Lama believes that interfaith activities are imperative in a globalised world where religious cultures interact with ever-greater intensity (Dalai Lama 2010).

Sentiments like these can give the impression that Buddhism is a purely benign force for tolerance and peace, and it can raise hopes that Buddhist influence in interfaith meetings can offset the tensions that exist between other religions. There is something in this, but the truth is more complex. Although Buddhist teachings reject violence in all forms, there are longstanding conflicts between Buddhists and Moslems in Thailand, Myanmar and Bangladesh, between Hindus and Buddhists in Sri Lanka and India and between Christians and Buddhists in Korea, Sri Lanka, Mongolia and elsewhere. Often these conflicts are more about ethnic tensions and the effects of nationalism, rather than religion per se, but the two are often hard to disentangle. Consequently, while some Buddhist movements such as Sarvodaya in Sri Lanka have led efforts to make connections across communal divides and to resolve conflicts nonviolently, other Buddhist leaders have been prominent advocates of nationalism and even ethnic violence.

Running alongside these political and ethnic issues, Buddhist teachings set it apart from most of the religious traditions that are represented in interfaith settings. Buddhism is not part of the Abrahamic family of faiths, and while Hindus sometimes consider Buddhism to be a part of the Hindu fold, most Buddhists hold that fundamental differences separate them. Above all, Buddhism is nontheistic, and this can lead to awkward moments in interfaith gatherings. At one meeting I attended a Bahá'í speaker informed us that, despite our differences, we were united by our devotion to God. I hardly liked to spoil the mood by telling her that Buddhism is not concerned with God whatever name He goes by.

While the early Buddhist scriptures portray the Buddha in dialogue with numerous celestial beings, one of whom (Brahma) is considered the most eminent, the Buddha denied that any of the gods, Brahma included, had any special significance from the perspective of Buddhist practice (Dharmasiri 1988). Buddhism is often called 'agnostic' in the sense that it does not explicitly deny the existence of God, but it is also nontheistic in the sense that God does not play a role in its teachings. So while most Buddhists, in my experience, are happy to visit places of worship belonging to other faiths, respect the rituals connected to them and participate in shared ceremonies, we are likely to disengage from prayers that assume a shared belief in God or acceptance of other non-Buddhist beliefs.

A further reason why Buddhists can find themselves in a distinctive position in interfaith settings is the place of Buddhism in British society. When the organisers' principal aim is allaying ethnic or religious tensions, Buddhists are likely to find that their presence is largely irrelevant. The 2011 census found there were 248,000 Buddhists in the UK, around half of whom were ethnically Asian (Office for National Statistics 2016). But ethnically Asian Buddhists are divided along both national and sectarian lines into fairly small groupings that in no way compare with large Hindu, Sikh or Muslim communities. Others are people of European descent who have converted to Buddhism, and interfaith representatives are often drawn from this group.

## WORSHIP IN BUDDHISM

Many people associate Buddhist practice with meditation, but a visit to a Buddhist temple will clearly show that we certainly do practise 'worship' (*puja* in Sanskrit). This is an important element of most Buddhist traditions and, in some traditions, such as Japanese Shin Buddhism, it is the main practice. But if Buddhists don't focus on God, what do we worship? The forms of Buddhist worship vary widely – think of the gulf between the mantras, incense and trumpets of Tibetan Buddhism and the formalised simplicity of Japanese Zen. But, for almost all Buddhists, devotional practices are directed towards the Buddha, Dharma and Sangha, which represent the highest values of Buddhism and are collectively known as the Three Jewels.

The golden Buddha Jewel is, in the first instance, Gautama, the historical individual who is known to history as the Buddha: 'The One who has Awakened'. For Buddhists, Gautama's Awakening or Enlightenment made him 'a teacher of gods and men'.[1] In the Mahayana Buddhism that prevails in Tibet, China and the Far East, Gautama (also called Shakyamuni) is just one figure in a pantheon that includes numerous archetypal Buddhas and other figures known as Bodhisattvas, all of whom represent Enlightenment in some way. Buddhists direct their devotion towards these figures and hold Enlightenment as a goal to which they themselves aspire.

The blue Dharma Jewel represents the Buddhist teachings and practices that lead towards Enlightenment. In addition, it is the reality, beyond words and concepts, which these teachings describe. The Sangha Jewel is red in colour. 'Sangha' often means the community of all Buddhists and sometimes the monastic order, but as an object of devotion it usually refers to all those who have gained some degree of Awakening and therefore embody the Buddhist path and guide others along it.

Buddhist ceremonies are sometimes very elaborate, but at their heart is an expression of commitment towards and reverence for the Three Jewels (often referred to as 'Going for Refuge'), accompanied by offerings and chanting of some sort. Buddhist shrines, which are the focus of Buddhist temples and centres, feature representations of the Three Jewels, often centring on an image of the Buddha himself. Buddhist worship therefore involves praise of spiritual exemplars, expressions of commitment to the Buddhist ethical precepts and

1   *sattha devamanussanam*; the epithet is found in the Buddhist chant 'The Tiratana Vandana'.

expressions of spiritual aspiration. This usually isn't prayer in a petitionary sense, but expressions of aspiration can take a prayer-like form.

## THE BUDDHIST CONTRIBUTION TO INTERFAITH WORSHIP

For all the differences from other faiths, I believe that Buddhism can make a distinctive contribution to interfaith dialogue and worship because at least some elements of Buddhist discourse offer a viable language for at least some of the values that the various faiths share in common.

### Compassion, ethics and common humanity

Compassion, or 'loving-kindness', is a core value for Buddhists, as it is for members of other faiths. All of us, Buddhist teachings say, want to find happiness and avoid suffering, and yet our lives are impermanent and insecure. The human condition, therefore, involves continually seeking to make sense of our experience – grasping on to things we find pleasant and pushing away what we find painful – and this causes us to suffer.

Compassion is the natural response to seeing this suffering and understanding the process that causes it. The Buddhist approach to compassion encourages us to see beyond the badges and identities (including religious ones) that keep us apart, so that we can meet simply as fellow human beings. Buddhist ethics starts with a sense of compassionate connection with others that prompts a wish to help those who suffer and to avoid causing suffering. Buddhist ethical reflection concerns what that means in practice.

The Dalai Lama has been a leading proponent of this approach, which is encapsulated in the titles of his books: *Ancient Wisdom, Modern World: Ethics for the New Millennium* (Dalai Lama and Norman 1999) and *An Appeal by the Dalai Lama to the World: Ethics Are More Important than Religion* (Dalai Lama and Alt 2016). He has made the annual Kalachakra initiation ceremony an interfaith event dedicated to world peace, and he leads compassion-based meditations at meetings of global faith leaders.

## Meditation and mindfulness

One important Buddhist teaching identifies five 'spiritual faculties'. Faith, which is fostered through worship, is one of these, but the remainder of Buddhist practice relates to the other four: energy, wisdom, meditation and mindfulness, and I suggest the last two offer the Buddhist distinctive contribution to interfaith worship.

While Buddhists of Asian descent are often most familiar with devotional practices, Western converts to Buddhism typically practise silent, contemplative meditation. There are many Buddhist meditation practices, but the most prevalent do not imply any particular set of beliefs. The Mindfulness of Breathing, the commonest Buddhist meditation practice, involves focusing on the breath and the body, and the Development of Loving-Kindness practice offers simple ways to foster kindly feelings for oneself and others.

Mindfulness is sometimes identified with meditation, but while a meditation practice is a particular technique that one engages in for a period of time, mindfulness is an attitude or faculty that one can use in any situation. A simple definition is that mindfulness is a way of paying attention, calmly and without judgements, in the present moment, to yourself, others and the world around you.

I think the resonance of mindfulness in society at large is a sign that it can also have a role in interfaith settings. Mindfulness practices derived from Buddhism have been integrated with modern psychological approaches and are widely taught in the National Health Service, schools and many organisations. They are often seen as a key to wellbeing, an antidote to the stresses of modern life and a gateway to spiritual experience. In addition, there are growing mindfulness movements in some Christian churches as well as in Jewish and some other faith traditions. Among the Christians, Richard Harries and Rowan Williams are both practitioners and advocates of mindfulness who connect Buddhist-inspired practices with contemplative aspects of their own faith.

Mindfulness practices are being successfully employed across these secular and religious settings because they speak to immediate experience without invoking particular beliefs or images. In Buddhist settings, mindfulness has a particular meaning and purpose but, because Buddhists see it as a human faculty, we understand that it has a role in any setting where people value calm and awareness. Even when mindfulness is stripped out of its traditional context a spiritual resonance often remains and this is significant in interfaith gatherings because most worship is intertwined with beliefs that are not shared by members of other faiths. Some faith representatives will undoubtedly view Buddhist-derived mindfulness practice techniques with suspicion, but the techniques themselves are accessible to all.

## INTERFAITH WORSHIP AT THE GIRLS' SCHOOLS CONFERENCE

In 2015 I was contacted by Alun Jones, the president of the Girls' Schools Association, in regard to their annual conference at The Celtic Manor, which is near my home in Cardiff. Around three hundred heads of the country's leading independent girls' schools attend the conference each year and the event has always included a Christian service. Alun wanted to enliven this element of the proceedings and told me that he was struck by the growing popularity of mindfulness within the schools. We agreed that the best approach would be for me to co-lead the service with a Christian minister and that together we would find a way to combine mindfulness practices, plus a little Buddhism, with more familiar Christian elements. Alun nominated Rev Dr Karin Von Harmuth, an Anglican priest in Cambridgeshire, to co-lead the service, and together Alun, Karin and I devised the programme.

The service was entitled 'Schooling the Heart', and we intended it as an opportunity for the participants to re-centre themselves in the midst of a hectic event. As well as offering an opportunity for Christian worship, it showed how a service can foster an atmosphere of calm and reflection; we hoped the heads would find this relevant to their schools.

The service started with music and a hymn. Then I gave an address on the theme of 'Schooling the Heart', which explored the importance of emotional development in education, and I led a period of guided mindfulness meditation. This introduced and set the mood for a reflective sequence of music, Biblical readings, hymns and a poem. Karin led the Christian elements and I led a short period of loving-kindness meditation. Finally, both Karin and I offered short prayers. My prayer concerned 'Transference of Merits', a reflection from Mahayana Buddhism, which expresses the altruistic desire that the benefits of one's actions are felt by all beings.

Around eighty head teachers attended the service. We had been concerned that some people would feel that a longstanding Christian element of the conference was being undermined by the introduction of non-Christian elements, but the responses were positive.

The service wasn't presented as interfaith worship. Other than the concluding prayer, the Buddhist material was implicit and placed in the service of the event itself. The intention was to deepen participants' engagement with their own experience and to place the Christian and secular elements of the service in that context. However, I was speaking as a Buddhist and offered Buddhist reflections.

## CONCLUSION

The resonance of mindfulness practice in this predominantly Christian setting raises a more fundamental question about interfaith worship: are we simply worshipping alongside each other, or are we seeking common ground in which we can practise together? Of course, the latter is more problematic but, from my perspective as a Buddhist, I think it is possible. It requires that we shift our focus from the object that we worship – for instance, God or the Buddha – to the subject who worships – that is, to ourselves and our immediate experience. Mindfulness, an offering from the Buddhist tradition, gives one way of doing that and it can happily co-exist with methods drawn from other faiths.

## SUMMARY

- Buddhists are active in interfaith settings and have been prominent advocates of religious harmony.

- However, globally Buddhists are also party to religious conflicts.

- Buddhism is set apart from many other faiths as a non-Abrahamic and nontheistic tradition with a distinctive view of the nature of religion.

- Buddhists also have a smaller stake in the communal and ethnic issues that often drive interfaith initiatives than members of some other communities.

- Buddhists do engage in worship and devotion, which focuses on the Three Jewels: the Buddha, Dharma and Sangha.

- Buddhism can make a distinctive contribution to interfaith gatherings through teachings and practices that don't imply a particular set of beliefs and offer a shared language for values that are common to all faiths.

- Buddhist resources that can be explored in this way include its teachings on ethics and compassion.

- There is a particular role for mindfulness practices as a part of interfaith worship because it offers a spiritual practice with which all participants can engage.

## REFERENCES

Dalai Lama (2010) 'Many faiths, one truth.' *New York Times*, 24 May.

Dalai Lama and Alt, F. (eds) (2016) *An Appeal by the Dalai Lama to the World: Ethics Are More Important than Religion.* Salzburg: Benevento.

Dalai Lama and Norman, A. (1999) *Ancient Wisdom, Modern World: Ethics for the New Millennium.* London: Abacus.

Dharmasiri, G. (1988) *A Buddhist Critique of the Christian Concept of God.* Kandy, Sri Lanka: Golden Leaves.

Office for National Statistics (2012) 2011 Census aggregate data, UK Data Service.

# Reflection

## The Editors

One of the benefits of interfaith contact is that it is full of surprises and challenges. What defines a religion? What of a great and ancient religion which is not theistic and therefore neither prays, at least in a petitionary sense, nor worships a god or gods? There are also shocks, for we are reminded by Vishvapani Blomfield that Buddhism, which has an enviable reputation for cultivating generosity and peace, can be and is caught up in nationalism and violence in common with other religions throughout history and all over the world. All religions exist embedded in human society and none can avoid being conditioned by their social and political context. Religions are very different, and each has a struggle to play to its strengths.

Or are they that different? This chapter on Buddhism comes just after one on Jainism and follows an earlier one on Hinduism. There are important similarities in the manner in which all three religions describe the route to spiritual perfection and also in their ethical teaching. That does not mean that all are 'going the same way', but there are links which can be seen as bridges enabling prayer and devotion to be explored jointly and then shared with others.

Buddhism, in its many varieties, has much to contribute to interfaith worship and prayer and there have been influential leaders, like the Dalai Lama, who are widely respected for their deep insights, especially in the practice of meditation as a route to wisdom and purity of life, on the path to the supreme goal of Enlightenment.

Taking prayer first, the two authors point out that they cannot participate in something which makes an assumption which they deny, namely that there is a god or gods. When meeting with Buddhists, there is no shared belief in God from which to start. Yet the focused use of silence and the practice of meditation and mindfulness bring an invaluable gift to those of other faiths. Practices such as the Mindfulness of Breathing relate to what are basic human experiences and therefore can be shared by all. Many of those who do not see themselves as religious, as well as those from religious groups, have found that the attentiveness of mindfulness improves attitudes both to self and to others. And the calm reflective nature of meditation contrasts with the words (and sometimes wordiness) of the practice of praying in other religions. Meditation may appear to be empty of content or even selfish, but Bogoda Seelawimala points out that meditation provides an opportunity to work hard to weaken greed, hatred and delusion, while strengthening the capacity for love and generosity on the road to Enlightenment. What is more, he quotes from writings on Buddhism containing poetry which, although not prayers to God, nevertheless chime in with the sentiment and language of prayer used by other faiths, for example: 'May I be a home for the homeless and a servant for the world.'

The question of worship also leads to a contrast to the activities of other faiths. What is it to worship without a belief in God? Yet Buddhists give great value to chanting (perhaps together with the spinning of a prayer wheel), both as a benefit to those who chant by protecting them from harm, and also, for example, as a help to someone who is ill or dying. Then there are prostrations in front of an image of the Buddha, in order to engender respect and humility in the believer and to give thanks for the teaching and example of the Buddha.

Both the 'prayer' and the 'worship' have clear ethical intentions. The aim is to purify the mind of the believer, creating a right attitude to others and a general sense of loving-kindness, harmony and compassion for the suffering. It is the duty of Buddhists to work hard to lead a good life and to awaken a capacity for giving loving help to others. Merit, which has been gained through generosity, is seen as being transferred to others, thus giving benefit to all.

Buddhists can bring much to interfaith prayer and worship, especially as they have a distinctive approach which can complement the practices of other religions. That is especially the case with meditation and mindfulness.

# Chapter 8

# ZOROASTRIANISM

## 1

## Moving Forward through Prayer and Worship Together

Jehangir Sarosh

### Greetings

*Hamazor hama asho-bed*, may all be united in strength and righteousness.

### THE NEED

Everything in creation is either evolving or dying, and the time has come to realise that and to accept that the only way forward is to acknowledge the interconnectedness, the interrelatedness and the interdependence of creation. Either we live well together or suffer and die apart.

I am considering the role of religions in our changing society, a society that is changing not only in the economy, but also culturally, demographically and religiously. Many factors are contributing to the rapid changes that are taking place: globalisation, climate change, movement of people, the demands of economic wellbeing, loss of trust in religious institutions. At the same time, there is a rise in the individual search for spiritual growth through practices such as mindfulness, meditation and yoga.

This desire for spiritual growth requires religious institutions to abandon their exclusiveness and grow, evolve and move forward as part of the family of humanity. Praying together is not just an approach for a few to follow while being ignored by the exclusivists; it is a moral decision that affects the wellbeing of the whole human family and especially of future generations.

The saying is 'don't curse the darkness; light a candle'. Interfaith prayer helps to light the universal light.

## HUMILITY AND COURAGE

Religions were the first international institutions and their unique asset is their transcending of ethnic and national borders. Today, however, they are often seen as divisive, creating a notion of the Other. So their transcending of borders has to be harnessed once again for the global community to flourish. This will require humility and courage.

It will require humility to acknowledge that my religion is good: good not better. Then it will be possible to accept that the other also has good within it, thereby recognising the worth of the other and our common kinship.

It will also require courage to recognise that the changes needed are applicable to each of our religious institutions, understandings and observances. It is vital that we stop thinking only of our own flock and recognise that 'we must be the change we wish to see in the world'. That change is within individuals and institutions: all open to growth and development, not losing our important foundations, but open to the Spirit.

Within our interfaith encounter, the concept of the 'Other' dissolves, as we give greater emphasis to the golden rule 'do unto others as you would have them do unto you' – a dictum that is in most, if not in all, of our religions. The Other will be one of us and yet each will still remain a Christian, a Hindu, a Jew, a Buddhist, a Jain, a humanist, an atheist.

Discipline, maturity and humility are required. I recall an interfaith meeting that was organised in London, where during the morning session the Abrahamic faiths (Jews, Christians, Muslims) offered their contribution and then left, missing the afternoon session which was to be the contribution of the other faiths. Perhaps they were not yet ready for a true dialogue, not ready to recognise the truth that Truth is not the exclusive possession of any single faith.

## PRAYING TOGETHER

Christians, Hindus, Jews, Zoroastrians and Muslims creating a larger circle of prayer

Credit: Jehangir Sarosh

If my religion does not help me to connect with the divine, the self within, with you, with mother earth, to me that is no religion. The religious tendency is to live comfortably within our own 'private' or exclusive communities, whether they be religious or ethnic. What we need to create is a larger circle that offers a sense of belonging to us all through prayer and worship together, opening our hearts and giving a soul to the community.

Christians speak of 'bringing the kingdom of heaven to earth', Jews speak of 'repairing the world'; in the Zoroastrian tradition we say 're-fresh the world'.

Common kinship within religions binds people together; common kinship through interfaith worship and prayer binds communities together. This sense of community can be further developed if each religion offers a positive word about the faith of the 'Other' during an interfaith service or prayer meeting, recognising and honouring the dignity and worth of the Other. For that to happen, we need to feel secure in our own faith.

During the troubles in Ireland, 'Religions for Peace' organised a multifaith event in Belfast. During the preparatory meeting we suggested that it was our usual practice for each of us to offer a prayer before the start. To this, one of the Northern Irish religious communities objected and said they would not pray together in the same room. One of our team members suggested that perhaps we could all sit in silence for a few minutes before we start. We were told that the silence would be considered to be prayer and therefore be unacceptable. We left it at that, and then had a successful interfaith meeting, sharing our common concerns while reflecting on our Scriptures. At the end of the meeting we were surprised and delighted when the same faith community that had objected to praying together suggested we ought to finish with silent prayer together. By working together, all felt secure. Even though it was silent prayer, it was a beginning. From small acorns do mighty oaks grow.

Over the course of the past forty years with 'Religions for Peace', we made it a practice to begin the day with prayers and meditations, offered by people of different faiths. Where appropriate others joined in, while those who found it uncomfortable just bowed their heads and remained silent. This practice enables people to enjoy the harmony of diversity during the rest of the day.

## A NEW SITUATION

We felt safe if our nations were a monoculture with a homogeneous single faith and a single ethnicity, offering a sense of belonging. It follows that religions cooperating together have an important task of creating a new environment that celebrates and recognises the changed religious and cultural context: one that perceives the humanity of the 'Other' thereby acknowledging our common vulnerabilities and our shared responsibility to address them. Prayer and worship together help in this task.

## SOCIAL RESPONSIBILITY

One driving force for interfaith worship and prayer is social responsibility. Here religions need to respond to the current situation by promoting freedom, wellbeing and justice for all. Religions have often failed to promote justice or have even promoted injustice and given religious justification for doing so. Here Zoroastrianism can play a crucial part, for ethics are at the heart of the religion. 'Listen with your ears to the best things. Reflect with a clear mind – each for herself/ himself – upon the two choices of decision…and

choose good' (Yasna 30.2), 'with responsible choice and free will at
your command' (Yasna 31.11). (Yasna is the primary collection of
Zoroastrian texts.)

We cannot abdicate responsibility. Asho Zarathushtra knew that
what he said might not be valid in the future, so he offers us the
responsibility for constant reformation, re-formation according to
the need/context of the moment.

Religions can work together, which also means talking, praying
and worshipping together, looking jointly at our institutions and at
the wider world to see where human rights are denied.

Zoroastrianism has at its centre the triple ethic of Good Thoughts,
Good Words and Good Deeds, where good is often described as
'Only that which is good for any body, is good for one's own self'.
Its dualistic philosophy is not of two gods but of good and not good,
alongside the gift of free will.

> Hearken with your ears to these best counsels,
> Reflect upon them with illumined judgment.
> Let each one choose his creed with that
> freedom of choice each must have at great events.
> O ye, be awake to these, my announcements.

In the next stanza Yasna says:

> In the beginning there were two primal spirits,
> Twins simultaneously active
> These are the good, and the not good, in thought, and in word,
>     and in deed
> Between these two, let the wise one choose good,
> be good, not base. (Irani 1994, HA 30. 1&2)

Hence the prayer:

> Remember Remember Remember
> Evil is not in the body
> Evil is in the mind
> Therefore harm no body
> Just change the mind
> Just change the mind
> Just change the mind

I am reminded of an example of changing the mind through a
multifaith encounter. The European Council of Religious Leaders

(ECRL) was asked by a United Nations agency, which was having difficulty in getting the Muslim and Christian communities to work with them, to help in rebuilding the mosques and churches that were destroyed during the fighting in Kosovo. Neither community would work with the UN agency, on the grounds that the UN was supporting the other side. ECRL called a meeting of the religious leaders of the two communities of Kosovo together with religious leaders from six other faiths. An agreement was reached in a safe multifaith environment: a classic example of where religion was a problem, but religions together was the solution.

There is a desire amongst many young people to experience the divine, the mystery of the self and the joy of being. The young are put off by the exclusivist way of thinking and living, which is seen by them as divisive, not leading to a more fulfilled life.

They wish to engage with the spiritual and also to be involved in humanitarian actions to heal the world. This is what makes them feel fulfilled and happy. Zarathushtra said, 'Happiness to the one who gives happiness to others' (Dhalla, no date).

Joint action enables people to feel empathy with the Other and to experience love and belonging. Participants connect with the human spirit: a spiritual experience.

If we accept that my religion is good and not better, then it is easier to accept that the Other also has something good within, thereby recognising the worth of the other and enabling joint prayer and worship to help integration.

Many communities are now free to discover new ways of being religious and of embracing diversity.

## THE ROLE OF ZARATHUSHTIES (ZOROASTRIANS) IN INTERFAITH WORK

The philosophy of Zarathustra offers a meeting of East and West. From the East: its encounter in India with the concept of Dharma – duty. Also, the Hindu notion of a God for each temperament, yet believing in one ultimate divinity with a thousand names. Zoroastrianism is entwined with the ancient Persian culture and values. From the West, the few hundred years of Christian education and influence has enabled Zoroastrianism to be more liberal, through the understanding of the various Christian reformations and the Enlightenment.

Yet we have retained the basic tenets of Asho Zarathushtra's philosophy, giving us the talent to integrate but not totally assimilate, thus maintaining our uniqueness (as many other religious traditions have).

## AN OPEN INVITATION

Interfaith organisations have the question of which groups can be considered a religion and whom to invite to the table. Perhaps one group is seen as a cult and another as 'too new'. More often the objection is from the so-called mainstream religion (mainstream because of their numbers) and thereby being divisive.

I remember well when, some forty years ago, interfaith groups were seen as a fringe element and the attitude of mainstream religious leaders was 'ignore them they will go away'. Today they are our presidents and patrons!

Religions offer hope of a better world to the whole of humanity through the philosophy of love, compassion, righteous action, charity, and so on. Therefore, I would invite all to the table while being mindful of the objective of that specific encounter. For example, if the issue is freedom of religion and belief, one could not leave out any faith. At the same time, one has to be pragmatic and may need to begin with a small group, earn their trust and then gradually expand.

On the point of trust, I am reminded of an incident during my tenure as chairman of our local interfaith group in Watford. During some riots in India there was an attempt to burn down the local mosque in Watford. This act of arson was perceived to have been carried out by some Hindus. The hotheads in the mosques were threatening to go out and burn the Hindu shops. A friend of mine called me from the mosque and asked me to come and try to calm things down.

I went to the mosque with the leader of the Hindu community. By then the police were already there. Through discussion, calm was restored, because the Hindu leader promised that if they found out who did this act, they would hand the culprit over to the police.

The imam accepted this, for he knew the Hindu leader through the interfaith group and they had prayed together. Peace was restored: an example of relationships building through interfaith prayer.

## WHAT IS PRAYER; WHAT IS WORSHIP?

- Religions cooperating together have an important task of creating a new environment – cooperation is prayer in action.

- Standing together showing solidarity with the other is prayer.

- Listening to the other is prayer.

- Understanding the other is worshipping with the other.

- Through interfaith prayer and worship we develop a spiritual community, an openness that brings about understanding of the other, recognition of her/his dignity and thereby respect for each other.

- Praying together is promoting integration that offers a sense of belonging.

- Praying together is a joyous healing experience of our interrelatedness.

- Common kinship through interfaith worship and prayer binds communities together.

- Caring for the other is worship.

- Sharing prayer and worship together, we communicate our feeling for each other.

- Worshipping is honouring and respecting not just the divine somewhere out there, but the divine in the Other and all elements of the creation.

- More and more governments, especially in secular Europe, are recognising the value of religions cooperating together, enabling religions to claim their appropriate space in the public square to safeguard common ethical values.

Zarathushies (Zoroastrians) are a minority community yet are involved in disproportionate numbers in interfaith and multifaith organisations. Perhaps because of their aim to make this a better world (added to which they, and their religion, do not threaten anyone) Zarathushties have had the honour to serve as officers (and still do) on local, national and international interfaith organisations.

Asho Zarathustra's ethical principle can be summed up as: may good thoughts be formulated into good words and may the good words manifest into good actions.

This prayer for peace is an example:

> Peace is for the hungry to be fed; feeding the hungry is prayer in action.
> Peace is for the sick to experience care; caring for the other is prayer in action.
> For the oppressed, peace is to be released; working for the freedom of the other is prayer in action.
> Allowing the voiceless to be heard is prayer in action.
> Bringing the marginalised to the centre is prayer in action.
> May our actions together be our prayers.

I began and I conclude with the Zoroastrian greeting that is itself a prayer:

*Hamazor hama asho-bed*

May we all be united in strength and righteousness.

May all be united

## REFERENCES

Dhalla, M.N. (no date) *As Homage Unto Ahura Mazda*. Karachi: The Karachi Parsi Anjuman Trust Fund & YMZA/Dastur Dr. Dhalla Institute.

Irani, Dinshaw J. (1994) *Understanding the Gathas*. Womelsdorf, PA: Ahura Publishers.

## FURTHER READING

Jehangir Jamshedji Motivala (1897) *Enlightened Non-Zoroastrians on Mazdayasnism*. Bombay.

Khosro Khazai (2007) *The Gathas: The Sublime Book of Zarathushtra*. Brussels: European Centre for Zoroastrian Studies.

### Websites

Avesta: Zoroastrian Archives (extant scriptures of Zoroastrianism and Pahlavi): *www.avesta.com*

European Zoroastrian Foundation: *www.gatha.org*

# 2

# Zoroastrian History and Beliefs Are Compatible with Interfaith Involvement

Behram Deboo and Maneck Bhujwala

## INTRODUCTION

The religion founded by Iranian prophet Zarathushtra (known as Zoroaster by ancient Greek philosophers like Plato, who studied his teachings and philosophy and incorporated some of his concepts such as rational thinking) is one of the oldest monotheistic, revealed religions of the world still very much alive and practiced, which has influenced Judaism, Christianity, and Islam. Zoroastrianism was the majority religion of three Persian empires for over a thousand years and has a small but dedicated following today.

Different modern scholars have placed Prophet Zarathushtra somewhere around 1700 BCE and Greek and Roman historians have dated Zarathushtra as living around 6000 BCE. US archaeologist scholar, Mary Settegast, a graduate of UC Berkeley and Columbia University, supports the earlier date (based on her archaeological research and the Prophet Zarathushtra's advocacy of a settled life and his praises for the farmer) and has explained her reasons in a book, *When Zarathushtra Spoke* (2005). So, over the centuries, traditions have evolved, influenced by different ethnic groups who followed this religion.

Zoroastrianism became prominent with the establishment of the first Persian empire by Cyrus the Great (who is mentioned as a savior of the Jews in the Old Testament). Briefly interrupted for around two hundred years by the invasion of Alexander the Macedonian and the rule of his generals, the religion revived under two other Persian empires for several centuries but declined under Muslim rulers after the Arab invasion of Iran in the seventh century CE, and committed genocide, forced conversions, slavery, and persecution of Iranian subjects for centuries after the invasion.

What makes Zoroastrians naturally comfortable with the concept of interfaith unity, prayer, and service is their belief that all religions that share common ethical values and goals were divinely inspired by the same source of all good creations, which is known by different names and is worthy of respect. In general, Zoroastrians are proud of their religion, but do not consider other religions as inferior or see the need to convert people of other religions; they do not have missionary programs for doing conversions. In the multicultural and multireligious society of India (where some Persians migrated in the tenth century CE, after the Arab Muslim invasion of Iran to escape genocide, persecution, and forced conversion to Islam), many Zoroastrians respectfully visit places of worship of other religions and sometimes even join in prayer with them.

Those Zoroastrians who are members of interfaith organizations or who attend interfaith events in the USA often participate in interfaith prayer and worship. Progressive Zoroastrians are usually open to joining interfaith organizations and attending interfaith events. Some other Zoroastrians believe that we have to faithfully follow the religion of our parents, and avoid getting distracted by other religions, and therefore these Zoroastrians will not join interfaith organizations nor attend interfaith events. Some other Zoroastrians are afraid of attempts by some interfaith members to try to proselytize, and therefore stay away from joining interfaith organizations. This is a valid concern, in spite of the fact that many interfaith organizations include a policy prohibiting proselytizing in their constitutions. Some organizations call themselves 'interfaith,' even though they may have different interpretations of that word, for example groups restricted to different types of Christian, or Abrahamic groups, and even these may be further restricted to mainstream religions. Sometimes the word 'interfaith' is used to attract people to a meeting where proselytizing is employed with a soft-sell approach.

## POSSIBILITY OF INTERFAITH PRAYER AND WORSHIP

Today we live in a world that is increasingly global in many ways. We work in many private companies and in city, state, and national government departments, with people of different ethnic and religious backgrounds. We see a diversity of people at grocery stores, shopping malls, movie theatres, restaurants, and often get to know something about their religious beliefs. With the internet we can also learn about other religions at the touch of a button, if we have the interest. So there is a strong possibility that we will not only learn something about other religious beliefs, but also realize that there are many things in common that different religions share. So it is very possible that at least some people will attend interfaith events or join interfaith organizations, and become curious to learn more from the internet, work colleagues, and friends. Eventually some of these people will find the opportunity to participate in interfaith prayer and worship, and potentially experience the feeling of brotherhood and sisterhood.

Different interfaith council meetings and events may have different customs involving prayers. In the interfaith council in Huntington Beach, California, which is an all-volunteer group that includes faith organizations and individuals as members, meeting once a month in the early morning, we usually ask the volunteer who brought the breakfast to lead a short prayer before the meeting begins. The South Coast Interfaith Council has representatives from different faith communities but is limited to a board of directors and maintains a paid administrative staff. It meets once a month in the evening, each faith representative taking a turn each month in giving a brief talk about his/her faith and/or a short prayer. Some people will use a specific name of God or the name of their religious founder in the prayer, and others will use a general term like 'God.' A genuine interest in learning about other religions and not making judgments about other religions makes it possible to have prayers from different religions recited at interfaith meetings. When any prayer is being recited by a faith representative, the rest of the members bow their heads and listen respectfully, joining in an 'Amen' at the end of the prayer. On some occasions, when the prayer is composed without specific names of God and is not directly from any one scripture, people of all faiths may join in reciting the prayer.

Music is known as a universal language, and when associated with prayer is often another popular form of interfaith prayer that attracts people of different faiths to join in, either in the form of songs or prayer accompanied by music. Some Christian groups will sing with a guitar and other Western instruments. Christmas carols are popular during holidays, often sung by diverse choral groups. Sikhs will sing with Indian musical instruments like the harmonium and tabla (small drum). The original teachings of Prophet Zarathushtra are known as 'Gathas' (meaning songs) that were composed in a unique poetic meter by the prophet himself, and therefore can be recited like a song with or without Persian or Indian musical instruments. Later compositions by his followers also include religious poems in praise of God or His messengers, known as 'Monajats,' which can be sung with or without musical accompaniment. Although originally composed in Persian languages, today there are also English versions which can be sung by English-speaking participants, and there are Gujerati language versions used in India.

Meditation is another form of interfaith prayer that is sometimes practiced by interfaith groups. Hindu representatives in interfaith meetings and events sometimes lead a short meditation reciting the word 'Om.' Prophet Zarathushtra told his followers to meditate on his teachings in order to properly understand their deep meanings, so that they can make the right informed decisions in their daily life. Rational thinking instead of blind faith requires meditation and understanding. So Zarathushtis can easily take part in a meditation form of silent interfaith prayer.

Yet another type of interfaith prayer and worship done by some interfaith organizations is service to the community. Prophet Zarathushtra taught his followers about good thoughts, good words, and good actions, to bring happiness to society. In our short prayer of Yatha Ahu Vairyo, one line reminds us that the kingdom of God can be established by giving help to those in need. On the service day, some local interfaith organizations carry out several projects such as providing medical and hygiene items, food, and other services to the homeless or tasks such as cleaning up parks and beaches, or painting fences. Visiting different places of worship is becoming popular, as it allows people to see how prayer and worship is done in different denominations, as well as seeing religious symbols and hearing a talk from an authorized representative explaining beliefs and worship style.

From extensive experience in the interfaith councils, in Washington State and California, respectively, by the authors of this article, it was noticed that what is normal behavior in one group might not be the same for other groups. It was noticed that some religions have some type of hierarchy which involves the priest class or caste and the laity. A line is drawn between them. In Hinduism and Zoroastrianism, the priest was traditionally born into the priestly family; the succession is hereditary. Daughters born of the priest family were not allowed to be priests. However, it was also learned that Hinduism has occasionally allowed women to become priests regardless of their birth origin, known as 'Purohits.' Similarly, today, in Zoroastrianism, men and women from the laity are being trained as assistant priests called 'Paramobeds' or 'Mobedyars,' in order to cope with the current shortage of practicing hereditary priests. Their role is restricted so as to maintain the privileged status of hereditary priests who undergo more rigorous training in India and Iran. However, in the past history of Zoroastrianism the separation of priests from laity was not always practiced strictly, and it was more of a social class, unlike the Hindu caste system. Even when it was occasionally strictly practiced, exceptions were made to allow qualified laypersons to enter priesthood. This is described in detail by Dr Sir Jivanji Jamshedji Modi in his book *The Religious Ceremonies and Customs of the Parsees* (1995; originally published in 1922), where the term Parsees (Persians) is used to refer to Zarathushtis who migrated to India from Iran. In more recent history, over the last few centuries, especially in Indian society where a caste system is practiced by Hindus, the separation between priest and laity has become strict again, with a difference that allows children of priests to take on other occupations but does not allow children of laity to become regular priests.

It was observed that in Islam, Christianity, Jainism, and Buddhism, a priest is not defined by birth origin but rather is one who can be qualified if that person meets the requirements outlined by each religion. Judaism is observed as being very demanding in following the commandments, which can count in the hundreds in some versions. The menstrual law is more or less similar in Zoroastrianism to Judaism, except the former does not require the white cloth checked by a rabbi.

It was noticed that there is missionary zeal among Mormons where young people serve in pairs and go to different parts of the world and serve the Mormon temple at the family's expense. Members of the Mormon church were observed to be very polite and pleasant in communication with visitors to their church.

The main aim of interfaith is to promote understanding of different belief systems, which may not be identical to one's own, but enable the realization that there are more things we share in common, such as belief in a common source of creation, honesty, compassion, charity, justice, human dignity, and so on.

Due to a general lack of knowledge about Zoroastrianism in the public sphere, an educational campaign was launched to make people aware that it is a vibrant living religion, in spite of its relatively small numbers. It had to be explained during talks, panel discussions, and person-to-person dialogues that Zoroastrianism teaches about free will, and that choosing between good and bad has good and bad consequences, respectively. It was learned in interfaith communication that this may not always be the case with the Semitic religions, depending on the interpretation, where God's will and predestination work hand in hand together.

It was learned that quite often religious beliefs tend to be explained in religious terms only. In past times, since theologians lacked scientific as well as astronomical knowledge, everything was explained in terms of stories, metaphors, and images, whether it was the origin of the universe, earth, or beginning of humanity. Natural disasters were blamed on the sins of the people and even epidemics of diseases. More and more of today's younger generation do not readily accept what is told to them without asking questions; they are open to receiving information from alternate sources including the latest scientific studies.

In the past many religions have been used by political and religious leaders to promote intolerance, hatred, violence, and force, taking advantage of ignorance of other religions to gain political power or convert people of other religions. Interfaith communication was noticed to serve the purpose of accepting each other's belief systems nonjudgmentally, the understanding of the belief system in question, and bringing about cooperation between people of different religions to promote a 'live and let live' policy. Thus interfaith gatherings are definitely beneficial to promote peace and harmony in increasingly global and multicultural societies of today. What politicians often fail to do, because of mistrust of their knowledge and intentions, interfaith organizations have succeeded in: bringing people from historically opposing religious faiths together for dialogue.

In logical succession to interfaith dialogue, it is further observed that interfaith prayer and worship adds an emotional and spiritual dimension that can be a great binding force, uniting people of different faiths in a spirit of humility, brotherhood, sisterhood, and service to humanity, with hope of a better future for mankind and all creations on our planet Earth.

## CONCLUSION

In our opinion, interfaith prayer and worship, if done sincerely by participants who truly respect the rights of followers of different religions to believe and practice their own faiths in their own ways, can serve to build stronger relationships based on mutual respect and trust, and promote interfaith harmony among different faith communities in societies where such prayers are done.

## REFERENCES

Modi, J.J. (1995) *The Religious Ceremonies and Customs of the Parsees.* Bombay: Union Press.

Settegast, M. (2005) *When Zarathushtra Spoke.* Costa Mesa, CA: Mazda Publishers.

## FURTHER READING

Kanga, M.F. (1993) *Khordeh Avesta.* Bombay: Bombay Parsi Panchayet, Jenaz Printers.

Kanga, M.F. (1997) *Gatha-Ba-Mayeni.* Bombay: Bombay Parsi Panchayet, Jenaz Printers.

Mistree, K.P. (1982) *Zoroastrianism: An Ethnic Perspective*. Bombay: Zoroastrian Studies.

Taraporewala, I.J.S. (1979) *The Religion of Zarathushtra*. Bombay: B.I. Taraporewala Publishers.

## Websites
Avesta: Zoroastrian Archives (extant scriptures of Zoroastrianism and Pahlavi): *www.avesta.com*

# Reflection

## The Editors

A mark of this ancient religion is to treat other religions with respect, as equals. Zoroastrians are inclusive when it comes to the question of those to whom they relate in interfaith activity.

The three contributors state clearly that the faith is centred on 'Good Thoughts, Good Words, Good Deeds' in the context of the free will of each person; there is an emphasis on faith at all times having an ethical outcome in good actions. The qualities of humility and courage converge on the main aim, which is to re-fresh the world in response to the writings of the prophet Zoroaster and in the service of humanity. It follows that prayer is for the good of all and especially for peace and for those in need. This emphasis brings shape and force to what is a characteristic of the religions already covered in this book and indeed also to those of later chapters. There is no religion which cannot learn from others and the manner in which Zoroastrians express their ethic and put it into practice is of significance to all. In an age of increasingly multicultural societies with their accompanying variety of faiths, the need to pray together for good thoughts, words and deeds becomes all the greater.

A vital point made in Jehangir Sarosh's contribution (and in other parts of this book) is that interfaith meetings enable participants to know and trust each other. That sounds satisfactory in a general sort of way, but actual examples demonstrate the social and political consequences of personal contact and friendship. As Sarosh says, religions were the first international institutions and they have the capacity to transcend ethnic and national divides (an ability, sadly, often neglected). He gives examples of specific social and political outcomes: first after the Kosovo conflicts in the Balkans and second in Watford, England. In Kosovo the context of many faiths meeting together enabled the Christians and the Muslims, who had been on opposing sides, to have discussions and reach some agreements. In the Watford example, during riots in India a mosque in the town had been attacked, leading to a threatened disturbance between Muslim and Hindu communities. Peace was brought about through a meeting of leaders. They were part of an interfaith group and, having prayed together, they had gone beyond learning about each other's customs and beliefs and were able to put mutual trust to use in the community. That example illustrates the fact that with social media and other forms of contemporary communication, news (both true and false) travels fast and interfaith crises and triumphs are global in significance.

Such cases exemplify the Zoroastrian willingness to share in interfaith prayer and worship. The only reason cited for avoiding interfaith interaction is the danger that it will be used as an explicit or covert means for evangelism. Indeed, there is some implied criticism of the so-called 'Abrahamic religions' both for their histories and for their contemporary exclusiveness and air of superiority. One could add that such treatment happens despite the probability that Zoroaster's teaching influenced Judaism, Christianity and Islam (and the Scriptures of two of those faiths praise the Zoroastrian Cyrus the Great as the Lord's anointed! (Isaiah 45:1)).

Zoroastrians realise that many know little about their religion, so among other interfaith activities they spend much time giving an account of their own faith. They have many gifts to bring and share, especially their particular ethical emphasis, with help to those in need being seen as itself a prayer. Also, as mentioned by Behram Deboo and Maneck Bhujwala, they bring 'Gathas' and 'Monajats', which are poetic songs, often recited with Persian or Indian musical accompaniment. Each faith learns from the worship and prayer of others.

Chapter 9

# SHINTOISM

## 1

### Peaceful Co-Existence: The Indigenous Religion of Japan

Yoshinobu Miyake

As is the case with many languages and cultures existing in the world, there are various religions. This is undeniable fact. Historically and currently, religious differences have often been a cause of conflict and warfare. What is the role of religion in helping to counter strife in the modern world? (See Miyake 1991.)

## HIDDEN ASSUMPTIONS AMONG RELIGIONS

In this respect the religions called 'monotheist', which belong to the traditions of Abrahamic religion, such as Judaism, Christianity and Islam, recognize that many religions in fact exist. However, there is often a hidden assumption that 'my religion is the only right one among many religions'. This way of thinking is directly linked to the idea of 'alternative facts' which emerged when elections were conducted around the world in 2016–2017. This way of thinking resulted in confusion for citizens in the United States and Europe.

I have attended interfaith dialogue and worship more than a hundred times as a Shinto representative in the years since 1980. Although the fanatical fundamentalist will not attend, most participants, who seemingly have an open-minded attitude, also privately think 'my faith is the only right one, though there are many religions in the world' or 'there may be a part of truth (revelation) in other religions, but my religion has the authentic truth (revelation)'. I understand people's feelings if we are talking about our own faith subjectively; for each person, it is essential to believe that one's own faith is the right one.

However, this way of thinking is clearly contrary to the objective facts. It is helpful in understanding if we use languages as an analogy. Although human beings have 6500 languages now, nobody would say, 'French is more correct than Arabic.' If we compare the population of native speakers, the biggest population is those who speak Mandarin (955 million), followed by Spanish (405 million), English (360 million), Hindi (310 million) and Arabic (295 million) (Parkvall 2007). Among these languages, there is no distinction of rank in a qualitative sense, simply a quantitative distinction of population numbers. In religions, we cannot compare the qualitative distinction even if we could compare the quantitative one, such as the number of congregants.

## SHINTO'S RESPECT FOR OTHER RELIGIONS

Among the religions in the world, there are believers who hold as a matter of principle that 'my religion is the only right one among many religions'. On the other hand, there are believers who think 'there are many deities in the world and we should show our respect for another's faith'. Shinto, the indigenous religion of Japan, is the latter type. If we follow the study of religion, Shinto is sometimes categorized as 'animism', as we find a spiritual being not only in Heaven and Earth but in mountains, rivers, gigantic stones, enormous trees, animals and also the tools used in everyday life. With regard to human beings, not only the hero known for tremendous achievements but also the horrible person has the chance to be revered as a deity after death, if s/he has been an extraordinary personality. There is also the possibility of being revered before death. Ancestors are also revered as 'Kami' (deity). Therefore, in Shintoism, the term 'Yaoyorozu no Kami' (numerous numbers of deities) has been used since ancient times. In other words, it is a major concern for Shinto that the 'world' is filled with 'others' and to mediate between them in order to promote good relationships. It is the same logic as the 'principle of biodiversity' (the existence of various organisms and species which have many functions and keep the ecosystem working over long periods).

## THE PLACE OF SHINTO IN JAPANESE SOCIETY

In the past, religions of bountiful forest 'animism' expressed the religious sentiment of human beings all around the world, but they were pushed to the margins by Abrahamic religions founded in the arid area which is now called the Middle East. Now we find animism only in minority tribes who maintain their own cultural tradition, living in areas such as sub-Saharan Africa, Latin America, Southeast Asia or in isolated small islands far from any continent. Although Japan is a country with advanced technology that has a population of 125 million, it may surprise people to learn that Japanese religious sentiment is based on the element of animism.

Shinto is deeply rooted in Japanese society; if you visit a famous shrine in the New Year, you can see a million people visit to worship. About five hundred years have already passed since Christian missions came to Japan, but the population of Christians has never risen over 1 per cent, due to its intolerance toward other religions. When Buddhism was introduced into Japan via ancient China 1500 years ago, the Japanese constructed many temples and worshipped many Buddhas and Bodhisattvas, but they have never forsaken the faith in Shinto which has existed since ancient times. Moreover, since the commemoration of a person's ancestors, which is an important element of Shinto, has been integrated into Buddhism, Japanese Buddhism has become different from the Theravada Buddhism of Sri Lanka and Thailand, or the Mahayana Buddhism of China and Tibet. The description of such a religion could be: 'Buddhism influenced by Shinto'.

Even Amaterasu, who rules the world as Sun Goddess, did not adopt the style of top-down decision-making. She listens to others' opinions (including conflicting opinions) carefully and puts the consensus of opinion into action. After Buddhism reached Japan from China, the Japanese adopted this method. For a thousand long years, Shinto priests from across the country have visited temples and offered Shinto prayers to Buddhas and Bodhisattvas. Also, Buddhist monks from across the country visit shrines and read their sutras for Shinto deities. This religious tradition of syncretism of Shinto with Buddhism was the rule for religions in Japan until the 'shinbutsu bunri' (the separation of Shinto from Buddhism) was issued by the modern nation-state in 1868 under the influence of Western rationalism.

Prayer involving Buddhists, Shinto and new religious movements during a visit of the
Dalai Lama, Todaiji Temple, Japan

Subsequently, against Western powers who invaded Asia, Japan modernized (= Westernized) rapidly to maintain its independence. In the process, Japan borrowed only traditional Shinto ritual, while it built an official religion called 'State Shinto' with a hierarchical system. This system, which was 'not like Japan', continued until Japan's defeat in World War II. During six years under the occupation of the Allies led by the United States, Americans did missionary work enthusiastically, using 'carrots' like food distribution, but hardly managed to increase the number of Christians, as was the case for the previous four hundred years. Probably the reason was the Japanese idea which has continued since ancient times – that the view of 'the many' is more likely to be right than the view of 'only one'.

According to the oldest constitution of Japan, 'The Seventeen-article constitution', established in 604 by Prince Shotoku, it is stated in Article 1 that 'Harmony is to be valued', and in Article 17 that 'Decisions on important matters should not be made by one person alone. We make a great deal of sense in reaching a decision if we consider it together.' The Japanese people have preferred the opinion that the majority ought to be right, even if there is doubt whether it is absolutely right, as opposed to following the opinion of a leader, whatever the leader's ability. The people chose the idea of 'democratic process' believing that the majority's decision would lead in the right direction. Although Prince Shotoku is well known as someone who had deep knowledge of Buddhism and introduced it to Japan, we can see that his idea stems from a Shintoistic perspective.

This history of Shinto, together with the character of the Japanese, enabled them to be one of the leaders of interfaith dialogue after World War II. It is more than a coincidence that the International Religious Fellowship was established in 1947, and the World Conference of Religions for Peace was established in 1970 in Japan. In fact, many religious leaders who have different religious and traditional backgrounds still work together for a common goal many years after the founding of these interfaith organizations. For example, since 1987, the Gathering of Prayer for World Peace has been held at the summit of Mount Hiei, where there is a sanctuary of several Buddhist schools, and many different religions' leaders join in this event every year to pray together. This meeting is attended not only by Japanese traditional religious people like Buddhists and Shintoists, but also by authorized representatives coming from the Holy See and Al-Azhar (Islam) who generally do not pray together with other religions.

I think that the Japanese religious model, where many different religions co-exist peacefully (though it is a social model established by Shinto in ancient times), may offer an exemplary answer to the issues of a world which is divided by religious hostility or ethnic antagonism. However, since Shinto has put more weight on its daily 'ritual' offering to the deities, rather than on having 'written texts', which is common among Abrahamic religions, Buddhism and Hinduism, we Japanese lack sufficient materials written in English. This makes it difficult to explain the value of the 'Shinto' model in universal terms to people who do not speak Japanese. With an interest among many people of the world in the model of Shinto, the Japanese traditional religion, Shinto becomes increasingly useful in recognizing the meaning of 'praying together' in the modern world where the level of religious (or ethnic) conflict is escalating.

## REFERENCES

Miyake, Y. (1991) *The Living of Peace*. Laporte, PA: Heiwa Press.

Parkvall, M. (2007) 'Lista över världens största språk efter antal talare [The world's 100 largest languages in 2007].' In *Nationalencyklopedin*. Höganäs: Bra Böcker.

# 2

# 'All the World under One Roof'

## Yasuhiro Tanaka

I served as a Shinto priest to Meiji-Jingu Shinto Shrine, located in Tokyo, for over forty years. During my service there, I experienced several interreligious meetings. Based on my experience, I would like to express my thoughts on interfaith prayer and talk about what is helpful and what is not helpful in this matter.

First, I would like to introduce to you a *waka* poem by Emperor Meiji:

> Yomono-umi, Mina-harakara-to, Omouyoni, Nado Namikaze-no, Tachi Sawaguram
> The seas of the four directions –
> all are born of one womb:
> why, then, do the wind and waves rise in discord?

I believe in the universal brotherhood of all countries in the world, but it is a sad fact that conflicts do exist among many countries. The *waka* poem above has been well known in Japan not only during the Meiji era, when the emperor lived, but also throughout the long history of Japan. The belief represented in this poem has been present in Japan's diplomatic relations with other countries as well. Thus, we, as Japanese Shinto followers, believe interreligious and interfaith dialogue to be both meaningful and practical.

'*Hakko-ichi-u* (八紘一宇)' is another phrase that has been important in Japanese history. It means 'All the world under one roof'. The origin of this idea goes back to the first emperor of Japan, Emperor Jinmu. The idea was followed in the *waka* poem of Emperor Meiji. And not only the Meiji-Jingu Shrine but other Shinto shrines apply and reflect on this idea today, including in their engagement in interfaith dialogue.

In addition, this basic idea and philosophy can be found in Japanese mythology. As you know, Shinto is polytheistic. So, in the mythologies, whenever *Kami*-deities face troubles or problems, they discuss them with each other and solve them. An example of this is a story where the deity *Amaterasu-O-mikami* suddenly hides in a cave of rocks with a thick door, called *Amano-iwato-gakure*. This deity symbolizes the sun, so after she hides herself, the world becomes dark. While the other *Kami*-deities worry about the situation, one strong *Kami* among them cannot make a decision, so another deity asks all of them for ideas and opinions. Eventually each *Kami* takes a role and they succeed in regaining the sunlight. This story teaches us the importance of dialogue, of the value of gathering together, and of drawing out the wisdom of people around the world to create a better world.

## THE VALUE OF DIALOGUE

For a long time Japanese society has built up resources for interfaith dialogue with a view to mutual understanding, and Shinto shrines have been a crucial part of this process. Examples are the establishment and work of the World Federation Movement (WFM) for Japanese religious committees, the World Conference of Religions for Peace (WCRP), the Mount Hiei Religious Summit, and other interreligious gatherings. With the network built through such efforts, when we face difficult situations and challenges, such as earthquakes and other major disasters, we collaborate with each other and dispatch rescue teams made up of different religious groups. This is a consequence of helpful interreligious and interfaith dialogue. One of the recent examples would be the 2011 great earthquake that took place in the northeastern region of Japan. The interfaith voluntary rescue team not only contributed to the removal of debris, but also provided therapies for the survivors, organized memorial services for the casualties, and was of general assistance.

Another good example would be the 75th Pearl Harbor memorial ceremony that took place last year. Some interfaith delegations attended a service organized by the US Navy, and, on behalf of all the interfaith delegations, a Shinto priest made a speech there. Interfaith delegations have been sent to the memorial ceremony every year for the last 35 years. According to the Shinto priest, in the first few years, they were booed with calls such as 'Jap! Go home!' The interfaith delegations, however, never stopped attending the annual ceremony. They kept going back and finally, last year, the US attendees said to the Shinto priest, 'Thank you for attending and praying.'

There is another grass-roots effort that my family experienced during World War II. My ancestors served as Shinto priests for generations at a shrine named Hyozu-jinja in Aichi prefecture. The period when my grandfather served as a priest there was during World War II. Right beside the historic shrine was a Buddhist temple, also with a long history. The shrine had built an evacuation building to protect their treasures from the bombing attacks of the US. However, the Buddhist temple did not have any evacuation buildings to protect its treasures. My grandfather had long been acquainted with a monk at the temple, so he offered the temple part of the shrine's evacuation building so that they could protect their treasures. Because of this, valuable treasures of both the Shinto shrine and the Buddhist temple have been preserved to this day.

## SOME DIFFICULTIES

On the other hand I would say that what is unhelpful for our interfaith dialogue is the very absence of it. It remains the case that different religions have not been able to reach a deep dialogue. That is especially when we are faced with – and are focused on – religious and dogmatic differences, rather than finding common denominators. We tend to stop our dialogue and never reach deeper communication.

The tendency to try to understand other religions within one's own frame of philosophy or values, I suspect, is another unhelpful idea in interfaith dialogue. The language used for interfaith dialogue, especially at international conferences and gatherings, is English. When we try to explain about Shinto myths and philosophy, it is extremely difficult to express something so Japanese, while using other languages, particularly English, for the religious and cultural background of the language is monotheistic. For example, the meaning of *Kami*-deity in Shinto cannot be accurately expressed using the English term God or gods. With careless use of such terms in international interfaith gatherings, we are always faced with a dualistic idea that attempts simply to compare monotheism to polytheism, and, furthermore, to understand Shinto using monotheistic values and a monotheistic worldview. This can lead to significant misunderstanding and can become an obstacle as we strive towards true and meaningful interfaith dialogue and prayer. As much as I believe that international and interfaith effort in this matter is quite important, since every religion has its own unique worldview and beliefs, I also believe it is our responsibility, as Shinto delegations (and a challenge for us), to work towards the future to overcome these linguistic barriers in order to communicate our own beliefs more effectively.

## MUTUAL RESPECT

Now I am serving as the 204th chief priest of *Kamigamo-jinja* (formally *Kamo-wake-ikazuchi-jinja*) Shinto Shrine. It has been over 13 years since I began my service at this shrine located in the northern part of Kyoto City. This Shinto shrine is recognized as a World Heritage Site by UNESCO. Today many groups from overseas visit us. Recently, the number of couples getting married at our shrine, in Shinto style, has increased dramatically. We understand and accept that these international people have their own faith. For example, their religions include Christianity, Judaism, and Islam. The reason why they choose to get married at our shrine is because they understand that Shinto belief does not require their religious conversion. They see and accept a Shinto wedding ceremony as a part of Japanese culture. This, we believe, is a result of the accumulation of effort made by many religious followers to recognize and accept religious diversities and to have mutual respect and understanding for each other.

# Reflection

## The Editors

Shinto is an *'indigenous religion'*, according to Yoshinobu Miyake. It is worth considering what that term means and what role a religion which is indigenous can play in interfaith worship and prayer, especially as we have a chapter (4) with the title 'African Traditional Religion', a description chosen after some discussion with the authors of two other possible titles: 'African Religion' and 'African Indigenous Religion'. Those who generalise have to deal with exceptions, but there are certain characteristics which are indicated when the term *'indigenous'* is used. The fact that an area or a country has a religion by which it is known (as in 'Georgia is a Christian country') does not make that religion indigenous. There, the reference is to the faith of the majority, but here the reference is to a religion which has grown up over an immeasurably long period, closely identified with the local culture, shaping and being given shape by the life of a people, in a manner different from that of a religion which has an identifiable origin or was 'imported' at a particular time. The term could be used more widely, for example of Hinduism.

Professor Norman Havens argues that definitions of Shinto range from 'the entire Japanese way of life' to 'a collection of elements from other religions' (Swanson and Chilson 2006, p.17). Our contributors take a midway position. Japanese culture is not reducible to Shinto, although Shinto is certainly characterized by the natural, the human and the spiritual worlds being intertwined in a distinctive manner. While it is true that Buddhism, Taoism and (to a much lesser degree) Christianity have influenced Shinto, it also has continuities of its own. It is distinctive.

Shinto's long history need not concern us here, except to point out the major change that took place in 1945. During the Meiji era and right up to the end of the war, there was what is called State Shinto; this means that Shinto was enlisted as the ideological underpinning of nationalism and of those in power, with emperor worship at its centre. Although Shinto since 1945 has been varied, there is no doubt that its main focus has been a return to the position of a religion of the people, community-based and oriented to nature and the environment. This contemporary phase is usually called Shrine Shinto. One of the contributors to this book, Yasuhiro Tanaka, is the chief priest of a great ancient shrine in Kyoto (*Kamo-wake-ikazuchi-jinga*) which has an emphasis both on the enshrined deity and on agriculture and nature. It is a part of a World Heritage Site. Shrine Shinto is our focus here, although there are many sectarian and folk streams of the religion; as with all religions there is variety.

Shinto wishes to be seen as an independent religion in its own right with its own special characteristics. That is true of a number of indigenous religions all over the world. Shinto does not easily fit in with some Western conceptions of what a religion is, for the West tends to regard religion as a matter of choice where followers engage with the divine and join a community of believers. In Japan, the person is already 'there' by virtue of family and nationality: as it were, immersed. This is an observation stressed by Yoshinobu Miyake who has had long experience of interfaith meetings and, as a result, is aware of those who are dismissive of religions which are markedly different from their own. Indeed, he comes up with the fascinating observation that indigenous religions all over the world, emerging from bountiful forests and having an element of animism in their beliefs and practices, have often been pushed aside by the more forceful Abrahamic religions, emerging from the arid deserts of the Middle East (and, one might add, dreaming of the Gardens given prominence in the Qu'ran and in Jewish/Christian scriptures!).

Prayer and worship in Shinto are directed to 'kami'. That belief makes for a further difficulty in interfaith meetings since there are real challenges of translation and comprehension, as pointed out by Yasuhiro Tanaka. Shinto is polytheistic and 'kami' is a fluid term referring to the life forces which exist within or behind many kinds of phenomena: spirits/gods/deities/numinous powers existing in nature, places, people, ancestors. The term is also used of some gods about whom mythological stories are told, such as Amaterasu, the sun goddess. The shrines have the role of housing or enshrining kami and are a conduit to kami, making them more accessible. There are the major shrines and also ones by the roadside. Indeed, many Japanese have a shrine in their home and almost all make an annual visit to ancestral graves. Prayers are offered during important rituals of purification when kami are asked for help and protection, given presents and placated.

Shinto is involved in interfaith relations and eager to overcome the misunderstandings and other difficulties which such involvement entails, while focusing mainly on concerns which are shared. It stresses our common humanity. Shinto is accepting of other religions and of its own longstanding relationship with Buddhism. To speak of this partnership as 'dual allegiance', however, may not be entirely appropriate. As already mentioned, there is a sense in which Japanese are culturally Shinto and may at the same time choose to be involved in another religion as well. Indeed, Japanese who have been involved in Shinto rituals often have a Buddhist funeral. Shinto representatives are committed to interfaith meetings and, as Yasuhiro Tanaka points out, have shown great determination to be reconciled to those who treat them with suspicion. He writes of 35 years of attending Pearl Harbour memorial ceremonies before being fully accepted.

One area of hopeful cooperative work and prayer in the future is ethical. There is the personal ethic which is focused on purification, leading to a life of sincerity, honesty and purity. Then there is a more collective ethic in relation to ecology and the environment, symbolized by the care taken of the gardens and woods surrounding shrines. Shinto respect for the presence of *kami* in nature reinforces this commitment. Reference is also made to relief work in which Shintos have been involved after natural and other disasters.

Shinto participation in interfaith worship and prayer may be seen as challenging, as it is a fully pantheist religion. However, the very fact that Shinto and African Traditional Religion are representatives of a distinctive strand within the religions of the world is a reason why their presence in interfaith work in general, and in worship and prayer in particular, should be welcomed.

## REFERENCE

Swanson, P.L. and Chilson, C. (eds) (2006) *Nazan Guide to Japanese Religions*. Honolulu, HI: University of Hawaii Press.

# Chapter 10

# CHRISTIANITY

## 1

## Abrahamic Faiths: Prayer, Worship and Working Together

Hugh Ellis

## INTRODUCTION

From my experience of interfaith worship and prayer here in High Wycombe (UK), particularly since 2014, I will reflect on the following issues: potential for misunderstanding and matters associated with:

- theological compromise

- religious territory

- boundaries

- synchronicity.

Each of these issues has come to light in the context of some extraordinarily moving experiences of Christian acts of prayer and worship in which there were Muslim participants, Muslim Friday Prayers in which Christians were participants, joint acts of prayer in which Christians and Muslims participated and Jewish acts of worship at which both Christians and Muslims were participants.

## CHRISTIANS AND MUSLIMS PRAYING
## AND WORSHIPPING TOGETHER

On 22 September 2013, a twin suicide bomb attack took place at All Saints Church in Peshawar, Pakistan, in which 127 people were killed and over 250 injured. The chairman of the Council of Christian–Muslim Relations (CCMR) and I decided that we should call a meeting of leading Christians and Muslims in the town to agree a statement for publication and to discuss any other response, as such an event had the potential to divide our communities and could lead to an increase in Islamophobia. As a number of us met, we heard accounts of Muslim relatives who had been killed by other attacks by the same terrorist group in Pakistan. In fact, there were a number of protest rallies in Karachi, Lahore, Multan and other cities to condemn the killing and evidence that it was Muslims who came out in support of the Christians who mourned their losses. So, it became evident that this was not, as the media had portrayed it, so much an anti-Christian attack by Muslims but more like an internal theo-political act aimed at destabilising the Pakistani government.

As a group we wanted to respond in such a way that both demonstrated our solidarity as Christians and Muslims in High Wycombe and spoke a different theological message. In the event, we decided that a number of us Christians, including our bishop, would join in Friday prayers at one of our mosques at which I was invited to preach alongside the imam and our bishop was invited to say a few words. Following an 'induction' into what was going on during Friday prayers we were invited to participate, which quite a few of us did.

We found the experience both moving and meaningful as Christians. Clearly, our Muslim friends were very moved that we had joined them. From our perspective as Christians there was no sense of betraying or compromising the integrity of our own faith. We prayed in faith to the God we knew and, together with our Muslim brethren, believed it to be the same God to whom we were praying. I experienced the lengthy time of open prayer just as I would in a Christian context as we all together made our private prayers to the living God.

The following Sunday, a similar number of Muslims joined us Christians at the main morning Eucharist at which I invited the same imam to preach alongside me (for just over five minutes each). We had agreed to root our preaching in a text from the Torah as the

Torah was acknowledged as authoritative in both our faiths. This was a direct consequence of doing scriptural reasoning together (a means of reflecting on excerpts from each other's scriptures based on an agreed theme) in a local Jewish, Christian, Muslim group which I formed to encourage positive relationships between Jews, Christians and Muslims and mutual learning. (This has been most successful apart from the time when the topic of the Israel–Gaza conflict arose in discussion of a chapter in a book we were studying together. Much one-to-one dialogue became necessary in order for the group to continue to work together in a positive way.)

The imam selected the following texts from the Holy Qur'an (4:36) echoing the text from the Torah:

> Worship God and do not associate anything with him and be kind to the parents and to the relatives and the orphans and the needy and the neighbour who is your relative and the neighbour who is not your relative and the companion by your side and the traveller and those whom your right hand possess, Indeed God does not love one who is proud and boastful.

And from the Hadith: 'Prophet Muhammad (PBUH) said, "None of you has faith until you love for your neighbour what you love for yourself."'

And I selected Deuteronomy (6:4–6):

> Hear, O Israel: The LORD is our God, the LORD alone. You shall love the LORD your God with all your heart, and with all your soul, and with all your might. Keep these words that I am commanding you today in your heart.

And Leviticus (19:1–4, 7, 18):

> The LORD spoke to Moses, saying: 'You shall not take vengeance or bear a grudge against any of your people, but you shall love your neighbour as yourself: I am the LORD.'

During the Intercessions the imam prayed for the Christians in Peshawar and I prayed for the Muslims there. The imam preached strongly, condemning the terrorist actions as contrary to the teaching of the Holy Qur'an.

My Muslim friends informed me that there was much more of the service with which they were comfortable to participate than we

had envisaged. Some came for anointing for healing and some went
up, to our surprise, to receive the consecrated bread (we had carefully
explained what was going on, using the printed order of service, and
its meaning during a run-through a few nights before).

These experiences for the participants were moving and bonding.
Since that time the sense of warmth between many Muslims and
Christians in town has been extraordinary and noticeably stronger. Of
course, participation in one another's main acts of worship were seen
as one-off events as a means of responding to the particular horror
in Peshawar; however, there have been requests to repeat the mutual
experience. In addition, as the parish church is commonly used for
civic services, it is usual for Muslims to be present and participate to
a degree. One fruit of our joint worship experience at these services
has been an increase in participation in both the worship and liturgy
by our Muslim friends.

## ACTING TOGETHER WITH LOVING KINDNESS (ATWLK)

The following account describes a joint Christian-Muslim response
to the terrorist attacks in Paris on 13 November 2015.

Late on 14 November 2014 I emailed some key links from the
local CCMR inviting them to join me in a prayer vigil the following
day at 12 noon at All Saints Church, with a view to doing something
similar the following Sunday afternoon for the wider community.
The vigil, comprising about twenty people, Christian and Muslim,
was deeply moving, during which tears flowed and one or two short
speeches were made. Immediately following, I invited those who were
willing to stay behind in order to consider what we could do together
for the wider community, which comprises approximately 20 per cent
Muslim population. The common theme arising expressed a strong
desire to do something which facilitated unity and acts of kindness as
a public response to the apparent aims of the terrorists to divide and
harm. The concept of acting together with loving-kindness was thus
articulated, and somehow it encapsulated the wishes of all present.
The title has become synonymous with a growing network of people
(mainly Christians and Muslims) seeking to work together for those
in need.

In the event, a public gathering was organised for the following
Sunday at which a Sunni Syrian refugee was invited to tell his (deeply
moving) story. Around two hundred people attended, despite the short

notice, and the proceedings commenced with a local imam reading a passage from the Qur'an, followed by a prayer for peace and unity, and then my doing likewise using Matthew's Gospel, Chapter 25. Both readings related the part in which the hearer asks, 'When did we see you naked and clothe you, hungry and feed you... As you did it to one of the least of these you did it to me.' Following the talk and questions addressed to our Syrian guest, I invited those present to pray in silence for peace and unity and to express that, if they so wished, through the lighting of a candle. Hundreds were lit, and tears flowed. The sense of the divine presence was extraordinary and led to many comments such as 'I've never experienced anything so moving before.' The gathering concluded with eating Asian food and home-baked cakes together as we freely mixed and chatted. Many described the gathering as a deeply moving, inspiring and delightful experience.

Lighting a candle for peace
Credit: High Wycombe Refugee Partnership

Similar gatherings have subsequently been repeated with more people from the town, and beyond, being drawn in, including some of other faiths and a few humanists. Each one was preceded by a mixed Muslim–Christian group, tasked to prepare for the gatherings and to work on a five-year plan to enable Syrian refugees to be housed and integrated into the local community. In response to many offers of help, a charity, Wycombe Refugee Partnership, has been formed which, at the time of writing, has housed and enabled wrap-around support for eight refugee families in the Wycombe area. The evolving model has drawn attention from bodies such as the National Refugee Council, as well as national media. In addition, a developing partnership with the District Council is helping to smooth the process of local integration.

Trustees who pray together

Each meeting has been opened and closed with a prayer, led by a Muslim and a Christian respectively. This experience was both unifying and bonding. On one occasion when this group was meeting in the church I was asked by the Muslim group secretary if it would be alright if they did their evening prayers at 4.30 pm (at a break in the meeting) in the church. I judged that it would be ok, being a private gathering. They asked me which way they should face towards Mecca, and so I explained how the church, as with many churches, was oriented east–west. They were amused that they had to ask a Christian priest which way to face for their evening prayers.

## RELIGIOUS TERRITORY

Within that context this seemed entirely natural and the right thing to do but, subsequently, I have been challenged on the controversial aspects surrounding the matter of Muslim prayers in a church. I have been informed that some Muslims see this as a territorial matter and that praying in a church was, somehow, claiming the ground.

However, this was so clearly not the case in this instance and context. This is a matter which could do with some careful examination and clarity over what would be good and acceptable and what could lead to misunderstanding. According to http:// www.nusseibeh.org/history the relevant episode from history seems to relate to the fact that, in the seventh century, on one occasion when the prayer time came in Jerusalem, the archbishop of the city, Sophronius, invited Caliph Omar, a leading companion of Muhammad, to pray at the Church of the Holy Sepulchre, Christianity's holiest site. Omar refused, fearing that future Muslim generations would claim the church as their own and turn it into a mosque. Omar instead prayed a few yards away from the church where a mosque is now built. The Mosque of Omar still stands next to the Church of the Holy Sepulchre as a reminder of the strong Muslim–Christian bond in the Holy Land. Upon entering Jerusalem, Omar signed what became known as the 'Covenant of Omar' with the Jerusalem Christians. It guaranteed protection for the Christians to live and worship freely and also protection for Christian places of worship.

## BOUNDARIES AND SOLIDARITY

Regarding interfaith prayers in a consecrated building: clergy in the Church of England have to consider a ruling called Canon B5, which permits variations from authorised forms of service as long as they are reverent, seemly and not contrary to, nor indicative of any departure from, the doctrine of the Church of England. Such doctrine requires affirmation of belief in one God who is revealed as Father, Son and Holy Spirit. This, of course, requires careful thought and judgement in interpreting that canon in relation to the particular context. For example, it raises the question, does my reading and scripture and a prayer alongside my imam colleague, who has just read a similar passage from the Qur'an and then prayed, constitute a departure from Church of England doctrine? Were the boundaries between the two faiths being blurred? All those who mentioned the matter only interpreted it as a sign of standing together in solidarity as Christians and Muslims in caring for Syrian refugees and, together, enjoining those present to be welcoming and kind towards them. There has been no evidence that our doing this was interpreted as a blurring of boundaries.

## An observation and comment

It just so happened that the Muslims engaged with ATwLK were predominantly from the local Wahabi-influenced mosque which, being more conservative in approach, would not permit any non-Muslims to worship with them or join in their prayers in their mosque (visitors could observe from behind a black line at the back of the prayer room). Also, the women and men were separated for their worship and prayer. Consequently, I was rather surprised when, in the church context during our prayers, the men and women sat together whilst their children happily played in the children's area. Also, I was not expecting the evening prayers to be led by our group's secretary, as she is a Muslim woman and there were Muslim men participating in those prayers. I can only conclude that the separation is more of a cultural matter which primarily holds sway in the mosque context.

Within the context of the members of this task group having got to know and trust each other, all seemed comfortable with the prayers happening in a church context. The permitting of this act has led to deep appreciation being expressed by our new Muslim friends and has proved to be an effective bridge-building experience.

Inevitably, as relationships have developed between Christians and Muslims through CCMR and ATwLK, and through participating together in a primary act of worship in a mosque and the town's Civic Church, so the sense of belonging to one another has increased. This has happened to the extent that a couple of our local Muslim leaders have described themselves as 'Sunni-Christians' and have said that they feel that All Saints is their church. On further exploration of the statements it is clear that these Muslim friends are not describing a synchronicity of being both Sunni and Christian at once, but appear to be articulating their sense of welcome and belonging. This appears to be the explanation as to why so many more Muslim friends than we expected have participated in civic services and in the one-off Eucharist. In neither circumstance was there any sense of either faith being compromised although as Christian hosts we were concerned that our Muslim brothers and sisters did not feel under any pressure to conform against their better judgement.

## CONCLUSION

My main comment in this brief reflection is that context is the primary factor in determining how a particular joint act of interfaith worship or prayer is perceived. Without the context of the Peshawar and Paris bombings deeply impacting our local community, praying together as Muslims and Christians in a church might easily be misunderstood and seen as a form of syncretism. However, in each of the cases mentioned, careful thinking, discernment and discussion between the principal Christian and Muslim leaders concerned enabled outcomes that were perceived as both sensitive and apposite. Furthermore, local reporters were very moved by these gatherings and warmly reported them. The impact on Christian–Muslim relations in the town has been exceptionally positive and members of other faith groups (Jews, Buddhists, Hindus and Sikhs) have supported the work with refugees through monetary or practical donations as a consequence.

Lessons learned include: talking about Middle East politics together can be problematic (mainly, it seemed, due to different narratives being believed through propaganda-driven social media reporting); doing charitable work with people of other faiths has a deeply positive impact on interfaith relations; informally praying together in relation to a common charitable work is both bonding and moving; reflecting on excerpts of each other's scriptures together with an open heart to the Divine is enriching, educational, unifying and inspiring; reflecting on unexpected outcomes, such as some Muslims wishing to receive the consecrated bread of Holy Communion, has led to a deeper cross-cultural understanding.

# 2

## Shared Rituals Encourage Interfaith Engagement

Sheryl A. Kujawa-Holbrook

### INTERFAITH PRAYER

Samir Selmanovic, a Christian minister, and the founder of Faith House Manhattan, writes: 'The sacrament of human life is the sacrament that supersedes our religions. We live before we believe, and we are human before we are religious. Our life together is a temple where we all meet' (2009, p.58). According to Selmanovic, 'the sacrament of human life' is the lived spiritual experience in which people of all traditions share, where we develop relationships across the boundaries of difference, and grow in mutual understanding. The work of Faith House Manhattan is to intentionally construct immersion experiences where people participate in the rituals from across traditions. Selmanovic said that he founded Faith House in an effort to build an inclusive church where Christians are not the only ones in charge, and where people from across traditions have a right to belong as interdependent partners, not as outsiders needing conversion. At Faith House Manhattan through shared rituals people from different religious traditions are enabled to 'actually learn to need one another' (Selmanovic 2009, p.58).

Every day billions of people throughout the world raise their voices in prayer, and, while the forms and languages differ, the human desire to communicate with the divine is a constant.[1] Shared prayer is already a major part of the activities of many local interreligious groups. A study released by the American Sociological Association in August 2017 finds that, in about 75 per cent of the faith-based community organizing coalitions studied, interfaith group prayer is considered a 'bridging cultural practice' that plays an important role in uniting people across racial and socioeconomic differences. Far from being a source of division, shared rituals that emerge from a group's cultures over time, and celebrate the diversity of the group, encourage individuals to interact with each other, and are a unifying influence. The study argues that the more diversity a group represented, the more likely the group was inclined to participate in interfaith prayer; such prayers were commonly perceived to both acknowledge and appreciate, rather than to avoid, the religious differences present (Fowler 2017; Pederson 2017).

---

1    As the sensitive use of language is integral to interfaith encounters, I want to note here that in my own work I tend to utilize the language of 'prayer,' rather than the language of 'worship,' when speaking about cooperative interfaith ritual practice. I find that 'prayer' translates more readily across traditions than the term 'worship.' In my contexts, feedback about using the term 'worship' often brings with it an assumption that the shared rituals are, in effect, based in forms of Christian worship. Both terms represent a multiplicity of definitions when considered across religious traditions, and those who claim no tradition. What is perhaps most salient about this discussion is that such terms are based in context, and that grappling with the meaning of such terms is a part of the interfaith encounter.

As an Episcopal priest and as a scholar active in interfaith engagement, I have prayed in a wide variety of rituals in settings where participants are from different religious traditions, and no tradition. I agree with colleagues who suggest that interfaith shared prayer needs to be conducted with great sensitivity. Religious groups have differing assumptions about the conditions under which shared prayer builds empathy across religious differences, as well as the circumstances under which ritual boundaries should be maintained. Certainly, all interfaith experiences do not mean the same thing to all participants. For some people an experience will constitute worship, for others it will build solidarity, or serve as an occasion of interfaith hospitality, and, for still others, it will be an educational experience. Joint spoken prayers are not encouraged by all interfaith groups because there is a danger of participants feeling pressured to join in what appears to be worship of a divinity not of their own tradition. Some groups are particularly sensitive to the appearance of religious syncretism or idolatry, for example. Other groups are wary of religious assimilation. Religious leaders of some traditions do not participate in public prayer with religious groups other than their own; other groups feel it is generally inappropriate to have visitors participate in worship. Nontheistic religious groups may have difficulty with prayer that assumes a divine being. Others may feel awkward or alienated by religious images in prayer or song which are not a part of their own tradition.

Much of Christian history has focused on the importance of right belief, or orthodoxy, and the importance of separating ourselves from adherents of other religions. There are many examples throughout Christian history where differences in belief caused violent conflicts between Christian groups, and between Christians and adherents of other religions. Within the history of interfaith relationships, Christian liturgies were used as a powerful tool against other religious groups. For example, a recent book, *Invisible Weapons*, by Cecilia Gaposchkin, argues that the liturgy was deployed during the crusades against Muslims by embedding a devotional ideology of crusading warfare in the heart of orthodox Christian identity (Gaposchkin 2017). Given the potential for devotional ideology to cultivate hatred among religious groups, how might we then use ritual's rich potential to cultivate mutual understanding and serve to unite humankind? In this spirit, in September 2016 a group of Muslim, Christian, and Jewish leaders in Israel planned an interfaith place of worship in

Jerusalem to allow people to pray together in the city where they prayed together for centuries, 'creating something religious and true against the lie that everything is a lie and only war exists' (Jewish News Service 2016).

## THE CENTRALITY OF RITUAL

Ritual is an essential part of human social experience, and thus it is integral to the rich diversity of humankind's religious traditions. As a Christian within the Episcopal/Anglican tradition, I am acutely aware of the central role of ritual within my own spiritual practice and have come to see it as a channel for deepening my understanding of other religious traditions. I experience my own tradition, as well as other religious traditions, as diverse and multifaceted, and thus am concerned when interfaith encounters are focused mainly on the de-ritualized, cognitive, aspects of religion, to the exclusion of the ritual, material, communal, and pre-colonial aspects of religious experience. As interfaith scholar Marianne Moyaert argues, the lack of emphasis on ritual within the study of religion may be attributable to both the way we define religion, and also to inherent biases which minimize the role of ritual practice (Moyaert and Geldhof 2015, Introduction). Protestant Christian biases of right belief and the supremacy of texts privilege understandings of religion that de-emphasize the ritual aspects of embodied practice. Such bias limits religions to intellectual content, and marginalizes elements that are about spiritual experience, such as mystery, beauty, and awe. While religion is certainly an academic discipline, it is more than that, and it encompasses more than the life of the mind. It is also about the spirit, and the search for meaning, and the yearning for connection. It is part of the work of interfaith engagement to challenge fixed, monolithic, and colonial definitions of religion in favor of approaches which recognize the hybridity and fluidity of religious experience. Rather than question if it is appropriate for people from different religious traditions to pray together, the question from the perspective of interfaith engagement is how do we construct experiences of shared prayer that both respect the deep commitments of individual traditions and at the same time are hospitable across religious differences?

As a Christian in the Episcopal/Anglican tradition I find unity and belonging with others across my tradition in the way we pray, but at the same time we relate to each other and negotiate through a spectrum of theological beliefs. Being a Christian is about more than following a set of beliefs; it is also about the way I inhabit the world. Interfaith worship challenges me in a similar way to negotiate the space between commitments to my own religious experience, and my desire to be open to others and their traditions. Appreciating the role of ritual within religious traditions leads me into a more complex understanding of interfaith relationships which considers more than our differences of belief and opens the way for healing and solidarity on the level of our shared humanity.

## VARIETIES OF INTERFAITH SHARED PRAYER

The growth in interest in interfaith shared prayer suggests a desire for deeper engagement, beyond the common levels of verbal dialogue and shared action. Perhaps the most commonly held forms of interfaith shared prayer focus on silent prayer and meditation, or prayers said in a pattern of sequential offerings by members of different religious traditions, where others listen. Just as Mahatma Gandhi believed that prayer was an expression of the longing of the soul, so does the sharing of silence serve as a bridge between people of different cultures and traditions who share in the same longing. For some prayer is communication or a relationship with the divine; for those who are nontheistic, prayer can refer to a transformation of consciousness.

In addition to silent prayer and meditation, interfaith prayer services usually take on one of four additional formats, all of which attempt to balance the deep commitment of individual participants, while creating hospitable space across religious differences (Kujawa-Holbrook 2014). The first format is a service grounded in one tradition, in which members of other religious traditions are invited to participate. For example, recently the Minnesota Council of Churches worked with local Muslim organizations to coordinate a series of interfaith iftars to decrease anti-Muslim sentiment and to bring local neighbors of all faiths together during Ramadan. In this case Muslims coordinated the iftars, while their Christian partners headed an outreach and education effort across the state. While the iftars honored the tradition of the Muslim participants, the intentional hospitality offered to participants provided an occasion to build and nurture relationships across faith traditions (Blumberg 2016).

A second format is that of an interfaith service that borrows from a variety of traditions. That is, representatives of local religious traditions work together on a shared format, and the occasion is hosted on rotation by different religious communities or at some 'neutral' site, such as a school or city hall. One example of this format is the Floating Lantern Ceremony organized by the Shinnyo-en (Buddhist) Foundation each Memorial Day in Hawaii. The Foundation intentionally invites participants from many different traditions to come together to make lanterns, and then float them and offer prayers for victims of war, natural disasters, famine, and disease. Prayers are also offered in gratitude for all life, including our ancestors in the past, as well as hopes for the future. The Floating Lantern Ceremony is an occasion of deep interfaith hospitality, where relationships were nurtured and valued. The ritual allows individuals to participate in their own way while upholding the values of the diversity and interdependence of the human family.

The third type of interfaith service has a 'serial' format where each religious tradition involved plans and executes a defined segment of the overall experience. Many civic religious observances utilize this format, for instance, when Jewish, Christian, Muslim, Buddhist, and other leaders each in turn share prayers, music, and ritual from their own tradition. The serial form of shared prayer is advantageous for promoting interfaith encounter for a variety of reasons. First, each faith community selects and presents its own material. Those in attendance are left free to participate in whatever ways they feel comfortable. An example of this model is an interfaith service held in New Orleans in 2016 with the theme 'bridges of mercy.' There adherents of five traditions gathered and shared their own prayers based in their desire for God, and intention to become peacemakers. 'Mercy is the bridge that allows us to pray together,' said a participant. 'And maybe, just maybe, we will imitate and share that mercy that God shows us, and God can use us to walk into the lives of others in their places of in-betweenness – when they are fearful or angry or hurt or experiencing xenophobia' (Donze 2016).

The fourth format of interfaith shared prayer, though not always acknowledged, are rites of passage such as marriages and funerals. Cultures and religious groups have diverse traditions to honor these occasions as well as other rites of passage. Although religious customs surrounding marriages and funeral vary, most people can identify with the emotions involved in these occasions. Growing religious pluralism in local communities means that there are an increasing number of interfaith families, often unacknowledged within faith communities.

In many Christian churches, Sundays are opportunities for interfaith hospitality where prayers are shared by communities of diverse faiths. The essence of pastoral ministry is relationship – relationship to God, to one another, and to the wider world. Christian pastoral ministry today requires sensitivity to the presence, needs, and gifts of the many persons of other religious traditions who inhabit our communities and the wider world.

## THE LANGUAGE OF FAITH

My Christian faith is inextricably linked to embodied practice. As a person of faith and a scholar, it is the language of ritual – symbols, texts, mystery – that leads me to God, and teaches me most deeply about my own tradition, as well as other traditions. When I first encountered other religious traditions, I thought dialogue was about conversation and exchanging information. While these remain invaluable dimensions of interfaith encounters, the vibrancy of lived religious practice opens me and challenges me to experience other traditions in multivalent ways, just as it opens me to go deeper into my own tradition.

Interfaith prayer is critical to deepening encounters across religious differences, and to widening our experiences of the holy. Religious leaders across the world believe that while there are many differences between religions, we also all support the work of peace and reconciliation for the sake of a better world and for the preservation of our planet. 'My humanity is bound up in yours,' says Desmond Tutu, Archbishop Emeritus of Cape Town, 'for we can only be human together' (Tutu 2011, p.22).

## REFERENCES

Blumberg, A. (2016) 'Interfaith iftars aim to bring communities together this Ramadan.' Huffington Post [Electronic], https://www.huffingtonpost.com/entry/interfaith-iftars-ramadan_us_573f58b8e4b00e09e89f0061, accessed on 20 May 2016.

Donze, B. (2016) 'Interfaith service hails our common "God of Mercy."' https://clarionherald.org/2016/11/30/interfaith-service-hails-our-common-god-of-mercy, 10 November, pp.1–3, accessed March 3, 2017.

Fowler, D. (2017) 'Study suggests prayer can build unity in diverse organizations.' American Sociological Association [Electronic], www.asanet.org/sites/default/files/savvy/documents/press/pdfs/ASR_August_2014_Ruth_Braunstein_News_Release.pdf, accessed April 10, 2017.

Gaposchkin, C. (2017) *Invisible Weapons: Liturgy and the Making of Crusade Ideology.* Ithaca, NY: Cornell University Press.

Jewish News Service (2016) 'Muslim, Christian, Jewish leaders plan interfaith worship center in Jerusalem.' Breaking Israel News, https://www.breakingisraelnews.com/70931/muslim-christian-jewish-leaders-plan-interfaith-worship-center-jerusalem, pp.1–11, accessed November 11, 2016.

Kujawa-Holbrook, S. (2014) *God Beyond Borders: Interreligious Learning among Faith Communities.* Eugene, OR: Pickwick.

Moyaert, M. and Geldhof, J. (2015) *Ritual Participation and Interreligious Dialogue: Boundaries, Transgressions and Innovations.* London: Bloomsbury Academic.

Pederson, T. (2017) 'The power of interfaith prayer to unite cultures in religion.' Spirituality & Health [Electronic], https://spiritualityhealth.com/blogs/spirituality-health/2014/11/05/traci-pedersen-power-interfaith-prayer-unite-cultures-and, pp.1–4, accessed March 20, 2017.

Selmanovic, S. (2009) *It's Really All About God: Reflections of a Muslim Atheist Jewish Christian.* San Francisco, CA: Jossey-Bass.

Tutu, D. (2011) *God Is Not a Christian and Other Provocations.* New York: HarperOne.

## FURTHER READING

Mosher, L. (2005) *Faith in the Neighborhood: Praying: The Rituals of Faith.* New York: Seabury Books.

Peace, J., Rose, O. and Mobley, G. (2012) *My Neighbor's Faith: Stories of Interreligious Encounter, Growth and Transformation.* Maryknoll, NY: Orbis.

# 3

# The Religion of Love Embraces All

## Marcus Braybrooke

As a growing number of countries become more multireligious, occasions for interfaith prayer are increasing: both as large gatherings after a disaster and as intimate family occasions, such as a marriage where the couple are of different faiths. Interfaith prayer, however, is not new. The Emperor Akbar dreamed of:

> A temple, neither Pagod, Mosque, nor Church,
> But loftier, simpler, always open-door'd
> To every breath from heaven. (Hayes 1954, p.29)

The elaborate ceremonies for the opening of the Suez Canal in 1869 'began with a Muslim prayer, followed by a Catholic mass, conducted by the Archbishop of Jerusalem'. It would seem that the guests were expected to be present at both.[2] There was also interfaith prayer at the World Parliament of Religions in Chicago in 1893.

Does attending worship of a faith community other than your own count as 'interfaith worship'? It may be you go out of politeness to the funeral of a friend who was Jewish; you may go as an observer to a gurdwara because you want to learn about Sikhism. But perhaps the ceremony moves you so that you sense the presence of God, as I did years ago listening to the chanting at the Rameswaram Temple in South India. In Galilee, a Ramakrishna Swami was a member of our pilgrim group. As we stood at the lakeside in a circle to share the bread and the wine, we both felt it was right for him to receive communion. Yet when I asked some Catholic priests in India who were joining in *bhajans* in praise of Krishna, they said, 'We just substitute mentally Christ for Krishna,' which I thought was cheating.

So as a guest, are you just physically present or also spiritually present? I have found it very moving to be asked to participate, for example, in a Shinto ceremony or to speak in a synagogue at a Shiva Remembrance, or to join the prayer line at a mosque. On one occasion, at a time when I was feeling depressed after being diagnosed with angina and being laid off work, I was at a conference in which

---

2    *The Illustrated London News*, 11 December 1869.

a priest of a new African religious movement arranged a ceremony. We were in a big circle and a cup of fellowship was passed around – as I drank from it, I experienced healing and peace.

Often when people talk of interfaith services they think of set pieces, but it is the unexpected moment which opens one's eyes to the universal presence of God. I have always believed that there is One God, who is creator and lover of all people. So, when a radio interviewer asked me how I could worship Muslim and Hindu gods, I replied, 'I am a monotheist and believe in the Oneness of God.' With this there is the mystics' awareness that God transcends all language and description – the '*Neti, Neti*, Not this, Not that' of Hinduism. Indeed, it is the mystics of every faith who seem closest to each other. Their experience of the Holy transcends words. George Appleton, a former Anglican archbishop in Jerusalem and editor of the *Oxford Book of Prayer*, said, at the start of one interfaith service, 'We stand in worship before the mystery of the final reality to whom or to which we give differing names, so great and deep and eternal that we can never fully understand or grasp the mystery of His Being' (Appleton 1970, p.13). This also means that doctrines and dogmas and indeed also scriptures are not the truth but pointers to a Living Truth that cannot be captured in words. They are like fingers pointing to the moon.

Some Christians would say that such an approach endangers both the claim that Christianity is the only true religion and that communion with God is only possible through the atoning death of Jesus, God's only Son. Too easily, however, Jesus becomes the focus of Christian worship instead of the One God whom Christians approach through Jesus Christ. The Cross for me is a symbol of the love of God for all people.

There is also a widespread fear of syncretism. The word is usually used in a pejorative sense of the artificial mixing of religions, which threatens claims of any faith to uniqueness. The *Oxford Dictionary of Religions*, however, says, 'All religions are syncretistic in the sense of absorbing and incorporating elements of other religions and cultures as they encounter them' (Bowker 1997, p.936). In my view religions are both means by which God reveals Herself or Himself to humanity and are also human responses, different and always inadequate, to God's self-revelation. This is not to say that all religions are the same. Rather, it is similar to the way that after a mother's death the siblings share their memories of her. Each child treasures his or her special memories; she loved them all, but in different ways. The sharing enriches each child's appreciation of her. In the same way, we can learn from anyone who shares his or her deepest spiritual experiences.[3]

Such a sharing allows interfaith services to recognise both distinctiveness and universality. At an All Faiths service at Bloomsbury Central Baptist Church, Rev Dr Trevor Howard welcomed participants by saying, 'No one would take me for a Tibetan Buddhist or the Dalai Lama for a Welsh Baptist.' Earlier, during his first visit to Britain, the Dalai Lama gave the address at the West London Synagogue, at an interfaith service, which included the opening of the Ark and a procession with the scrolls. This recognised the particular witness of the host community as well as the values shared by all.

This may be obscured in those interfaith observances (sometimes called 'serial') in which a member of each faith community reads a prayer or passage of scripture relating, perhaps, to the environment or human rights, but there is nothing said together. It is, again, not clear whether those of other faiths are observing or praying. For some, it is only an expression of our common humanity and does not imply giving any spiritual value to other religions. At the first day of Prayer for Peace at Assisi in 1986, convened by Pope John Paul II, after an introductory gathering, members of each faith met separately to pray, but then came together outside the Basilica of St Francis. Once again, a leader of each religion offered a prayer. Official Roman Catholic accounts explained that this was 'being together to pray' rather than 'praying together'. Some participants said they did not think the Holy Spirit was aware of the difference! The formula, however, was designed to placate those who said Roman Catholic claims to be the one true church were being endangered.

Serial interfaith observances are an important way of bringing together a community after a disaster. It was very moving after the London bombings to share in interfaith gatherings at a synagogue and then at a mosque.

Even more moving was participating with members of the International Peace Council in an interfaith Act of Remembrance in the remote village of Acteal in Chiapas, Mexico, where six months earlier nearly fifty women and children were massacred by a paramilitary

---

3    There have been numerous reports on the subject, which I discuss in Chapter 13 of *Widening Vision* (Braybrooke 2016). They include British Council of Churches reports (1968, 1983); Braybrooke 1974; a report by The Archbishops' Consultants on Interfaith Relations (Schneider 1980); and another by the Church of England's Board of Mission (1992). There are also a number of publications details of which are available on the web under 'Interfaith Prayer'.

group who wanted to drive the villagers off the land so that the natural resources could be exploited. Afterwards one mother, who had lost three of her children, said, 'My sorrow has not gone away, but the prayers have given me hope.'

Interfaith service on the site of the massacre of Christians in Acteal, Mexico
Credit: Peace Council; Daniel Gómez-Ibáñez

Interfaith services also witness to the shared concern for peace and human rights to be found in every faith. To me, however, besides often being rather 'wordy', they are like paddling on the seashore rather than immersing oneself in the ocean of Divine Love. As the Sufi Jalal-ad-Din ar-Rumi wrote, 'God's lovers stand beyond all faiths' (Jalal-ad-Din ar-Rumi 2008 [1529], p.103).

The services I have arranged have been attempts to create a cohesive whole – or shared liturgy – drawing on material from different religions so that there is a sense of cohesion and movement. For example, at the Barcelona Parliament of World Religions, where environmental concerns were high on the agenda, the World Congress of Faiths (WCF) arranged an interfaith celebration on 'the Gift of Water'. After some introductory remarks, the first part highlighted the symbolism of water in the sacred traditions: its place in the creation of the world, the dependence of all life on water, its use to symbolise spiritual cleansing, or the crossing of water to a new life. The second part looked at water as a symbol of compassion and a reminder of human responsibility to protect the environment. Then, in a time of silence, participants were asked to reflect on what action they could take to protect the environment or help those who do not have good water. The service ended with Donald Swann's 'Pilgrim's Hymn', which includes the verse,

> We work for the end of disunion in truth, in truth
> That all may be one communion in truth, in truth
> We choose the road of peace and prayer
> Countless pilgrims trod,
> So that Hindu, Muslim, Christian, Jew
> We all can worship one God. (Braybrooke 2005, p.145)

At the Melbourne Parliament of Religions, the theme was 'Respect for the Earth', and at Salt Lake City the devotion took the form of a multimedia reflection on 'Peace in Our Hearts, Peace in Our World'. In both cases quotations from different traditions were woven together in a way that most participants found enriching. In Melbourne, at the end we joined hands in a circle to share a Prayer to the Four Winds.

Great care needs to be taken in the preparation of such services. If possible, I have always tried to get participants to meet before the service or at least circulated a draft to ensure there is nothing unintentionally offensive. Do you mention God? Yes, but not in any congregational response which everyone is invited to say. As a Buddhist monk said to me, 'If you speak of God, I cannot come, if you speak of Truth, I will.'

The most difficult question, because of the numerous sects in every religion, is whom to invite to be leaders of the service. At a public occasion, such as Remembrance Sunday at the Cenotaph, it is easy to find recognised leaders, but jealousy is not unknown amongst the faithful and, for example, Muslims may have difficulties in joining with Bahá'ís, or Anglicans with members of the Unification Church.

Even with music, such services easily become too wordy. Now, like the Peace in many churches, early on I ask people to greet those around them. This creates a sense of community. Sometimes, at smaller events, everyone is given a flower; sometimes there is liturgical dancing. Almost always there is a lighting of candles. The United Religions Initiative has arranged ceremonies at which every nation is prayed for by name as its flag is taken to a central podium.

The question of interfaith prayer is not confined to public occasions. Once, a telephone-caller asked: 'Would you arrange a cosmic celebration for the birth of our child, please?' The caller was a Christian woman, who was married to a Muslim. The family was about to go back to their home in Malaysia, but the mother wanted a ceremony to welcome her new son. One of her best friends was a Hindu and another was Jewish. With the parents, I worked out a liturgy, beginning, as I said in my introduction, with the premise that 'in every culture and religious tradition the birth of a child is a time for rejoicing and thanksgiving'. We included readings from several scriptures and invited members of the congregation to greet the new baby and if they wished to offer a prayer or blessing. We ended with the words of Rabindranath Tagore that 'every child comes into the world with the message that God does not despair of humanity' (Tagore 2017 [1916], no.77).

When the family went home to Malaysia, the child was likely to receive Muslim rites of initiation, but I think the 'cosmic celebration' was meaningful for the parents and Christian family members. The Muslim rites affirmed the child's identity as a member of a faith community, but the cosmic celebration was a reminder that every child is first of all a child of God before he or she is a member of a faith community.

The issue of particularity also confronted me when a dying Jewish friend, whom I had visited almost every day, asked me to take his funeral. It did not feel right. Instead Rabbi Hugo Gryn took the service and I gave the address.

When two people who belong to different religions decide to get married there are many questions – not just about the ceremony. To which faith community will the children belong, or will they be left to decide for themselves when they are older? Would a Christian mother want her child to be circumcised? Would a Muslim father be happy with a Christmas tree in the home? And when one of them dies can they be buried together? – some cemeteries are only for members of one religion.

In terms of the wedding ceremony and leaving aside the various legal constraints,[4] there seem to be three options. First, a ceremony of one religious tradition, which may be modified to try to make the other partner feel included; second, two ceremonies – one from each

---

4   The legal requirement that a service in a parish church has to be according to the rites and ceremonies of the Church of England raises the question 'Can a Muslim or a Jew in giving the ring omit the words "God, Father, Son and Holy Spirit" and just say "God"?' The legal position seems unclear, but integrity would seem to require this. In some cases, a prior civil marriage may be required. Gay marriages are not allowed in most churches, but interfaith weddings and interfaith blessings raise similar issues. Weddings at a hotel are required by law to be non-religious although some couples want some form of blessing afterwards.

tradition; third, a ceremony specially designed with material from both traditions. I have officiated at each of these. The most interesting was a Christian–Jewish wedding at which the couple made their vows according to the required Church of England wording, and then a *chuppa*, the traditional Jewish wedding canopy, was lifted up in the centre of the church. The bride's mother gave a glass of wine to the bride, who, after drinking, gave it to the bridegroom, and the groom then placed a ring on the bride's finger – all with the traditional accompanying blessings.

Although many clergy are reluctant to participate in interfaith marriages, the theological justification for doing so is the Christian belief that marriage is a gift of God in creation. The introduction to the Anglican Church of Canada's liturgy for 'The Celebration and Blessing of a Marriage Between a Christian and a Person of Another Faith Tradition' says, 'It is better to speak of a "Christian understanding of marriage" rather than of "Christian marriage"' (Anglican Church of Canada 2018). This includes at least the free consent of a man and a woman to a loving relationship, which is lifelong and exclusive. It is therefore open to all, whether or not they are Christians. The report *Marriages between Christians and Muslims* makes the same point (Lamb 1998). It goes on to say difference should be seen not as a threat but an enrichment and concludes:

> Some years ago mixed marriages between Protestants and Roman Catholics were not highly valued…but they have become important meeting points for the spread of ecumenism. Is it possible…that some Muslim-Christian families may lead the way forward and become a pattern of future developments in Christian-Muslim relations? (p.30)

In the same way, the hope is that interfaith prayer will help to unite people of all faiths to join in the search for peace, the protection of human rights and care for the environment, as the whole congregation sang at the 'Go for the Golden Rule' service, held at St Martin-in-the-Fields to mark the start of the London Olympic Games:

> This is my song, O God of all the nations,
> A song for peace for lands afar and mine.
> This is my home, the country where my heart is
> Here are my hopes, my dreams, my holy shrine:
> But other hearts in other lands are beating
> With hopes and dreams as true and high as mine…
> May truth and freedom come to every nation;

May peace abound where strife has raged so long;
That each may seek to love and build together,
A world united, righting every wrong
A world united in its love for freedom,
Proclaiming peace together in one song.[5]


# REFERENCES

Anglican Church of Canada (2018) 'The Celebration and Blessing of a Marriage Between a Christian and a Person of Another Faith Tradition.' Accessed on 7 December 2018 at www.anglican.ca/faith/worship/resources/marriage-other-faith.

Appleton, G. (1970) 'The Mystery of Being.' *World Faiths 81*, 13–19.

Bowker, J. (ed.) (1997) *Oxford Dictionary of Religions*. Oxford: Oxford University Press.

Braybrooke, M. (ed.) (1974) *Inter-Faith Worship*. London: Galliard.

Braybrooke, M. (2005) *A Heart for the World*. Winchester: O-books.

Braybrooke, M. (2016) *Widening Vision: The World Congress of Faiths and the Growing Interfaith Movement*. Braybrooke Press at lulu.com.

British Council of Churches (1963) *Can We Pray Together?* London: British Council of Churches.

British Council of Churches (1968) *Inter-faith Worship?* London: British Council of Churches.

Church of England's Board of Mission (1992) *Multi-Faith Worship?* London: Church House Publishing.

Hayes, W. (1954) *Every Nation Kneeling*. Meopham: The Order of the Great Companions.

Jalal-ad-Din ar-Rumi (2008 [1529]) *The Masnavi*, trans. J. Mojaddedi. Oxford: Oxford University Press.

Lamb, C. (1998) *Marriages between Christians and Muslims*. London, CBCI.

McKenna, P. (n.d.) *Guidelines for Designing a Multifaith Prayer Service*. Scarboro Missions. Accessed on 16 November 2018 at www.scarboromissions.ca/interfaith...interfaith.../guidelines-for-de.

Schneider, P. (ed.) (1980) 'Report by the Archbishops' Consultants on Interfaith Relations.' *Ends and Odds* [Newsletter]. London: Lambeth Palace.

Tagore, R. (2017 [1916]) *Stray Birds*. New Delhi: Alpha Editions, Vij Publishing.

---

5   Verses 1 and 2 (omitted) are by Lloyd Stone (1912–1993) and verse 3 is attributed to Georgia Harkness.

## FURTHER READING

Braybrooke, M. (2003) *1,000 World Prayers*. Winchester: O-books.

Clark, S.J. (ed.) (1992) *Celebrating Earth Holy Days*. New York: Crossroad.

Cornille, C. (ed.) (2013) *Inter-religious Dialogue*. Chichester: Wiley Blackwell.

Potter, J. and Braybrooke, M. (eds) (1997) *All in Good Faith*. London: World Congress of Faiths.

Romain, J. (1996) *Till Faith Us Do Part*. London: Fount.

# Reflection

## The Editors

Christianity plays a leading role in interfaith activity. Yet there are many Christians who adopt an exclusivist stance, the extreme version of which is that the Christian way is the sole path to God and that any form of joint work or prayer leads to syncretism. It is therefore especially important to learn from the views of these three Christian contributors, since they have extensive experience of interfaith worship and prayer and reject such an exclusivist position.

Context is of particular significance in the inspiring story which Hugh Ellis tells of work in relation to two other religions that contain a wide range of opinions among their believers, most contact being with Islam, but also some with Judaism. Hugh Ellis notes that religions can be aloof and rigid, for example over boundaries, yet when confronted by tragedies in the wider world and the crying need for good relations at home, he demonstrates how much can be done together, without compromising one's own faith. They meet, with purpose.

As has already been observed by other contributors, Ellis believes that there is no substitute for frequent contact and for informed friendship. Those who study together (in this case, Muslims, Jews and Christians doing scriptural reasoning) and work jointly on community projects such as the housing of refugees should be able to worship and pray in a manner which will deepen their relationship and lead to new initiatives. If that means bending the rules of a particular faith community (for example, with Muslims participating in a Christian service more than had been foreseen) that is acceptable; all are praying to the same God who loves them; their intentions are founded on that fact and on their common humanity.

Common humanity is Sheryl Kujawa-Holbrook's starting point: the spiritual experience of shared human life, known especially in rituals from different traditions, thus acknowledging and appreciating diversity. She uses the example of the Buddhist Floating Lantern Ceremony that allows believers to participate in their own way, while at the same time being a time of prayer for those who suffer and an opportunity to give thanks for the gift of life. She goes on to explore the different motives and attitudes which surround interfaith prayer and makes the important point that ritual should have a central place. Emphasis on belief and on texts tends to bias religion towards the intellectual, devaluing the mystical and spiritual.

A focus on silent prayer and meditation, however, can unite people across many human differences such as those of race, socio-economic position and faith. Further, such activity can serve to express the human longing for healing and for solidarity.

Marcus Braybrooke brings wide-ranging experience of interfaith matters; he knows the joys and the risks, writing movingly about the sense of the holy that transcends the words of all the religions. Religions point to a truth which is beyond everyday language and participants in interfaith worship and prayer need to recognise that fact.

While seeing the value of 'serial' events, where each faith contributes in turn (for example, after a disaster), he favours the challenge of devising occasions which all those present can 'own'. Examples from his own experience include 'The Gift of Water' and 'Respect for the Earth'. He thus has a different emphasis to Kujawa-Holbrook's endorsement of 'serial' prayer, while agreeing with her enthusiasm for ritual: the use of flowers, candles, music and silence.

Both those contributors emphasise the crucial part played in interfaith relations by rites of passage, with Braybrooke going into useful detail from his experience. Interfaith marriage is often treated as problematic but is on the increase in many places and can be seen as a wonderful adventure where love has brought two people together and where special arrangements need to be made. Increased pastoral sensitivity is desirable from those religious representatives who see such a marriage as compromising the unique position of one religion or the other. Again, the birth of a child is an occasion for rejoicing in all faiths and can be a creative occasion for interfaith prayer. Such 'mixing' brings new insights and both Kujawa-Holbrook and Braybrooke write about the value of a representative of one faith speaking at an event of another: perhaps at a special 'rite of passage' such as a funeral, but also during normal worship.

In conclusion: first, the comment that some strands of Christianity are preoccupied with words and can discover insights from other faiths. Being silent, crying together, eating together and lighting candles can often be more effective than words.

Then, second, the hard point that Christianity's relations with other religions have often been disastrous in the past, especially in its contact with Judaism and Islam but also, for example (as mentioned in Chapter 4), in missionary contact with traditional or indigenous religions. Now it can use opportunities to continue an important role in good interfaith relations, as expressed in this chapter.

Chapter 11

# ISLAM

## 1

## Praying with Others

Ibrahim Mogra

For a number of decades Britain has been and continues to become more and more multiethnic, multicultural and multifaith. It is common to find places of worship of the many religions that are now flourishing in this country in close proximity to one another. There are some that stand just a stone's throw away, across the road or even side by side.

There are occasions, festivals and celebrations during the year and especially during interfaith week, when friends and neighbours of the many places of worship are invited over to attend events or share food together. It is not just happy and joyous occasions that bring diverse faith communities together in each other's places of worship, but also tragedies, as we have seen happening more and more often.

I felt privileged to have been invited by the Speaker of the House of Commons soon after 9/11 to the historic Chapel of St Mary Undercroft within the Palace of Westminster. The chapel is a Royal Peculiar, which means it is not under the jurisdiction of a bishop but is controlled by the monarch. There I joined a rabbi and a Christian priest to offer prayers for peace and harmony. Many members of parliament from different political parties joined us. All three of us prayed from our own scriptures and within our own distinct faith traditions; we were not active participants in the prayers of the others. It was a most moving and memorable experience. Later, I was told that this was the first time that Muslim prayers had been offered there.

I am in favour of praying 'with' others and in the company of others, including those with whose beliefs Islam fundamentally disagrees. The space in which the prayers are offered also does not pose me any challenges. As Muslims we have two distinct understandings of prayer. One is prayer in the sense of worship and ritual prayer. For example, the five daily prayers (*salah*) are seen as a direct form of worship. The other is supplication (*du'a*), praying to God for one's needs.

Often when Muslims think or talk about prayer they mean worship and ritual prayers. These prayers are obligatory on all adult Muslims and must be prayed during specified times in a specific way, having performed ablutions beforehand. There are many rules that must be followed in these prayers. These prayers are addressed and offered only to God. They are performed collectively in a mosque but may also be offered individually if circumstances do not permit this. This form of worship (*salah*) is only to be offered by Muslims. Non-Muslims should not join in or participate, although they are welcome to observe. I have observed, albeit rarely, when a well-meaning but poorly informed Muslim has invited a non-Muslim to join in. I have also observed some non-Muslim visitors to mosques who feel that they should, or that they can freely, join the Muslim congregational prayer, either to make their hosts feel honoured or because they subscribe to an unregulated idea of inclusivism, believing that all religions are the same as they all lead to God. Both situations need correcting.

## THE ROLE OF A GUEST

I believe Muslims must not invite non-Muslim people to join in *salah* but instead should help them to observe the prayers. And as for non-Muslim visitors I would say that they must refrain from joining the *salah* even when invited to do so; they should politely decline. I believe this is more respectful and will certainly not offend anyone. In fact, one may cause offence to many by joining in what is meant to be a Muslim-only act of worship and prayer. According to many Muslim jurists, such participation of non-Muslims can also impact on the validity of the prayer for the Muslim worshippers.

With the same token, I believe Muslims must never join, as active participants, in the ritual prayers of other religions whether in their place of worship or in a neutral space. For example, it is allowed, if a group of Muslims chooses, or is invited, to visit a church for a Sunday service or for Midnight Mass on Christmas Eve, but only to observe Christians at prayer. Islam does not allow them to participate in any of the Christian worship, especially receiving communion or blessings in the name of the Father, the Son and the Holy Spirit. I believe priests must spell out to all non-Christian visitors that the Christian worship is only for Christians and no one should feel obliged to join in. I have experienced, for example, many a Christian worshipper enthusiastically handing me a book of the service and pointing out the relevant page. Whenever I have accepted or picked up any prayer book from my seat in the pews, it is only to learn and know about what is being said, but never to participate. In churches with which I work and am known to the congregations, I remain seated whilst the Christian worshippers stand to pray. Needless to say, no one has ever insisted that I stand. I always aim to sit in the last row, except when the hosts want me to be in the front row. In circumstances where I feel my remaining seated may be seen as being disrespectful, and certainly in the presence of Her Majesty the Queen, or if the service is being broadcast on television, I do always stand, although I do not use the service book. Instead, I always say Muslim prayers and quietly recite the Qur'an, sometimes from memory and occasionally on my mobile Qur'an app, when appropriate.

## SHARED EVENTS

Westminster Abbey organises a Commonwealth Day Service that is attended by the Queen and the royal family and also by ambassadors and dignitaries from all the Commonwealth nations. I am regularly invited along with other faith leaders and representatives to pray for the Commonwealth. Each of us takes it in turn to pray in our own tradition and from our own scriptures, although the rest of the service is Christian in nature. The prayer book contains all of our prayers, which we write in a most inclusive way touching our common humanity and our collective need for peace and prosperity. Some of the prayers, which are addressed to God Almighty directly, are the ones to which I am able to say *amin* (amen). Those that are addressed to other deities or offered in the Trinitarian way, I do not participate in or say *amin* to.

Westminster Abbey recently celebrated the Queen's diamond jubilee and held a Service of Thanksgiving. They prepared prayers that were inclusive and addressed to God alone and all of us faith representatives were able to say in unison after each prayer words of thanks to God.

St Margaret's Church, Westminster Abbey organised a service for the new parliament to which faith representatives were invited. I stood in silent observation throughout, as it was a wholly Christian service. I prayed silently, as a Muslim, for our new parliament.

I have been attending the annual Holocaust Memorial Day observance for many years and was honoured to light a candle on one occasion. This year, when all the speeches and presentations were done, the attendees were told that to conclude the day's events a Jewish prayer in Hebrew would be offered and we were invited to stand. I did not know what the prayers were saying so I remained seated and did not stand or participate. I prayed silently, as a Muslim, for peace, justice and prosperity for all.


## RESPONSE TO A TRAGEDY

Some years ago, there was a tragic murder of an African Caribbean young man in Leicester. A revenge attack got addresses mixed up, an innocent family of four perished in the arson attack and their whole house was gutted. This tragedy involved the Christian, Muslim, African Caribbean, Somali and South Asian communities. Emotions and tensions were naturally running high, with a real possibility of further violence and of a breakdown in the good community relations which Leicester is very fortunate to enjoy. I was personally involved in working with Leicestershire Constabulary, the Bishop of Leicester and other faith community leaders to ensure that peace prevailed and that all of us remained united as 'One Leicester'. Prayers were organised at churches and mosques and, as faith leaders, we went to each other's places of worship. At the young murder victim's church, I, along with three Muslim community leaders and representatives, were given a place in the front next to the altar. I was invited to say a few words after which I took my seat. When the Christian service and prayers began, I remained seated and did not participate. My Muslim colleagues were unsure and I could clearly see that they were feeling uncomfortable, because the whole church was standing, including some other Muslims in the congregation, whilst I remained seated. I felt pleased that these Muslims sitting next to me on the stage took the cue from me and remained seated. This happened three times as the congregation stood and sat for various hymns being sung. Eventually it was all too much for them and the next time the congregation stood the three Muslims also stood up. I believe this was precisely the wrong time to stand and that they should have remained sitting because the bishop was now sending the congregation home with blessings in the Trinitarian formula.

## ISLAM AND TRUTH

Islam is a religion that makes a truth claim. The Qur'an declares that Islam is the only way of submission, and of life acceptable to God. God will reject all other ways. Muhammad's preaching (peace be upon him) about the one and only God was not acceptable to his tribesmen, the Quraysh. They tried to negotiate with him and offered him a deal. The deal was that for six months in a year they would all pray together to the idols and other deities and for six months they would all pray to the one God. God commanded Muhammad to declare to the disbelievers:

> Say, 'Disbelievers: I do not worship what you worship, you do not worship what I worship, I will never worship what you worship, you will never worship what I worship: you have your religion and I have mine.' (Qur'an 109:1–6)

There are several other instances when Muhammad ensured the Muslims did not even imitate or pray at the same time as non-Muslims, let alone praying together with them by participating in their rituals. For example, fire and sun worshippers in his time used to worship when the sun was at its zenith. Muhammad instructed Muslims to wait until the sun had passed its zenith and only then perform the *Zuhr* (afternoon) prayer.

When Muhammad migrated from Makkah to Madinah as a refugee, he saw that the Jews were fasting on a day that corresponded to the 10th of Muharram, the first month of the Muslim calendar. He asked them why they did this and was told that they were fasting in order to thank God for saving Moses and the Israelites from Pharaoh. Muhammad said that we have more right to do that and recommended Muslims also fast on the 10th whilst stressing that they must add one day before or after, just to be different from the Jewish practice of fasting on that single day.

Following from this guidance, Muslims would not be allowed to wear a crucifix as it is a distinct symbol representing a Christian belief, nor would they be allowed to grow side locks like some in the Jewish Hasidic communities do, as it is a distinct expression of their Jewish faith and of their love for the Commandments.

## CONCLUSION

I feel truly privileged to have experienced very moving emotions when praying with and in the presence of non-Muslims. I have seen and heard the appreciation of non-Muslims for the prayers that I have offered, which I always ensure are inclusive of the needs of all of humanity, whilst ensuring they are wholly Islamic in nature. I have seen how many non-Muslims have ensured that their prayers are also such that Muslims are able to feel included and perhaps also be able to say amen. This I believe is the right way for all. May God Almighty bless us all, amin.

# 2

# Uniting for Peace

## Monawar Hussain

We are living through one of the most exciting times in human history. Modern forms of transportation, communications, social media platforms, a proliferation of satellite channels and a host of e-technologies have transformed our world into a global village. But all is not well. There has been a worrying rise of nationalism worldwide, including in Europe and across the Atlantic, far too often emboldening extreme far-right groups and individuals into violent action (Benhabib 2017). Violent extremists, employing Islamic symbols, have carried out appalling attacks on European streets and beyond, in the name of Islam. Both use the violent actions of the *other* to generate, often within their own communities, fear and mistrust of the *other*. What should we do in the face of narratives of hate, division and violence? Can we, as people of faith, bridge the gap of misunderstanding and misperception in order to advance a narrative of mutual love, respect and understanding? I believe we can, we should and we must.

## SPIRITUAL AND PRACTICAL UNITY

It is true that the orthodoxies of the world's great religious traditions often seem triumphalist and exclusivist. However, I take the view that when we dig deeper, penetrating the surface, we discover that there is a shared spiritual essence and it is this that will enable the great traditions to reformulate in the twenty-first century, producing narratives of tolerance, love and understanding in an ever-changing world. This is precisely what I try to do through my interfaith and community work, and also through my national initiative entitled *United for Peace: Communities United Against Extremism*.[1]

In a multifaith and multicultural society such as the contemporary United Kingdom, the coming together of faith communities for interfaith prayer becomes an imperative, especially at moments of national commemoration such as Remembrance Day and Her Majesty's ninetieth birthday celebrations, or at times of terrorist outrages. Such meetings affirm national unity and articulate a collective will to stand united both at times of heartache and of celebration. This might seem a commonsense approach and something that adherents of diverse faiths would welcome but that is not always the case.

## THE TEACHING OF THE PROPHET

Following one of our *United for Peace* events at the University of Birmingham, I shared our booklet for the event with a young Muslim. He was articulate, British born, and I thought would be receptive to the initiative. His reaction was one of horror. He could never envisage sharing the same space for prayer with people of other faiths and a number of quotes from Islamic scripture followed – all aimed at justifying his position. By way of illustration, I note below one of the Qur'anic verses he was citing:

---

1    An example of a number of *United for Peace* service booklets providing detailed sets of interfaith prayers and messages can be downloaded at www.theoxfordfoundation.com/united-for-peace.

> You who believe, do not take the Jews and Christians as allies: they are allies only to each other. Anyone who takes them as an ally becomes one of them – God does not guide such wrongdoers. (Qur'an 5:51)[2]

This young man had been told that friendship with Christians and Jews was not permissible, and this was the verse that justified that position. The idea of coming together for prayer was a total anathema. But I said to him, if we read surah 5, we note that, at verse 5, God had given Muslim men permission to marry women from the 'people of the Book', that is Christian and Jewish women, so how can you argue that we cannot be friends? Marriage in Islam not only brings together two people, but it brings together two families at the very least, perhaps even two tribes as at the time of the Islamic revelation, creating thereby strong bonds of mutual love, respect and social cohesiveness. In Qur'an 60:8–9 Muslims are ordered to deal with people of other faiths with kindness and justice. There are other verses of the Qur'an that can be interpreted in a positively pluralist way:

> But they are not all alike. There are some among the People of the Book who are upright, who recite God's revelations during the night, who bow down in worship, who believe in God and the Last Day, who order what is right and forbid what is wrong, who are quick to do good deeds. These people are among the righteous and they will not be denied [the reward] for whatever good deeds they do: God knows exactly who is conscious of Him. (Qur'an 3:113–115)

> We have assigned a law and a path to each of you. If God had so willed, He would have made you one community, but He wanted to test you through that which He has given you, so race to do good: you will all return to God and He will make clear to you the matters you differed about. (Qur'an 5:48)

> [Believers], argue only in the best way with the People of the Book, except with those of them who act unjustly. Say, 'We believe in what was revealed to us and in what was revealed to you; our God and your God are one [and the same]; we are devoted to Him.' (Qur'an 29:46)

---

2     All Qur'anic quotes are from Professor M.A.S. Haleem's translation (Haleem 2008). For a discussion of misinterpreted verses, see Imam Monawar Hussain's OMPEP programme (Hussain 2013), available for download at www.theoxfordfoundation.com.

I also cited the story of the Christian delegation from Najran, visiting the Prophet in his mosque in Medina. When the time for prayer came, the Prophet gave them permission to pray in his mosque facing towards the east (Lings 1991). In addition, *A Common Word: Between Us and You*, an international initiative by Muslim leaders recognised for their religious authority, drawn from diverse strands and denominations from across the Islamic world, and addressed to the main worldwide religious leadership of the global Christian world, states that the two 'foundational principles' common to Muslims and Christians are:

> love of the One God, and love of the neighbour. These principles are found over and over again in the sacred texts of Islam and Christianity. The Unity of God, the necessity of love for Him, and the necessity of love of the neighbour is thus the common ground between Islam and Christianity. (MABDA 2012, p.53)

Arab Muslims and Christians use the same term for God, Allah. They might conceive this Infinite, Absolute being differently but nonetheless worship the same One God, that is what our scriptures affirm. There are plenty of other examples of common ground that can be cited here, but this should be sufficient to demonstrate that the position I take is rooted within the mainstream Islamic tradition. What should be our guiding principles for a positive encounter for praying together?

## RELIGIOUS INTEGRITY

This is best illustrated through a meeting with a Christian gentleman who had come to speak with me to learn more about how the *United for Peace* service works. Some 40–45 minutes into the conversation, having gained a degree of empathy, he said, 'Monawar, let me cut to the chase, are you trying to create some universal religion?' His primary concern was that coming together for prayer with people of other faiths would breach the integrity of his faith tradition, as well as that of those participants from other faith traditions. Many adherents of other faiths share this view too. Shafiq and Abu-Nimer (2007, p.13) note that one of the fears of Muslim interfaith participants, particularly those from South Asia, is that it will result in a 'new, diluted "Abrahamic" religion'. This was an experiment carried out by Akbar (1542–1605), the sixteenth-century Mughal ruler, who had 'sought to create unity and reach out to many religions by creating a new religion – *Dini-Ilahi* – through combining Islam, Brahmanism, Christianity and Zoroastrianism'. Siraj (2008, p.324), however, has called this claim 'a fantastic fallacy of history' and argued that at the most Akbar had developed 'a basic belief in the commonness of all religions, but never to the extent of heresy against Islam or coercing his citizens to follow a new faith'.

What I mean by religious integrity is that, for any encounter of praying together to succeed, I must recognise that each person of another faith will be as committed to his or her faith as I am. This recognition has to be the foundation for a productive and fruitful encounter, always being alert to those who might wish to use a shared space for prayer in order to proselytise or score points, who must be stopped at the first instance. We realised this principle by ensuring that the planning committee for our events was inclusive, representing all the major traditions within our city; our first event, held in Oxford, was delivered in partnership with the Oxford Council of Faiths. It is also worth noting here the backdrop to this first *United for Peace* service. The group calling itself 'Islamic State' had brutally murdered a number of Western hostages, including two British humanitarian workers – David Haines and Alan Henning. I was devastated and wanted to do something that would unite all our communities. I emailed a group of interfaith colleagues in our city; the response was immediate and overwhelming, in support of a coming together. We gave ourselves six weeks!

## THREE FAITHS OR MULTIFAITH?

There were a number of issues we needed to address. Although we took as a given the multifaith nature of the service, should we include a reading from the humanist/atheist community, so that all the different strands of Oxford were represented? Clearly, this would no longer be a multifaith service, but we would need to change the title to something that would reflect and also ensure inclusion of nonfaith members. We decided to run with the title *United for Peace: Oxford's Communities United Against Extremism*, with a subtitle reflecting what we were doing: *A service with readings and silent reflection*. We were coming together to offer prayer for those brutally murdered by 'IS' and for their families; we were affirming the dignity of the human person, love, compassion, understanding and mutual respect – values that we all felt were common to all our traditions.

## THE QUESTION OF LANGUAGE

What language should we use for the readings and prayers? Each of the major traditions might wish to offer prayer in their particular sacred language, without which it might not be considered authentic to that tradition. The downside to this approach was that the audience would not follow what was being said and, if each tradition chanted a prayer together with a translation, the duration of a service could become onerous. Having considered this, the planning committee decided that we should confine all readings to the English language, thereby enabling the language itself to become a terrific unifier. This also had the consequence of almost all the readings using 'God' or 'Lord', instead of their equivalent in their sacred language.

## CONTENTS OF PRAYER

What should the content of the prayer be for each religious tradition? Would this need to be distinctive or universal? Would the universality of a prayer compromise the integrity of that tradition because it would privilege an inclusive reading over an exclusivist? Conversely, would the distinctiveness of a reading compromise the universality and the common ground between the diverse faith traditions? There was a sense here that the purpose of our coming together for prayer was to offer a prayer together and share the silence, so, by digging deep within each tradition, each member would bring forth a prayer that was authentic to that tradition, while at the same time affirming each other. By way of example, I note here four prayers from out of seven – Christian, Jewish, Muslim and Hindu – respectively, in a shorter form to provide an idea of some of the contents of the prayers.

### Christian

Dear Lord, we thank you for bringing us here together. Thank you for the chance to worship and pray for peace and understanding between all religions and all people. Give peace to all the aching hearts of humankind, stir us all to seek your compassion in everything we do and so establish a way of life that is according to Your kingdom and Your love.

Lord in your mercy, hear our prayer.

## Jewish

At times like this, we all need to recognise the potential for extremism in every faith and political system, including our own. Rather than pointing the finger, we need to draw close together and reaffirm our values of peace, justice and compassion. We need to renew our determination to help the victims and to promote our joint human values together, as people of all faiths and none. We as Jews can reaffirm and contribute our belief that every human being is created in God's image. We aim to see the divine in the person very different from ourselves.

Song, led by Adele Moss (based on verses from Micah 4). All join in.

And everyone 'neath his vine and fig tree Shall live in peace and harmony. [repeat]

And into ploughshares beat their swords, Nations shall make war no more. [repeat]

A pause for silence and personal reflection

## Muslim

In the name of God, the Infinitely Good, the Most Merciful

Praise be to God. Oh my Lord You are the Most Kind, the Most Compassionate, the Ever-Forgiving, the Most Merciful of the Merciful.

Oh my Lord, strengthen those who are working for peace, reconciliation and healing wherever they may be in the world.

Oh my Lord, bless this beautiful city of ours with every blessing and make this event today an inspiration for others, to be voices of love and peace.

Oh my Lord, grant us always to be united against the voices of hatred, division and violence.

A supplication repeated after prayer:

O God, You are Peace, From you comes Peace,
And to You returns Peace, Enliven us with Peace, Our Lord.
Enter us into Paradise – the abode of peace.
You are the Most Blessed, Our Lord,
Most Exalted, Possessor of Glory and Nobility. O Most Merciful of the Merciful, Have Mercy upon us. Pardon us, O You, Who are Most Generous.

## Hindu

In the Rig Veda the Mantra reads:

Only One God exists eternally BUT wise persons call Him by Many Names.
Om Shaantih, Shaantih, Shaantih, Om (O, Peace; Peace; Peace).
O Lord, Let there be peace in the Heavens; Peace in the Atmosphere; Peace on Earth;
Let the waters be cooling, the herbs healing and the plants enhancing Life.
Let there be Harmony between, and peace for, all beings in the Universe.
With perfection in Knowledge let peace pervade everywhere.
May this Peace be within me as well!

In our discussions, we took the view that a common song and a common Pledge for Peace would enhance the service by engendering a shared group-feeling. Some faith groups might be reluctant to participate in a common song but that would be alright too, as we sought to hold together people from differing starting points in this kind of a shared service. Adele Moss, who was an established storyteller and singer, led the chorus and it must be said that this was a very powerful, moving and unifying moment for the service. It worked well! The Pledge for Peace is the final moment in the service, when all congregants stand up to affirm their commitment to live in respect, peace, harmony and understanding:

We have come together today as citizens of Oxfordshire and the
   United Kingdom.

We pledge to stand united
against those who propagate hate and violence towards others.

We pledge to stand united
against all forms of violent extremism.

We pledge to live by the values that are inherent within our
   traditions – values of compassion for the needy,
      love for our neighbour
and respect for one another.

We pledge to do all we can
to promote understanding, respect and mutual love for all.

## MUTUAL RESPECT

What kinds of food should be provided? I had on one occasion
been at an interfaith gathering at a leading UK institution where
the participants had been assured that all food was vegetarian,
only to have the organiser announce later that the food was not all
vegetarian! This did not go down well. Some of us wanted to offer
both vegetarian and meat options, others took the view that we should
restrict ourselves to vegetarian, thereby being as inclusive as we could
be. Does this privilege vegetarian eaters over meat eaters? I suppose it
does, but that would be asking the wrong question. When individuals
come together in the spirit of love, compassion and understanding,
all seeking to create a shared space that embodies these values and
recognises our diversity as well as our shared common humanity,
people are always much more willing to seek out common ground
even when it comes to food. This is not a place for competition or
one-upmanship.

Since our first event in Oxford, we have held a number of events
in Birmingham and the Thames Valley. We have experimented with
music and poetry, including singing in different languages, also
with personal testimony from victims of racial or terrorist violence,
combining sacred language with English translation – doing all this
carefully, sensitively and at all times with the participation of many
different faith or nonfaith adherents. For this to be a successful
endeavour, it must articulate and be a voice drawn from the depth

of all our spiritual traditions. I conclude with one of many messages, this one received after our service at Eton Dorney:

> The atmosphere of love and mutual respect that you created… was extraordinary. I do congratulate you on bringing us all together, it was a marvellous idea in the first place, and I thought it succeeded in a wonderfully heart-warming way. And there was no doubt that God was blessing our endeavours in that fabulous sunset as we all left.

## REFERENCES

Benhabib, S. (2017) 'The return of Fascism.' *New Republic 248*, 11, 36–43.

Haleem, M.A.S. (2008) *The Qur'an: A New Translation*. New York: Oxford University Press.

Hussain, M. (2013) *Oxford Muslim Pupils' Empowerment Programme (OMPEP)*. Oxford: The Oxford Foundation.

Lings, M. (1991) *Muhammad: His Life Based on the Earliest Sources*. Cambridge: Islamic Texts Society.

MABDA (2012) *A Common Word: Between Us and You*. Amman: The Royal aal Al-Bayt Institute for Islamic Thought.

Shafiq, M. and Abu-Nimer, M. (2007) *Interfaith Dialogue: A Guide for Muslims*. Washington, DC: The International Institute for Islamic Thought.

Siraj, M.A. (2008) 'India: A laboratory of inter-religious experiment.' *Religion and the Arts 12*, 319–328.

# 3

## Inclusivist Islam

### With the Name of God, the Merciful, the Compassionate

Usama Hasan

I certainly subscribe to an inclusivist view of Islam. In fact, I go further: the essential message of the Qur'an, for anyone who cares to study it carefully, is a universal one, and Islam by its nature is a universal religion. Numerous Qur'anic verses are addressed to 'people' or 'humanity', as well as those addressing the 'believers' specifically. Although most of the prophets in the Qur'an are Biblical, Israelite or Arabian, the Qur'an also affirms that God sent divinely inspired messengers and prophets to every people and nation on earth, so that they could not plead ignorance of God's word on the Day of Judgement, whether these prophets are named in the Qur'an or not. Accordingly, the hadith traditions speak of thousands of such prophets. History is witness to the Islamic teaching that Muhammad is the 'Seal of the Prophets', for all the major founders of religions appeared before him. The only major world religion that appeared after Islam is Sikhism, which explicitly draws on previous Islamic and Hindu teachings and traditions.

## PEOPLE OF THE BOOK: NOT JUST JEWS AND CHRISTIANS, BUT FOLLOWERS OF ALL MAJOR WORLD RELIGIONS

Contrary to popular misconception, the Qur'anic term *ahl al-kitab* ('People of the Book') is not limited to Jews and Christians only. Had it been, it would have been a redundant term, since the Jews and Christians are already known by specific terms in the Qur'an: *yahud* and *nasara* respectively. But 'People of the Book' is a universal term, encompassing followers of any scripture, and therefore applicable to all the major world religions. It is for this reason that many of the early Muslims, including Ali bin Abi Talib, a leader revered by Sunnis and Shias alike, and Imam Shafi'i, founder of one of the major schools of

Sunni jurisprudence, regarded the Magians (Zoroastrians) of Eastern Arabia and Persia as 'People of the Book'. I discussed this in more detail in a previous work (Hasan 2015). Similarly, Ihsanoglu (2004) relates that Muhammad bin Qasim, the first Muslim conqueror in India, granted Hindus the status of *dhimmis* (protected 'People of the Book') by declaring that 'Hindu temples are just like Christian churches, Jewish synagogues and Zoroastrian fire-temples' (p.15).

## UNIVERSAL SYMBOLISM OF ISLAMIC PRAYER RITES

This universal aspect of Islam is reflected in its modes of prayer. Now, when Muslims speak of 'prayer', there are at least three senses to this:

1. *Salah* or *salat*, the ritual prayer, consisting of cycles of highly symbolic postures of standing, bowing, prostrating on the ground and sitting. There are five daily *salat* prayers at different times of the day, as well as special forms of *salat* for Fridays, Eid celebrations, funerals, eclipses and other signs of nature.

2. *Du'a* or supplication, usually accompanied by a raising of both hands, cupped slightly and open towards the heavens. This may be done at any time but is especially practised at times and places regarded as particularly sacred or holy.

3. *Dhikr* or remembrance (of God). Remembrance may be done by every limb of the body when engaged in devotion to God, but *dhikr* usually refers to that of the tongue, in the form of formulas that are repeated. These may be general glorifications of God, or be expressions of wonder, praise, thanks or prayer related to specific actions that comprehensively cover daily life: sleeping and waking; eating and drinking; entering and leaving homes, toilets, markets and mosques; making love; witnessing natural signs such as thunder and the new crescent moon.

### *Salat*: the Islamic ritual prayer and its sacred symbolism

The most prevalent practice of Islamic prayer is the *salat*: it is experientially the richest, since it comprises numerous cycles of standing, bowing, prostrating and sitting, with each posture having its own prayers (*du'a* and *dhikr*). When we go from standing to prostrating, we also briefly kneel in prayer, and the hadith traditions speak of kneeling also. *Salat* is a universal form because its postures are found in different ways in the earlier religious traditions, each representing a major world religion. Thus, the Bible records that Moses, Aaron and Jesus Christ (in the Garden of Gethsemane), amongst others, all 'fell on their faces' in prayer: this practice has been preserved through prostration on the ground in Islam, the posture in which a person is most humbled, yet nearest to God. The Eastern religions also include similar prayer postures, such as in the practice of yoga and tai-chi, both of which were originally sacred practices.

## A striking example of sacred symbolism across different religions

In another example of sacred symbolism across religions that may seem trivial but actually signifies deeper mysteries, a striking part of the daily Muslim *salat* prayer is the raising of the forefinger whilst seated, indicating the Unity of God. Imams preaching the Friday sermon will also often raise their forefinger. Both practices are narrated directly from the Prophet, peace be upon him. But this instruction of his sparked a debate about interfaith matters: one of his wives, Umm Salama, who had participated in the first sacred migration (*hijra*) from Mecca to Christian Abyssinia, reported that she had seen statues of prophets in the churches there, represented with their forefingers raised in monotheistic belief (see al-Albani 1993). There is no doubt in my mind that this Islamic practice, like many others, evokes a continuation of previous monotheism. And it is intriguing that the forefinger occupies a central place in Michaelangelo's masterpiece on the Sistine Chapel ceiling, *The Creation of Adam*.

## Similarities to Islamic ritual prayer in other religions

Once, when looking to sight the new crescent moon marking Ramadan next to the Royal Observatory in Greenwich, I noticed an Orthodox Jewish man offering sunset prayers in the royal park, and his prayer included standing and bowing in a way very similar to Islamic practice. I mentioned this to a Jewish university student, and he told me, speaking historically as he saw it, that 'we used to bow and prostrate also, but our rabbis told us to stop doing so when you guys arrived on the scene'.

## My experience of allowing non-Muslims to join Islamic *salat* prayer

In 2013 I visited Israel and Palestine as part of a group of about 25 Jews, Christians and Muslims. This was a 'dual narratives' tour, with both an Israeli and Palestinian guide. At the 'White Mosque' in Nazareth, I was honoured to lead the Muslims in the afternoon prayers. Our Israeli guide, a Jewish woman, told me that she had not prayed in a long time and wished to reconnect with the Divine: she requested to join the Muslim prayer, and even to take part in the sacred washing (*wudu'* or ablutions) beforehand. Of course, I welcomed this, because in my view she was simply reconnecting with her own Jewish heritage through Islam, and indeed she told me afterwards that she thoroughly enjoyed the prayer and felt refreshed. God created humanity to know, love and worship God, and it would have been absurd of me to refuse our guide's request, based on some excessively rigid, legalistic approach. *Do they distribute the mercy of your Lord?* (Qur'an, Gilded Adornments, 43:32).

When the Prophet Muhammad received new converts to Islam, they would not know the formulaic prayers (*du'a* and *dhikr*) accompanying the postures of *salat* prayer, so the Prophet asked them to simply remember, praise and glorify God in their own way, whilst following the rest of the community in the physical postures of *salat*. I gave similar advice to our Jewish friend who joined us for the Islamic *salat* prayers. On another occasion I was asked to lead Friday prayers at a Muslim congregation in Oxford that is open to non-Muslims, and I invited the latter to also join the Friday prayer. Again, our non-Muslim friends expressed gratitude for being included, and commented on how refreshing it felt to place their foreheads on the ground in submission to God.

In similar vein, by the grace of God, I have presided over three of what I would call 'Muslim humanist' funerals in the past few years. These were for deceased Muslims who had a universalist outlook on life and religion, and there were many mourners present who were not Muslim. Now, the Muslim funeral *salat* prayers involve standing only, with no bowing or prostration in case this is mistaken as worshipping the dead. For these funerals, I actually led a traditional Muslim funeral prayer, but invited our non-Muslim friends present to join in, if they wished, by joining the rows of the worshippers and remembering the deceased in their thoughts and prayers, whilst we Muslims recited our prayers in Arabic and quietly, in the traditional way. The overwhelming response I had to these funeral prayers was that people felt included, and everyone was very happy that our non-Muslim friends were not excluded from the most intimate and sacred part of the proceedings.

## CHILDHOOD: MUSLIM EXPERIENCES OF CHRISTIAN WORSHIP AT SCHOOL

My approach has not come out of nowhere: I became used to interfaith prayer from a very young age, since my siblings and I attended Christian-ethos primary and secondary schools in the UK. My puritanically devout Muslim parents were happy that we had daily prayer at school, and only cautioned us against praying to Jesus: we were to pray only to God. Thus, we thoroughly enjoyed singing Christian hymns, although we would skip phrases such as 'Lord Jesus' and replace 'Father' with 'Lord' in the Lord's Prayer. My secondary school did not have a school hall, and we used the Anglican church across the road for school assemblies: again, I became used to Christian prayer in church. 'Hands together, eyes closed!' is an instruction I remember well from Christian prayer at primary school. My father used to joke that whilst Muslims pray (*du'a* or supplication) with palms open to the heavens, Christians clasp their hands together. 'We receive God's mercy descending into our cupped hands facing upwards, but it cannot get into Christian palms, since each hand closes off the other!'

## RECITING MUSLIM AND CHRISTIAN PRAYERS ON OFFICIAL BUSINESS

In 2017 I was asked to say the opening prayers at an official (government) event in Kenya: in this devout country, I was told that this was standard practice, just as in Pakistan. The meeting was attended by Muslims and Christians only, so I recited the opening prayer-chapter of the Qur'an (*Surat al-Fatiha*) in Arabic and English, and also recited the Lord's Prayer, explaining that I had to replace 'Father' with 'Lord'. I was very pleased to find that our Muslim and Christian colleagues joined in with me for their respective prayers.

## ISLAMIC BLESSINGS FOR INTERFAITH MARRIAGES

Another area of life in which I regularly participate in interfaith worship is when, as an imam, I bless interfaith marriages, which I do with increasing frequency, averaging almost weekly now. I do a traditional Islamic wedding blessing (*nikah*), sometimes before or after a civil registrar or Christian priest. I may soon officiate alongside a rabbi for a Jewish–Muslim marriage. Obviously, marriages are happy occasions and I use the most inclusive Qur'anic passages and prayers – the audience have always received these warmly. Recently, a Muslim–Christian couple asked me to conduct their *nikah* on Good Friday, a day that was especially holy in different ways to both traditions. In the most striking example of an interfaith wedding in which I have been involved, a German Lutheran Pastorin (female pastor) and I devised a truly interfaith wedding service, with Christian and Muslim hymns, readings, recitations and prayers intertwined. This was delivered in the Great (Marble) Hall of Hatfield House, once owned by King Henry VIII and where the monarchs Elizabeth I, Mary I and Edward VI played as children. The date happened to be September 11, and it was fitting that on an anniversary of a major spark of conflict, the Pastorin and I were able to show, in a historic hall, that great religions can come together in love, rather than instigating and perpetuating war.

## INTERFAITH PRAYERS

In conclusion, I would like to reiterate that believers in the major world religions can, and indeed must, pray together: this should be relatively easy, not only because we have a common source, the Divine, but also because practically our ways of praying have much in common. And just as when Sunnis and Shias, Catholics and Protestants or Orthodox and Reform Jews pray together, we avoid divisive language, true interfaith worship must also be sensitive in its choice of words, readings and liturgies. The Islamic modes of *du'a* and *dhikr* prayer are easily adapted to interfaith contexts, but let us reflect further on the ritual *salat* prayer.

## FURTHER REFLECTIONS ON *SALAT* PRAYER AS A TEMPLATE FOR INCLUSIVE, INTERFAITH PRAYER

The specific form of the Muslim ritual prayer (*salat*) is transmitted in great detail from the Prophet Muhammad, peace be upon him (see al-Albani 1993 for an example). Thus, Muslims will not agree to modify it – this would be a bit like changing the words of the Qur'an, simply inconceivable. However, although the *salat* prayer is nearly always recited in Arabic, it does not have to be so: Imam Abu Hanifa (2nd–3rd Islamic centuries or 8th–9th centuries CE), founder of the largest Islamic school of jurisprudence in terms of following, famously ruled that the *salat* prayer would be valid in Persian or other local language. Indeed, a group of 'progressive' Muslims in the USA recently broke this Arabic-only taboo: a female imam led a group of Muslims standing in mixed-sex rows in Eid *salat* prayer, reciting the Qur'an in Arabic along with English translation. The video of this historic act had over a million views on the internet and may serve as a template for interfaith worship in the future. Non-Muslims would be invited to join the rows for prayer, just as I have done for at least three different types of Muslim *salat* prayers, as described earlier.

Just as our non-Muslim friends are welcome to join the Muslim *salat* prayer, which I see as inclusive in nature, Muslims should feel comfortable in joining other prayer services, since we are used to standing, bowing, kneeling, prostrating and sitting in prayer on a daily basis. The only restriction would be that we worship God alone, something to which no major world religion will object.

Above all, it is the spirit of love and remembrance of God in community that should be the guiding principle for continued interfaith worship:

> The remembrance of God is truly greater. (Qur'an, The Spider, 29:45)

> Lo! It is through the remembrance of God that hearts find satisfaction. (Qur'an, Thunder, 13:28)

> Remember God: standing, sitting and reclining on your sides. (Qur'an, Women, 4:103)

Finally, I would like to note that, far from promoting rigid and literalist intolerance, I believe that if the vast hadith corpus is read holistically, with careful sifting out of genuine narrations from fabricated ones, we arrive at a liberal or generous reading of hadith that reflects the merciful and compassionate character of the *Sunnah*, the Way of the Prophet Muhammad, may peace and blessings be upon him and all his fellow prophets.

Dr Irfan Ahmad Khan, Founder of the World Muslim Council for Interfaith Relations, at prayers with Buddhist and Christian colleagues, Mexico 1999

Credit: Peace Council; Daniel Gómez-Ibáñez

## REFERENCES

al-Albani, M.N. (1993) *The Prophet's Prayer Described from Beginning to End, as though You Were Watching It*, trans. U. Hasan. Ipswich: JIMAS.

Hasan, U. (2015) *From Dhimmitude to Democracy: Islamic Law, Non-Muslims and Equal Citizenship*. London: Quilliam.

Ihsanoglu, E. (2004) *A Culture of Peaceful Coexistence*. Istanbul: Research Centre for Islamic History, Art and Culture (IRCICA).

# Reflection

## The Editors

With the chapter on Islam following that on Christianity, it is tempting to draw parallels. Both religions have a history of treating followers of other faiths as heretical, heathen or (in the case of 'First Nation' or indigenous people) as primitive or backward. Both, as with all religions, yet here more markedly, have allowed their religion to be so entangled with politics and nationalism that they have endorsed violence, often against each other. What is more, extreme exclusivism, resulting in an opposition to any contact with other religions, is widespread in both Christianity and Islam.

Yet there are many signs of hope, and the contribution from Hugh Ellis in the previous chapter, telling of the experience of one town in the UK, shows what can be done when occasions of sorrow and joy, accompanied by the camaraderie of cooperating in valuable community projects, bring people of different faiths together.

Ibrahim Mogra, with his involvement in the Christian–Muslim forum and his past experience of the Muslim Council of Britain, is representative of those Muslims who work in the public sphere for the good of people of their own faith and of the wider society, in the context of a particular nation. As a 'faith leader', it follows that he has a careful attitude to relations with other faiths: he is willing (and indeed keen) to be present at events, yet he makes sure that he is firmly within the bounds of what might be called an official line, namely that Muslims should not participate in the prayer and worship of other faiths and only pray with others through the medium of special prayers written to be acceptable to all. That point raises a question which can be put in the form: 'Where does authority lie?': something experienced in all faiths but especially in Islam where there are many points of tension between different groups and little in the way of an authority structure or indeed of an 'ecumenical movement'. It is crucial that faith leaders set an example of learning about other faiths and interacting with them as Ibrahim Mogra does. Is it also true that progress is often made by people stepping out of line?

Monawar Hussain starts from the exciting and dangerous state of the world, demanding change in the great religious traditions in the form of greater cooperation. He supports this view with references to the Qu'ran and the statements of Muslim leaders, while at the same time strongly opposing anything which appears either to lead to a 'universal religion' or to provide an opportunity to proselytise. There are examples of prayers written for a time of crisis and which are suitable for people of a number of faith groups. What is more, there is a discussion of that great unifier: eating together!

Usama Hasan starts from the position that the message of the Qu'ran is for all people, not just for the 'believers'. He appropriately challenges the usual understanding of the term 'People of the Book' (as being limited to Jews, Christians and Muslims) by giving examples of the inclusion of Zorastrians and Hindus in the past. His position is to be accepting of those who wish to worship in the context of another faith. He also uses his experience of the increasing number of 'rites of passage' which involve people of different faiths and which he believes are not difficult to arrange, for the participants have so much in common.

The profile of Muslims in the world is so high that it is hard for anyone to make comments. In part that is a matter of the violent extremists who misuse the term 'Islam', but it is also down to the confusion resulting from the sheer scale and variety of Muslims (Wahabis and Sufis, for example) and the complexity of the relationships between them. Add to those factors the difficulty of interpreting the Qu'ran and the Hadith on subjects as important as violence and the position of women, and it is not unreasonable for people to find difficulty in arriving at appropriate responses (Lewis and Cohn-Sherbok 2016). Some more liberal Muslims find the Hadith (authorised statements and actions of the Prophet which have become part of Muslim tradition) unhelpful and wish to concentrate on Islamic teaching derived from the interpretation of the Qu'ran alone (Mustafa 2017).

All these factors make for urgency both on the part of Muslims and also of those of other faiths. All over the world, there are fine examples of interfaith work and of the part played by interfaith worship and prayer. As has been pointed out in numerous places in this book, meeting together, eating together, learning about the faith of other believers, working on projects together, praying and worshipping – all these are routes to a more godly and peaceful world for everyone.

## REFERENCES

Lewis, C. and Cohn-Sherbok, D. (eds) (2016) *Sensible Religion*. London: Routledge. On the position of women see the chapter by Sara Khan; on violence see the chapter by Dawoud el-Alami.

Mustafa, P. (2017) *The Quran: God's Message to Mankind. New Millenium Exposition. An Exegesis for the 21st Century*. London: Xeitre-Signat.

Chapter 12

# SIKHISM

## 1

## 'The Whole World Sings Your Glory Day and Night': Sikh Response towards Interfaith Worship and Prayer

Pashaura Singh

Interfaith worship and prayer are deeply linked with the idea of 'religious pluralism', a phenomenon that refers to the co-existence of many religions in the society where we live and our reaction to that fact. It may be defined as the simultaneous existence in a single social arena of a number of different worldviews (or systems of thought, life and action) that are considered incompatible with one another. It has always been a fact of life, but its awareness has become more evident in recent times as a result of the process of globalization. The founder of the Sikh tradition, Guru Nanak (1469–1539), encountered diverse religious traditions of Hindu, Muslim and Nath origins. He was strongly opposed to an exclusive claim that a particular tradition might make to possess the sole religious truth. Indeed, the spirit of accommodation had always been an integral part of his attitude towards other traditions. He acknowledged the usage of different names of *Akal Purakh* ('Eternal One') across religious boundaries: 'What can the poor Nanak say? All the [devout] people praise the One Lord. Nanak's head is at the feet of such people [in reverence]. May I be a sacrifice to all your Names, O Eternal One!' (Guru Granth [GG]: 1168). Guru Nanak showed equal regard to the devout people of different religious traditions. For instance, the *So Dar* ('That Gate') hymn presents his personal experience of heavenly joys in the company of all liberated ones, who sing in eternity the praises of Akal Purakh's glory at the door of his ineffable court (GG: 6). In Guru Nanak's mystic vision, the saintly people of all continents enjoy the 'Realm of Grace' (*karam khand*): 'They know eternal bliss, for the True One is imprinted on their minds' (GG: 8). Such people speak with the 'authority and power' of the divine Word. On the other hand, the Guru frequently condemned the contemporary religious leaders – especially the Brahmins, Qazis and Yogis – as hypocrites for the way in which they divorce moral conduct and religious practice. This double focus must be maintained in order to appreciate Guru Nanak's response to religious pluralism. The early successors of Guru Nanak met the challenge of the religious pluralism of the sixteenth century by establishing a clear basis for a distinct Sikh identity. This sense of distinct identity was marked by a distinctive belief system, modes of worship, socio-religious institutions and an overarching organization with the Guru as its pivot. Indeed, the institution of the Guru carried an aura of divinity for the Sikhs.

One might raise the question that the consciousness of a unique superiority of one's own tradition does not naturally encourage a genuine acceptance of religious pluralism. The answer to this question may be found in Guru Arjan's *Ramakali* hymn where he celebrates colourful diversity by accepting the fact that many 'voices' speak to explore the deeper aspects of religious truth in their own way:

> Some call Thee, 'Ram, Ram', and some call Thee, 'Khuda'i'.
> Some serve Thee as 'Gusain', others as 'Allah'. (1)
> You are the Cause of all causes, O Gracious One.
> You shower your grace and mercy upon us. (1) Refrain.
> Some bathe at sacred places of pilgrimage,
> Some make the pilgrimage to Mecca.
> Some perform devotional worship (*puja*),
> While others bow their heads in prayer. (2)
> Some read the Vedas, and some the Qur'an.
> Some wear blue robes, and some wear white. (3)
> Some call themselves Muslim, and some call themselves Hindu.
> Some yearn for paradise, and others long for heaven. (4)

> Says Nanak: One who realizes the divine Order (*hukam*),
> Knows the secrets of one's Lord and Master. (5) (M5, *Ramakali 9*,
>      GG, p.885 [bracketed numbers are verses in the 'Four-Verse'
>      Hymn])

Indeed, the plurality of religious expression deepens our own sense of wonder and commitment. In this context Diana Eck makes an important observation: 'To recognize this plurality of religious claims as a profoundly important fact of our world does not constitute a betrayal of one's own faith' (Eck 1993, p.14). That is why Guru Arjan defines his own path of liberation in the last verse of this hymn, a path based upon the recognition of the functioning of the divine Order (*hukam*) in human affairs. Not surprisingly, while appreciating the different ways of the Hindu tradition and of Islam in his own days, Guru Arjan made a direct assertion of independent identity elsewhere: 'We are neither Hindu nor Musalman' (GG: 1136).

In response to religious pluralism, therefore, Guru Nanak and the succeeding Gurus were consciously involved in the process of establishing the distinctiveness of a relatively new and developing religious community (*Panth*) as well as their vision of an ideal spiritual life for that community. They were attempting to establish the self-identity of the Sikh community through the creation of their own canonical scripture, the Adi Granth ('Original Book'). Indeed, the compilation of the Adi Granth in 1604 was the most significant development that took place during the period of the fifth Guru, Arjan (1563–1606). The Adi Granth provided a framework for the shaping of the Sikh community and hence it was a decisive factor for Sikh self-definition. It achieved further dignity when Guru Gobind Singh (1666–1708), the tenth and the last human Guru of the Sikhs, closed the canon in the last decades of the seventeenth century. Before he passed away, he terminated the line of personal Gurus and installed the Adi Granth as the eternal Guru for Sikhs. Thereafter, the authority of the Guru was invested in the scripture (Guru Granth) and in the corporate community (Guru Panth). As the source of ultimate authority within the Sikh tradition, therefore, the Guru Granth must be viewed as providing the authoritative Sikh response to the challenge of religious pluralism. It should, however, be emphasized that each generation will have its own view of that authoritative understanding based on its particular interpretation of the text in light of the spirit of its age.

## THE *BHAGAT BANI* IN THE SIKH SCRIPTURE

A distinctive feature of the Sikh scripture is that it contains the compositions of 15 non-Sikh poet-saints from both Hindu and Muslim backgrounds, along with the compositions of the Sikh Gurus. Most of these compositions were first introduced in the early Sikh scriptural tradition during the period of Guru Amar Das. Later on, Guru Arjan extended the precedent of the third Guru and made the *Bhagat Bani* ('utterances of medieval poet-saints') part and parcel of the first canonical text in 1604. This was done in the historical context of the Mughal emperor Akbar's rule. In a sense, Akbar was a true pluralist who was born a Muslim but who married a Hindu wife. His curiosity about other religions led him to build the 'House of Worship' (*Ibadat-khana*) at Fatehpur Sikri where interreligious discussions were held among the scholars of all the major religions. He used to preside over these debates, which resulted in the formation of his own syncretistic religion, the *Din-i-Ilahi* or the 'Divine Religion', aimed at the unification of Hindu and Muslim thought. However, Akbar's pluralism must be understood as part of the large process of state formation in Mughal India. His liberal approach was much despised by his more aggressive co-religionists. For instance, Emperor Aurangzeb (reigned 1658–1707) imposed increasingly restrictive policies of Sunni orthodoxy that included enforcement of Islamic laws and taxes and sometimes the replacement of local Hindu temples by mosques.

The inclusion of the *Bhagat Bani* in the foundational text of Sikhism is, therefore, historically linked with a genuine experiment of religious pluralism in India in the late sixteenth and early seventeenth centuries. Although the effect of this experiment did not last long after Akbar's death, perhaps we can draw some inferences from this original impulse and develop a theory of pluralism that may be useful in the present-day interfaith dialogues, worship and prayer. The evidence of the *Bhagat Bani* certainly highlights the point that some forms of religious expression from outside the tradition were meaningful enough for them to be preserved along with the compositions of the Gurus themselves. The case of the *Bhagat Bani* may thus offer the following four-point theory of pluralism in the context of interreligious worship and prayer. First, one must acknowledge that all religious traditions have gone through the process of self-definition in response to a changing historical context.

Thus, the dignity of the various religious identities of individual participants must be maintained in a dialogue. In other words, one must be able to honour one's commitment as absolute for oneself while respecting the different absolute commitments of others. Therefore, the quest for a universal religion and likewise the attempt to place one religious tradition over and above others must be abandoned. Second, the doctrinal standpoints of different religious traditions must be maintained in mutual respect and dignity. Third, all participants must enter into a dialogue with an 'open attitude' which allows not only true understanding of other traditions but also disagreements on crucial doctrinal points. Finally, the 'other' must somehow become one's 'self' in a dialogue so that one's life is enriched with that spiritual experience (Singh 2003, pp.25–28, 170–175, 191).

## THE SIKH CONGREGATIONAL PRAYER AND INTERFAITH WORSHIP

Sikh worship consists mainly of the congregational singing of devotional hymns (*kirtan*), led and accompanied by musicians (*ragis*) playing harmoniums and the small drums called *tabla*. Through *kirtan* the devotees attune themselves to the divine Word and vibrate in harmony with it. People of all castes and creeds are welcome to participate in Sikh worship at the gurdwara ('House of the Guru', Sikh place of worship). The Sikh congregational prayer begins with the following stanza from Guru Arjan's *Sukhmani* ('Pearl of Peace'):

> You are our Lord and Master, and we make supplication to you. Our soul and body are all your gifts. You are our Mother and Father, and we are your children. Numerous joys lie in your grace. No one knows your extent. You, the Lord, are beyond all imaginable heights. All existence is strung on your thread. It is created by you and is compliant to your Ordinance. You alone know your reality and extent. Your servant, Nanak, is ever sacrificing to you, O Lord! (8) (M5, *Gauri Sukhmani* 4, GG, p.268 [bracketed number is stanza 8 of this astapadi ('Eight-Verse' composition)])

Most instructively, this stanza has become part of Sikh liturgy and is recited immediately before the congregational prayer. It is addressed to *Vahiguru* ('Divine Sovereign'), who is God of Grace, speaking the

Word of divine understanding to all who are prepared to shed their self-centredness (*haumai*) and listen in humility. By addressing the One as 'Mother and Father' simultaneously Guru Arjan stresses that *Vahiguru* is without gender. In fact, the performance of this prelude to the Sikh prayer appeals to *Vahiguru* for protection and guidance. It denotes total surrender, and humility and, above all, delineates the world as one family, with no distinctions whatsoever. The performance of Sikh congregational prayer repeats the common rich heritage of the Sikh tradition within five minutes. It recalls the past trials and triumphs of the *Panth* in a most profound way. It reaches its climax with a universal longing for the 'welfare of all' (*sarbat da bhala*) when it ends with the standard mandatory couplet: 'Nanak says: May your Name exalt our spirits with boundless optimism; and in your grace may peace and prosperity come to one and all.'

Following the example of the sixth Guru, Hargobind (1595–1644), who founded a village known as Sri Hargobindpur – in which he built at his own expense both a mosque, *Guru Ki Masit*, for Muslims and a temple, *Hanuman Mandir*, for Hindus – Sikhs are always ready to open their gurdwaras for people of other faiths to worship in their own way. On 20 August 2012, for instance, 'about 800 Muslims offered *Eid* prayers at a gurdwara in Joshimath in Uttarakhand on Monday after incessant rainfall prevented them from praying at a ground which they normally used for prayers in the absence of a mosque there' (Gopal 2012). Similarly, the first gurdwara built in 1912 at Stockton in California was the 'Model of Interfaith' where Sikh, Hindu and Muslim immigrants from pre-partition India used to worship together at weekends. Over the next three decades the Khalsa Diwan Society of Stockton hosted Hindu and Muslim spiritual leaders alike to build support for the Indian freedom struggle, especially those involved with the Ghadar movement (Balaji 2015). For Sikhs, all sacred spaces in both private and public spheres deserve equal respect and dignity. They enthusiastically participate in ecumenical gatherings around the world. In this regard the *Nishkam Sevak Jatha* of the United Kingdom is at the forefront of interreligious dialogues, including interfaith worship and prayer.

Sikh *langar* feeding thousands at the 2015 Parliament of World Religions
at Salt Lake City, Utah

Credit: Corey Barnett

An integral part of Sikh worship is the institution of the community kitchen (*langar*), the inter-dining convention that requires people of all castes and creeds to sit in status-free lines (*pangat*) to share a common meal. In fact, the establishment of a community kitchen at Kartarpur in the early decades of the sixteenth century was the first reification of Guru Nanak's spiritual concerns to reorganize the society on egalitarian ideals. In this setting of the partaking of food in caste-conscious India, anyone could be sitting next to anyone else, female next to male, socially high to socially low, and ritually pure next to ritually impure. The institution of the community kitchen promoted the spirit of unity and mutual belonging, and struck at a major aspect of caste, thereby advancing the process of defining a community based upon Sikh ideals. In plain ritual language, this egalitarian human revolution proclaimed explicitly that there would be no discrimination of high caste or low, no male or female, no Muslim or Hindu, no Sikh or non-Sikh. More recently, the Guru Nanak Darbar Gurdwara in Dubai hosted about 120 Muslim residents of over thirty nationalities to celebrate the holy month of Ramadan and support the Muslim community in breaking their fast in a multicultural setting. As the call to *Maghreb* prayers rang inside the Sikh temple, Muslims broke their fast over water, dates, *Rooh Afza* milkshake and Indian dishes of dal served with naan bread, paneer and biryani, followed by *ras malai* for dessert. Later, they offered their *Maghreb* prayers inside the Sikh temple, facing the *Qibla* direction, in Jebel Ali. For the Year of Giving, the Sikh temple held the Guinness World Record for serving a free continental breakfast titled 'Breakfast for Diversity' to the maximum number of people from diverse nationalities (Zakaria 2017).

## CONCLUSION

In response to the challenge of religious pluralism there has always been a process of self-definition in the major textual and institutional developments in Sikh history. Notwithstanding the emphasis on the protective Sikh attitude (which at times becomes militant defence of the tradition in the face of persecution), the spirit of accommodation has always been an integral part of the Sikh attitude towards other religious traditions. Any change in the religious and political situation calls for a new response to religious pluralism, not only from the majority of the Sikhs in the Punjab but also from the diaspora Sikhs who continue to face new situations as immigrants in other countries. Thus, each generation of Sikhs has responded to the question of self-definition in the light of its own particular situation. In fact, they rediscover their identity in cross-cultural encounters as well as their interaction with other religious and ethnic communities within the living context of interfaith worship and prayer. In this context it may be noted that the Sikh institution of community kitchen (*langar*) provided food to thousands of participants from different faiths at the 2015 Parliament of the World's Religions Conference in Salt Lake City, Utah.

## REFERENCES

Balaji, M. (2015) 'Model of interfaith: The history of Stockton Gurdwara.' 22 May. Accessed on 16 November 2018 at www.sikhnet.com/news/model-interfaith-history-stockton-gurdwara.

Eck, D.L. (1993) *Encountering God: A Spiritual Journey from Bozeman to Banaras*. Boston, MA: Beacon Press.

Gopal, N. (2012) 'Muslims offer Eid prayers at gurdwara in U'khand town.' *Indian Express*, 23 August.

Singh, P. (2003) *The Bhagats of the Guru Granth Sahib: Sikh Self-Definition and the Bhagat Bani.* New Delhi: Oxford University Press.

Zakaria, S. (2017) 'Muslims have Iftar, pray in Sikh temple in Dubai.' 16 June. Accessed on 16 November 2018 at www.khaleejtimes.com/ramadan-2017/ramadan-news/muslims-have-iftar-pray-in-sikh-temple-in-dubai.

# 2

# Sikh Interfaith Experience

This contribution relates to two interfaith experiences. Professor Nikky Singh from Colby College, a Punjabi Sikh academic, attended Sikh worship conducted by and with non-Sikhs in Fresno. Her non-Sikh American student, Religious Studies major at Colby College Lucy Soucek, attended Sikh worship and a traditional Sikh wedding. Here we have two entirely different entry points and yet there is a profound collective effervescence that each experienced in their unique interfaith encounter.

## CELEBRATING ANEW

### Nikky-Guninder Kaur Singh

### SEEING SIKHISM IN A NEW LIGHT

The weekend of April 8–10, 2016 in Fresno was packed with interfaith events. I had been invited by Director Jim Grant of the Social Justice Ministry, Diocese of Fresno, to be the Interfaith Scholar for their annual program. Throughout this memorable weekend, I was showered with warm hospitality, incisive questions, and ineffable shared experiences. The events took place at three religious spaces: Sikh Gurdwara Sahib, Temple Beth Israel, and the Unitarian Universalist Church.

On Saturday I led discussions at Temple Beth Israel. This was my first time giving a talk at a synagogue, but I felt totally comfortable. The openness of the aniconic space, the concept of one God, the reverence for scripture, the *I-Thou* relationship are common to both Jews and Sikhs. Even the momentous Aqedah event of Abraham sacrificing Isaac has a parallel in the creation of the Khalsa by the Tenth Sikh Guru.[1] I have been teaching at Colby College for over thirty years, so I was quite used to the general, academic-styled environment. We had rich discussions throughout the day and fun-filled conversations over meals.

The two bookends of the weekend were a different matter. For me, born and raised in a Sikh home, it was the familiar space of the Sikh Gurdwara Sahib on Friday evening and the equally familiar Sikh service on Sunday morning at the Unitarian Universalist Church that ironically took me aback. Here *my* everyday prayers and worship *with* my fellow Americans came across as radically different. The two events had a huge impact on me personally, and, the more I think about them, they have a wider significance as well. In fact, in our dangerously divided and polarized world, they serve as useful models for interfaith relationships. I am grateful for the opportunity to reflect on those moments.

Seeing forty or so non-Sikh men and women sitting reverently at the gurdwara on Friday evening in the presence of 'my' holy text with their bare feet and heads covered in an American town participating in 'my' daily evening worship was indeed out of the ordinary! These included Muslim, Roman Catholic, Unitarian Universalist, Hindu, Latter Day Saints, Congregationalists/ United Church of Christ, Christian Scientists, Mennonites, Methodists, Episcopalians, and Presbyterians. When did I ever pray and worship *my* way in my language with such a large number of people from so many *other* faiths? Sikh scripture (the Guru Granth Sahib) is the focus of Sikh ethics, philosophy, and aesthetics. The 1430-page text is draped in silks and brocades, has a canopy above it, and is attended by a person with a whisk. The holy volume is the living Guru for the Sikhs, and presides at all their public and private ceremonies, rituals, and worship. This evening men and women across faiths came together to hear its sublime songs, recite passages, and take part in the ceremony of putting the scriptural Guru to rest for the night (*sukhāsan*). At the conclusion we had the *langar* meal together. Our 'togetherness'

---

1    For details see Kaur Singh 2005, chapter 2.

was extremely special, for the bond of community expanded from just the Sikhs living in Fresno to the wide-ranging communities in the area. The spiritual energy in the Sikh gurdwara acquired a whole new dimension.

Likewise, I found the Sikh service at the Unitarian Universalist Church mesmerizing. I have never been to another's place of worship and perceived the very different congregation doing *my* worship! Rev. Tim Kutzman led the service he had so beautifully and thoughtfully orchestrated. It began with the reading of the essential Sikh prelude: 'There Is One Being Truth by Name' and the gathering then burst into a harmonious chant. Passages from the morning hymn Japji resonated in the stylistically modern church. Rev. Kutzman also spoke on Guru Nanak, the founder of the faith. He shared the narrative of Guru Nanak coming out of the river after disappearing for three days and proclaiming 'There is no Hindu, there is no Muslim.' Guru Nanak said these words in a religiously divisive medieval India where the major tradition of South Asian Hinduism and the West Asian Islam were in conflict. The Sikh founder's message that humanity go beyond the institutionalized categories and become more fully human was insightfully conveyed by Rev. Kutzman. Singing of Sikh scriptural hymns followed with melodious vocalists and instrumentalists directed by Mr. Lorenzo Bassman. The finale was a popular hymn that left a magic of infinity in the air:

> The sky is our platter; the sun and moon, lamps,
>     it is studded with pearls, the starry galaxies,
> The wafting scent of sandalwood is the incense,
>     the gentle breeze, our fly whisk,
> All vegetation, the bouquet of flowers we offer to you.
>     What a worship.
> This truly is your worship, you who sunder life from death.
>     The unstruck sound in us is the drum to which we chant.
>         (GGS: 663)[2]

From the beginning to the end of the service, these are the basics of the Sikh faith that I have been hearing and singing and reciting since I was a kid. However, in the ambiance of the Unitarian Universalist Church, spoken and sung in different accents with different instruments and

---

2    The translation of the verses from the Guru Granth Sahib (GGS) is by Nikky-Guninder Kaur Singh.

different juxtapositions and translations, they became absolutely extraordinary.

## THE FRESNO MODEL FOR INTERFAITH WORK

The premise of the revolutionary moments was simply the shattering of the binary *us versus them*. In Durkheim's expression it would be 'collective effervescence.' This exhilarating feeling is not simple toleration of people of other faiths, it is not adding aspects from diverse faiths into a syncretic blend; to the contrary it is real respect for and rejoicing in difference and distinctive richness of our shared humanity. In the twenty-first century how easily we connect over email, Twitter, Skype, Facebook, Instagram... But do we connect emotionally and spiritually? According to the Fresno model, a strong and enduring infrastructure with fellow humans embraces the following activities.

### 1. Experience the sacred places of one another

What are we afraid of? Of not being welcome? Of losing our faith? Sikhs (like other minorities) have been a part of the American mosaic for over a century, when they first came to work on the railroad, lumber industries, and farms. Today there are over half a million Sikhs in this country with almost three hundred gurdwaras, but how many non-Sikhs have actually visited a gurdwara? The result has been stereotyping, prejudices, mistaken identity, and hate crimes. Just a few years ago a white supremacist went on a rampage and killed innocent devotees doing their Sunday morning worship at the Gurdwara Sahib in a Milwaukee suburb. The blueprint of the Sikh sacred space designed by Guru Arjan had four doors to welcome all people equally from the traditional four classes of Indian society. That structure in the modern day is the Golden Temple in Amritsar. To maintain its open spirit, Sikhs should try their best not to be insular, and outsiders should shake off any trepidation about losing commitment to their faith. The togetherness in a sacred space is different from that in a plane or office or classroom or museum. I feel any sacred place permeates with an ineffable extra that enables us to retreat inwards, reach out to others around us, and return with a renewed strength. Sacred space is necessary for us to embrace our enormous diversity as an intimate togetherness, a togetherness that inspires us to resolve our social, economic, political, and religious problems. Only by realizing our shared purpose can we work together to eliminate environmental degradation, sexism, poverty, and all sorts of social inequities and religious hostilities.

I want to share my childhood example as testament that we do not compromise by worshipping in another's holy space. During my formative years in India, I attended a convent school where we daily recited the prayer 'Our Father' during the morning assembly, and took courses in moral science. I loved going into the convent, where we sang psalms and collected images of Christ and of Our Lady of Fatima, after whom my school was named. At home of course the centre of life was the Guru Granth Sahib. And yet life was not schizophrenic, for the two worlds with their different languages, different histories, and different styles of worship co-existed colorfully. Together they became an essential part of my psyche. The 'question' of identity never came up; just as I knew my name, I knew I was a Sikh. But that did not stop me from participating excitedly in the religious space of my Catholic teachers. I can still feel the fervor with which I would sing 'The Lord is my shepherd nothing shall I fear' in spite of my terribly poor musical talents. My childhood experiences in the Catholic church solidified my Sikh identity. Nothing diminished; I added something extra to my very being.

## 2. Read one another's scriptures

Scriptures are the quintessence of every religion. They express the deepest moral and philosophical values of a faith. Reading itself is complex, comprising the visual, perceptual, syntactic, and semantic processes. Therefore, reading 'Scripture' – especially another's – becomes a daunting affair. Often those within the tradition hold such reverence for their holy book that they fear any intimacy with it. Priests, along with scholars and exegetes, officiate as readers, which only increases the insecurity of those outside of the tradition. The result clearly leaves everybody alienated and impoverished. In their own and different ways, the Vedas, the Hebrew Bible, the Tao Te Ching, the New Testament, the Dhammapada, the holy Qur'an, the Shobogenzo, and the Guru Granth Sahib provide us with kaleidoscopic glimpses into the beyond, and simultaneously make us feel much more at home on our planet Earth. I value my liberal arts college for it gives me the opportunity to teach and read various

Asian scriptures with my students. Sikh scripture itself is an interfaith archive, including not only the verses of the Sikh Gurus but also of Hindu and Muslim saints. The different worldviews, images, and symbols were consciously compiled in the Sikh canon, and each author is clearly identified. The goal was to familiarize readers with difference and diversity and to promote pluralism in an essential way. Guru Nanak even laments, 'What can the poor Vedas [Hindu sacred texts] and Kateb [Muslim sacred texts] do when nobody recognizes the singular One – *bed kateb karehi kah bapure nah būjhehi ikk ekā*' (GGS: 1153)? The problem of 'inter' and 'intra' religious conflicts does not lie in the sacred scriptures of others but in us humans who neither reflect (*bicārai*) on them nor recognize (*būjhehi*) the singular One (*ikk ekā*). Readings from other religious texts not only give us an awareness of what is important to them, but we also expand our imagination, and end up getting a better sense of *ourselves*, of our neighbors, and of the globe we inhabit.

### 3. Hear the sacred music of others

Music has a reverberating quality that has a universal impact. It dissolves semantic disputes and differences and promotes arabesques of mutuality. A major portion of the Sikh scripture has been put into musical melodies. Sacred music has a mnemonic appeal, it has the capacity to bond people across different regions speaking different languages, and it strikes us with an aesthetic force crucial in shaping our worldviews, attitudes, and behavior.

### 4. Share our stories

The American poet Muriel Rukeyser perfectly said, 'The universe is made of stories, not of atoms' (Rukeyser 1949). In our multireligious, multicultural world we need to hear and read a wide variety of stories for that is how we make sense of the lives we live. For children's liturgy (and bedtime stories) faith groups could introduce protagonists who look and speak differently so they feel comfortable with difference, and grow up secure rather than afraid of 'strangers.' Hearing gospel narratives was a meaningful part of my primary education. The case of Rev. Kutzmark telling stories about young Guru Nanak highlights the fact that it is most enlightening to have one's *own* stories told by *another*.

## 5. And pray together!

However it is defined, prayer is the mode of remembering, celebrating, connecting with the One – a theistic or even an atheistic principle – from somewhere deep inside us. The Divine constantly articulated as the numeral '1' in Sikh scripture is imagined not only in polyphonic Hindu and monotheistic Islamic terms, but also as Buddhist nirvana (GGS: 97). Yet categorically, 'Always, always you alone are the One Reality – *sadā sadā tun eku hai*' (GGS: 139). Enclosed in our exclusivist ideologies we overlook the intrinsic 'oneness.' We get caught up in *my* One, *your* One, *his* One, and lose out on our capacity to experience our togetherness in all our multiplicity. Addressing the Divine, physically side by side with people from various faiths, helps us put aside our tensions and strengthen our horizontal human ligaments. So our veins flow with 'collective effervescence.' While praying together in the Sikh gurdwara and the United Universalist Church in Fresno, the verse that echoed in my mind was:

> Paradise is where we sing your praise
>
> *tahān baikhunth jaha kirtan terā* (GGS: 749)

The paradise or the kingdom of God imaginary from my convent school prayer had to be right here and now – sitting amidst a vibrantly diverse congregation. That sense of largeness with fellow beings was thrilling indeed. It was mysterious and enchanting. For those moments I became utterly oblivious to the 'isms' of our global society – racism, classism, sexism, and religious fundamentalism.

## SIKHISM EXPLORATION: A PERSONAL GLIMPSE INTO INTERFAITH LEARNING

Lucy Soucek

### INTRODUCTION: LEARNING TO LOVE DIFFERENCE

I am a white, middle class woman who grew up in rural Maine. I was homeschooled with my sisters for many of my formative years, until I attended a high school that mainly comprised white, middle class students. My family and I attended Episcopal services on most Sundays and holidays, until my Christian faith and spirituality dwindled when

I became more involved with the drama and excitement of high school activities. After graduating from high school, I moved to the mainly white, small, rural community of Waterville, Maine, where I studied at Colby College. Needless to say, I was not exposed to many different cultures, ethnicities, or religions during my adolescent years.

Therefore, I was intimidated when I attended a Sikh wedding for the first time. My biggest worry was that I would say something wrong or do something to offend someone. Entering a new place with people of a different religion was frightening, because I was never exposed in person to their specific and different customs. I was afraid of asking the wrong questions, of being offensive without knowing, or of giving someone a negative impression.

Walking amongst the wedding party, smiling faces surrounded me. As I stepped into the kitchen area of the gurdwara, the fragrant smell of warm chai tea, freshly baked naan bread, and spicy curry instantly wafted through the air. The long open benches fostered an open and welcoming environment, and guests were laughing and chatting around me. In each of the gurdwaras that I visited afterwards, I witnessed the same environment. I could sit down with anyone and they would make conversation with me. They genuinely wanted to know about me, where I was from, and what I was interested in. It was one of the most welcoming environments I have ever entered.

Can I say that I enter the same environment in many public spaces, regardless of religious affiliation? Sadly, I can't. We are separate. We keep to ourselves. We are secluded. Why don't we want to know about each other? Why don't we ask questions? Why don't we consider those feelings that are different from our own? After eating *langar*, the Sikh community meal open to anyone regardless of religion, I not only felt full through consuming mountainous amounts of rice, but I also felt full of love and appreciation for the people with whom I'd shared the meal. I was full of care and understanding for people whom I had just met. I am forever thankful to those who welcomed me into such inclusive environments, and I want others to be able to experience and learn in the same way that I did. We must learn about how loving people can be and engage each other in our differences so that we can learn and grow as a human race.

## SIKHISM JOURNEY: COLBY COLLEGE
## TO VANCOUVER BC

How do we share this environment with others who are unaware of the fact that Sikhism even exists? What are some ways to foster a pluralistic society, and appreciate people of different religions? We can start with spreading this knowledge through study. Academies in the USA are trying to foster interreligious understanding. In fact, Colby College was the first college in the USA to offer a full seminar on Sikhism when Professor Nikky-Guninder Kaur Singh joined the faculty in 1986. I created a survey to collect information about the depth of student knowledge on Sikhism on the Colby College campus. Out of the 91 people who took the survey, one third said that they did not know what Sikhism means; 49 people said that they had heard of it, but did not know much about it, and only 11 people said that they were quite familiar with it. Only 12 percent of the students who took the survey were confident in their knowledge about Sikhism. To me, this number is extremely low. The study of the scriptures and core values and practices of Sikhism and of other religions should be included in the curriculums of grade and high schools to spread knowledge about these belief systems, and to decrease the assumptions and judgments that we make out of ignorance. In effort to learn more about how much non-Sikhs know about the Sikhs who are living in the same community, I traveled to Vancouver funded by the Compagna-Sennett Fellowship from Colby College.

Vancouver contains generations of people related to the first Sikh immigrants, and is therefore home to a huge Sikh population, so I expected that many non-Sikhs would have a substantial knowledge of Sikhism from their surroundings, neighbors, and community members. However, this was not the case. I spent hours in local food courts asking local non-Sikhs similar questions to those that I asked at Colby, but the overall knowledge almost paralleled that of the Colby students. Out of the 88 people who took the survey, 22 people said that they did not know what Sikhism means; 59 people said that they had heard of it, but did not know much about it, and only 7 people said that they knew a lot about Sikhism.

Although this aspect of my trip disappointed me, my experience meeting several Sikh families in Vancouver is one that I will never forget. During my trip, I met my professor's friend Neelu Kang, who was friendly, loving, and willing to invite me to her house. She cooked for me, made wonderful tea, introduced me to her family, and provided me with the love and support that I had been craving after my time alone. Additionally, Barj Dhahan, another of my professor's connections, welcomed me into his home, and gave me an extensive picture of the Sikhs who migrated to Vancouver. He invited me to attend a political gathering, and his whole family was welcoming and pleasant.

Not only did I visit gurdwaras, but I also explored several events that exemplified the multiculturalism and pluralism that Vancouver celebrates. I learned that academia is not the only field that must be ready to facilitate a pluralistic society for there are many ways in which our communities can create more inclusive environments. I attended the Surrey Fusion Festival, which was a celebration of music, food, and cultural aspects from about forty cultures. At the festival, there were different booths from different countries, and I was able to try on local clothing, try different foods, and listen to music from different countries. The literary, artistic, and commercial fields can work towards expanding the reach of religious encounter as well. Films, novels, shows, lectures, and other aspects of the American public sphere can include Sikh and other minority protagonists, performers, and artists. This celebration and exploration of multiculturalism and pluralism helps to expand the public understanding of these different religions. Additionally, the study of the scriptures and core values and practices of Sikhism and other religions should be included in the curriculums of grade and high schools to spread knowledge about these belief systems, and to decrease the assumptions and judgments that we make out of ignorance.

## FRESNO, CALIFORNIA: AN INSPIRING INTERFAITH COMMUNITY

There are model towns that have created strong interfaith communities, such as Fresno. In Fresno, I not only met with Sikh locals, but I also met with locals of many other religions. By meeting with religious leaders of different faiths, I found that the interfaith relationships in Fresno work to break down misperceptions in order to make positive change and create understanding. Each leader that I met with generously shared information about their belief system and traditions and about what they do to forward interfaith understanding within their own communities. Along with several other organizations, I visited and learned about the Islamic Cultural Center, the Unitarian Universalist Church of Fresno, Temple Beth Israel, the United Japanese Christian Church, the St. Paul Newman Center, and the Selma Gurdwara, all of which were aware of and respectful of each other. When I met with Amrik Vik, a Sikh from Fresno, he gave me an extensive background about Sikhism and the values that are important to Sikhs. He was different from the other religious leaders whom I met with, in that he felt the intense need to share with me his values and the reasons why Sikhism is inclusive and focused on equality and social work. He showed me several different gurdwaras, all of which were welcoming and beautiful. I ate *langar* and drank tea with Sikhs of the different gurdwaras, and Amrik even insisted that I take extra food home. He not only welcomed me into several gurdwaras, but he brought me into the holy space where the Guru Granth, the Sikh holy book, is located. He answered all my questions; when I asked him if there were many non-Sikhs who came to have *langar*, he said that it is open all day and every day, but they don't get many non-Sikhs. He said that they do not want to impose their religion and their beliefs on others, but that they are always open, and are always there for anyone who want to visit and learn.

Additionally, I meet with Naindeep Chann (Deep), who is a leader of the Sikh Youth Council, a Sikh youth group in Fresno committed to social justice. They can be exclusive but are expanding the ages that they are trying to reach with camps and conferences for high school and college students. Deep opened my mind to the idea of spreading awareness through social justice work. He said that you can change the mindset of a people if those people are engaged and making a difference in a local community. Deep drove me around town, and showed me the location of a recent hate crime against a Sikh.

## CONCLUSION: LISTENING IS LEARNING

Being exposed to these different Sikh spaces and being amidst different Sikhs gave me the people-to-people interaction that we need to enhance understanding and appreciation. It is one thing to hear about a certain people or to read about them, but it is another to actually meet them and experience how loving and open they can really be. Feeling the love from Neelu, the enthusiasm from Amrik, and the dedication from Deep enabled me to recognize these humans as people who love, struggle, and care in the same ways I do. Interfaith scholar Diana Eck (2007, p.758) writes:

> Pluralism is not just the enumeration of difference, and pluralism is certainly not just the celebration of diversity in a spirit of goodwill. Pluralism is the engagement of difference in the often-difficult yet creative ways that we as scholars can observe, investigate, and interpret. In investigating the deliberate construction of multi-religious relationships, we might find a set of paradigms for pluralism, a set of practices, each of which expands the social space of religious encounter.

At the moment, our American society is becoming increasingly polarized. Especially in this day and age, with our increasing trend to close the borders of this country, ironically founded upon religious freedom, to those who are seeking refuge from their current situations, it is important to recognize the possibilities of a more pluralistic society. How can we, as a multireligious country, investigate the deliberate construction of (and appreciation for) multireligious relationships and forward a more pluralistic society? Through my travels and explorations learning about different religious groups and the ways in which they interact with each other, I have found that listening to and learning about other people's experiences and beliefs is the first step. When I started my studies at Colby College, I was a naive student who signed up for 'Global Sikhism' on a whim, without even knowing what Sikhism was. Now, I have traveled to several places to learn about how Sikhism can be understood and appreciated by surrounding communities and am hopeful that we can create more places that foster interfaith understanding and appreciation.

Exposing oneself to new traditions is intimidating. However, it is necessary in our multireligious society, if we are to live with a mutual understanding of our diverse global reality. The experiences of this professor and her student were different, but each fostered new relationships, found a sense of profound belonging, and were welcomed with open arms and warm smiles. Each discovered a sense of home amongst these new communities, realizing that difference should not lead to exclusion but to exciting new beginnings...

## REFERENCES

Eck, D. (2007) *Prospects for Pluralism: Voice and Vision in the Study of Religion*. Oxford: Oxford University Press.

Kaur Singh, N.-G. (2005) *Birth of the Khalsa: A Feminist Re-Memory of Sikh Identity*. New York: SUNY Press.

Rukeyser, M. (1949) *The Life of Poetry*. New York, NY: Current Books.

## FURTHER READING

Eck, D. (2001) *A New Religious America: How a 'Christian Country' Has Now Become the World's Most Religiously Diverse Nation*. San Francisco, CA: HarperSanFrancisco.

# Reflection

## The Editors

Pashaura Singh raises the question of how different religions with their differing theological assumptions can harmoniously co-exist. Religious pluralism, he states, can be defined as the simultaneous existence in a single social arena of different worldviews that are potentially incompatible with one another. Guru Nanak, the founder of the Sikh tradition in the sixteenth century, was well aware of this phenomenon. According to Singh, he was strongly opposed to an exclusivist claim that a particular tradition is the sole repository of religious truth. The spirit of accommodation was a central feature of his understanding of religion. As a consequence, he showed equal regard for the devout adherents of different religious traditions. At the same time he condemned contemporary religious leaders as hypocrites for the way in which they divorced moral conduct from religious practice.

Later, the successors of Guru Nanak met the challenge of religious diversity by establishing a clear basis for Sikh identity. This was marked by the formation of a distinctive belief system, modes of worship, religious institutions and an overarching organisation with the Guru at its head. Such a development might appear to undermine a general acceptance of other faiths. Yet, as Pashaura points out, this was not the case, as is evidenced by Guru Arjan's Ramakali hymn in which he celebrates religious diversity. In his view, the adherents of different faiths seek to explore the deeper aspects of religious truth in their own ways. According to Pashaura, the plurality of religious expression deepens our own sense of wonder and commitment. Here he cites the scholar Diana Eck who contends that the recognition of the plurality of religious claims does not constitute a betrayal of one's own faith. In Sikh practice today, there is a marked openness to other religions which is expressed in interfaith enthusiasm, in invitations to Sikh worship and prayer and in the realisation that eating together has a vital part to play: the Sikh *langar* (community kitchen).

In her contribution to this chapter Nikky-Guninder Kaur Singh similarly extols the virtues of religious encounter. Discussing her own experiences in three religious places: Sikh Gurdwara Sahib, Temple Beth Israel and the Unitarian Universalist Church, she describes how the spiritual enters in the Sikh gurdwara, acquiring a new dimension. In this context she cites the narrative of Guru Nanak coming out of the river after disappearing for three days and declaring that 'There is no Hindu; there is no Muslim.'

In making such a claim, Guru Nanak emphasised the need for humanity to go beyond institutionalised categories.

In this context Nikky refers to Émile Durkheim's expression of 'collective effervescence'. Such a feeling is not simply a toleration of members of other faiths, nor is it adding aspects from diverse faiths into a syncretic blend. Rather, it is rejoicing in difference and distinctiveness, and she goes on to outline four key religious activities. The first concerns shared experience of sacred places. Members of faith communities should not be fearful of such exposure. Sikhs, she states, should maintain an open spirit; they must not be insular. Any sacred space is characterised by a spirit that enables worshippers to retreat inwards while reaching out to others. Sacred space, she asserts, is necessary for humans to embrace the diversity of religious faith.

The second imperative is to read one another's scriptures. Scriptures, Nikky contends, are the quintessence of every faith, expressing moral and philosophical values. Such works as the Vedas, the Hebrew Bible, the Tao Te Ching, the New Testament, the Dhammapada, the Quran, the Shobogenzo and the Guru Granth Sahib provide kaleidoscopic glimpses into the Infinite. Readings from such religious texts provide an awareness of the central teachings of each faith and expand our imagination – they enable us to gain a better sense of ourselves, of our neighbours, and of the world.

The third quest is to listen to the music of other faith traditions. Music dissolves semantic disputes and differences. It has a universal impact, and the capacity to bond believers across different regions. The fourth quest is to share stories. And finally: we must pray together. However prayer is defined, worship provides a mode of remembering, celebrating and connecting with the other. By addressing the Divine together with members of various faiths, we can put aside our tensions and reach out to others. Such a spirit of largeness with fellow human beings is of vital significance in our global society. Echoing this view, Lucy Soucek describes her own spiritual journey in the Sikh community, an encounter which deepened her awareness and appreciation of the multifaceted character of religious experience.

These contributions advocate an acceptance of religious diversity, and the need for members of different faith traditions to engage in interfaith worship and prayer, together with the strong Sikh emphasis on sharing food.

# Chapter 13

# UNITARIANISM

## 1

## Unitarian Universalist Affirmations of Interfaith Worship

Feargus O'Connor

Gather us in, thou Love that fillest all:
Gather the rival faiths within thy fold;
Throughout the nations, sound the clarion call:
Beneath Love's banner all shall be enrolled!

Gather us in: we worship only thee;
In varied names we stretch a common hand:
In diverse forms a common soul we see;
In many ships we seek one promised land. (after George Matheson,
    1842–1906)

This interfaith hymn was sung in October 1903 at the inaugural service of my Unitarian congregation, originally called, significantly, 'All Souls', not 'All Saints'. The inaugural address was preached by Dr J. Estlin Carpenter, a Unitarian minister known for his dedicated work as a pioneer of comparative religion. I would like to think that at its best the congregation has stayed loyal to the sentiments of Matheson's hymn and Estlin Carpenter's broad, generous and inclusive vision.

## THE IMPERATIVE OF INTERFAITH
## DIALOGUE AND WORSHIP

My ministry at what is now called Golders Green Unitarians (GGU) in North London began on 1 September 2001. Within ten days the atrocities of 9/11 occurred. On 13 September I chaired and led the devotions at a meeting of Unitarian ministers. Among those present were three American Unitarian Universalist ministers, including a Jewish ministerial colleague from New York who had lost friends in the bombing of the Twin Towers. Suffice it to say that this meeting was the most difficult that I have ever faced. My original prayers and readings had to be abandoned, a new prayer composed and new readings adopted. We had to articulate together the grave consequences of what came to be called 9/11 for the world and interfaith relations worldwide.

Being already active in interfaith relations, I decided that I would hold regular interfaith events and reach out to as many people of other faith traditions as possible. As a committed member of the Unitarian Peace Fellowship, I felt it was particularly important to hold interfaith peace services. At both my ministerial induction service and first interfaith peace service, in which several Muslims participated, the voluntary collection was donated to UNICEF's Afghanistan emergency appeal, giving succour to the first victims of that ongoing war.

So, 9/11 and later the Iraq war overshadowed and helped shape my early, indeed all my subsequent, ministry in Golders Green, an area of London with the largest Jewish community in Britain. I decided to visit, with Dr Roohi Majid, a Muslim friend of my Unitarian congregation who has regularly participated in our services and other congregational activities, Leo Baeck College, the Reform and Liberal Jewish theological seminary, and Rabbi Lionel Blue, with whom we spent two pleasant amusing hours.

I became convinced that not only was interfaith dialogue morally and religiously imperative if we were to counter dangerous religious bigotry and communal hatred but interfaith worship itself was not only desirable but necessary if we were to create a peaceful community and a harmonious world for this and future generations. I have been confirmed in this view by all that has happened ever since in Afghanistan, Israel/Palestine, Iraq, Syria, Libya, Yemen and other countries torn by internecine religious conflict and war.

In that spirit we have raised funds for and awareness of the important mission of the School for Peace at the Israeli–Palestinian peace village of the 'Oasis of Peace', Neve Shalom-Wahat al-Salam, founded by a Jewish Roman Catholic priest, Father Bruno, and held peace services at which Israeli Jewish and Palestinian residents spoke and prayed together. Such encounters have been moving and empowering.

## TOWARDS A UNIVERSALIST IDEAL

> Be ours a religion which, like sunshine, goes everywhere: its temple, all space; its shrine, the good heart; its creed, all truth; its ritual, works of love; its profession of faith, divine living. (Theodore Parker, 1810–1860)

I invoke these inspiring words of the radical nineteenth-century American Unitarian minister Theodore Parker because they express the Universalist ethos which guides me in my ministry. I placed them on the front page of the first edition of our congregational newsletter and used them at services as a Universalist affirmation and declaration of faith. It is in this spirit and from that theological perspective that I write this contribution, which presents the values that characterise one Unitarian congregation and its efforts to witness to the vision that inspires its worship, social ideals and Universalist religious ethos.

What, it may be asked, does 'Universalist' mean in this context? Is the word being used in a 'Humpty Dumpty' sense?

> 'When I use a word', Humpty Dumpty said in a rather scornful tone [to Alice in Looking-Glass Land], 'it means just what I choose it to mean – neither more nor less.'

As even some Unitarians seem averse to this use of the word 'Universalist' in this context I invoke the authority not only of Rev. Dr Arthur Long, a revered doyen of British Unitarian Christian theologians, but also that of Humpty Dumpty himself, who was fond of using 'portmanteau' words. 'You see, it's like a portmanteau – there are two meanings packed up into one word.'

In his *Current Trends in British Unitarianism* (1997) Arthur Long sanctions the use of the word to describe not only the Christian belief in universal salvation for all humanity but also that strand of Unitarian thought and belief which searches for wisdom and enlightenment not solely in the Judaeo-Christian tradition but in the entire worldwide religious heritage of humankind. That belief and outlook go back at least to the period of the Enlightenment. They were evident in the writings of several prominent nineteenth-century Unitarian thinkers and were characteristic of Emerson and several other Unitarian Transcendentalists. Jenkin Lloyd Jones, the advanced Unitarian radical thinker and secretary of the 1893 World Parliament of Religions, dreamed of building 'a temple of universal religion dedicated to the enquiring spirit of progress, to the helpful service of love'.

Such a significant, albeit minority, strain of Universalist Unitarianism was evident too in the twentieth century, notably in the writings of Will Hayes (1890–1959), a British Unitarian minister who was inspired by the wisdom of many diverse religious traditions. His articles, prayers and services were highly regarded by early members of the World Congress of Faiths. His pioneering work of interfaith prayer, *Book of Twelve Services*, originally published in 1924, subsequently revised and published in 1954 as *Every Nation Kneeling*, was much admired by Sir Francis Younghusband, the founder of the World Congress of Faiths. Hayes argued that there were two kinds of Unitarians: the 'Unitarians of the United World', the Universalists, and those then in the majority, whom he termed 'Christocentric', who adhered primarily to the liberal Christian tradition.

So I am conscious that even in my own broad faith tradition, Unitarian Universalism, there are deep-seated differences between those whose approach is primarily a Christocentric one and those whose Universalism makes them particularly sympathetic to multifaith prayer and worship. I personally am so used to multifaith worship I find it hard to understand why others could object to it. I have a peculiarly Unitarian difficulty: participating in worship in which Trinitarian language is used by those who seem insensitive to the fact that people of other faiths may find this theologically objectionable.

## IS A TRULY UNIVERSALIST RELIGIOUS COMMUNITY PRACTICABLE?

'A Universalist spiritual community without walls'. These words are inscribed on the front page of my congregational newsletter. So, what are the characteristics of a truly Universalist congregation? It must surely embrace an inclusive religious ethic which nurtures and values each and every one of us as the unique souls we are. A congregation which recognises no dogmas and creeds imposed by the dead hand of past authority and no dull conformity with beliefs and conventions (however venerable and comforting) which our conscience and reason cannot accept. One which unites our diverse strands and heartfelt individual ideals in a higher unity, which brings together all that is of abiding worth in our own tradition and the traditions of other faiths in a strong sense of common purpose: a liberal religious idealism which accepts and values all that is precious and true in our common worldwide spiritual heritage and discards all that is narrow, sectarian and divisive. All that matters is surely the ceaseless search for truth?

Closed-minded 'sceptics' and religious dogmatists alike express disbelief that this bold ideal of Universalism can be translated into reality but many Unitarian congregations, here and in the USA, prove that it can be realised and indeed it may be seen to inspire their congregational life and worship. The question remains, however: how inclusive can such a congregation actually be? Can it really unite Universalist Theists, liberal Christians, pan-religionists, religious Humanists, Pantheists and other defenders of what American Unitarian Universalists call the 'interdependent web of all existence of which we are a part'? Can it bind us together in a spirit of free religious fellowship and mutual respect and serve to expand our spiritual horizons so that we may embrace what we perceive to be authentic and valuable in every religious tradition, East and West?

## GOLDERS GREEN UNITARIANS: STRIVING TO A UNIVERSALIST IDEAL

In reflecting on these challenges, I look to my own congregation at Golders Green and the diverse religious origins of our members and friends. I should explain that we have two categories of membership: full members and registered 'friends', the latter choosing to give moral and financial support without being entitled to exercise full voting rights. We have several members whose family origins are in the Brahmo Samaj, a Universalist liberal Hindu movement founded by Rammohun Roy in the earlier part of the nineteenth century; among its adherents were the father and grandfather of Rabindranath Tagore, who was raised in that tradition. A previous secretary comes from a Hindu family and our interfaith community coordinator is a practising Muslim who has been an active friend and regular attender at GGU worship for several years.

We have Jewish, Muslim, Hindu, Buddhist, liberal Christian and Humanist friends whose moral support and goodwill we value immensely. Several of these regularly attend our services and support our various community, humanitarian and charitable activities. A practising Muslim was co-opted to serve on our management committee, regularly comes to worship and actively supports our charitable and interfaith outreach work. Practising Liberal and Reform Jewish friends have loyally maintained their links for several years; another, now sadly deceased, was well known locally and in the pages of the *Jewish Chronicle* for his dual attendance at the local Reform synagogue and GGU. Evidently, he himself saw no conflict between being a committed but questioning Jew and a loyal and well-loved friend of our congregation, which he regarded as a community of open-minded fellow seekers after truth. All these attenders share a sense of gratitude that our congregation has a Universalist ethos which transcends any narrow and constraining 'Christian' perspective.

GGU may be taken as an example of a London congregation inspired by such an ideal: we try to rise to the challenge of making all comers welcome by using truly inclusive forms of worship, especially Universalist hymns, and everyone is made to feel welcome at our social, charitable and outreach activities. Like other Unitarian congregations, we make every effort to be truly sensitive to the diverse needs of our multicultural society: we have had evenings of Iranian classical poetry, Irish harp and folk music and multilingual poetry readings featuring Arabic, Hebrew and Urdu poets reading their original works. Having friendly relations with the local Jewish community, we have hosted the rabbi's classes, choir practice and other religious activities when the local Reform synagogue was being refurbished and we welcome many Jewish visitors. Like some American Unitarian Universalist congregations, we would warmly welcome into full membership more Jewish Unitarians ('Jewnitarians') and happily integrate them into our congregational life. Because there is no adherence to a specifically 'Christian' ethos Jewish friends feel that there is no psychological barrier to their full acceptance of our Universalist values, outlook and religious practice.

## IS THERE A LIMIT TO UNIVERSALIST TOLERANCE?

Although some may argue that our Unitarian movement should be open to all religious currents, it is surely important to distinguish between welcoming all comers and having a syncretistic and uncritical approach to all religions. I would argue that no Unitarian congregation should accept into full membership fundamentalist religious believers who declare an allegiance to dogmas and creeds which claim an exclusive revelation that are not open to reasoned examination and the scrutiny of our critical intelligence.

A real and serious conflict arises only when there is dogmatic adherence to a belief system which does not respect the liberal spiritual values that we proclaim and try our best to live by. Herein lies the fundamental importance of the supplementary clause in our Unitarian General Assembly Object, which, in the spirit of Universalism, affirms our liberal religious heritage and encourages us to 'learn from the spiritual, cultural and intellectual insights of all humanity'. In the spirit of the Jewish sage Maimonides, we should 'seek the truth from every source'.

## AN AFFIRMATION OF TRUE RELIGIOUS UNIVERSALISM

I am the fourth Unitarian minister to serve as secretary of the World Congress of Faiths. Like my predecessors, Arthur Peacock, the last Universalist minister in Britain who joined our Unitarian ministerial ranks in the year he became secretary (1951), Tom Dalton and Richard Boeke and a distinguished former WCF Unitarian chair, Lord Sorensen, I see liberal religion in a Universalist light and view all authentic faiths as temporal and transient manifestations of that perennial religion spoken of by mystics and sages down the ages.

Lord Sorensen was convinced that all faiths taught certain essential moral values vital to the future progress of humankind. Among these are 'justice, mercy, compassion, integrity, courage, sacrifice, fidelity and fraternity'. Only global religious unity and interreligious cooperation and agreement on such essential religious values could, in Sorensen's words, 'enable [humankind] to dwell on this Earth in co-operation, amity and peace'.

It is this deep conviction that inspired Sorensen's own work as a friend of Gandhi, chair of the National Peace Council and an ardent supporter of a host of humane and progressive causes.

'Universalism – Universe religion – the unity of all things. Why it's the greatest word in the language.' I am truly inspired by these words of Elizabeth Barrett Browning in all I do as a minister, whether in our special interfaith peace and animal welfare services (we host the only multifaith animal celebration in the UK) or our Sunday services, where the same Universalist ethos is always implicitly and explicitly present. If Universalism, imbued with those values of universal compassion and wisdom embodied in the world's great religions and our noblest literary heritage, is our guiding principle how can it be absent from all our worship? Should it not inspire us in all our words and deeds?

## REFERENCES

Hayes, W. (1954) *Every Nation Kneeling*. London: The Lindsey Press. Originally published in 1924 as *Book of Twelve Services* and subsequently revised.

Long, A. (1997) *Current Trends in British Unitarianism*. Belfast: Ulster Unitarian Christian Association.

## FURTHER READING

Bharat, J. and Bharat, S. (2007) *A Global Guide to Interfaith: Reflections from around the World*. Winchester: O Books (John Hunt Publishing).

Boeke, R. (2002) 'Ugly duckling or swan? Is Unitarianism a universal religion?' In M.F. Smith (ed.) *Prospects for the Unitarian Movement*. London: The Lindsey Press.

Braybrooke, M. (1992) *Pilgrimage of Hope: One Hundred Years of Global Interfaith Dialogue*. New York: Crossroad.

Braybrooke, M. (2003) *1000 World Prayers*. Winchester: O Books (John Hunt Publishing).

Braybrooke, M. (2004) *365 Meditations for a Peaceful Heart and a Peaceful World*. London: Godsfield Press.

Knight, S.H. (1985) *Hymns for Living*. Worldwide Heritage section of interfaith hymns (119–132). London: The Lindsey Press.

Marshall, V. (1999) 'Unitarians and other religions.' In G.D. Chryssides (ed.) *Unitarian Perspectives on Contemporary Religious Thought*. London: The Lindsey Press.

Marshall, V. (2007) *The Larger View: Unitarians and World Religions*. London: The Lindsey Press.

Smith, M.F. (ed.) (2006) *Being Together: Unitarians Celebrate Congregational Life*. London: The Lindsey Press.

2

# Unitarian Universalist Interfaith Worship and Prayer

Jay Atkinson

## A TRADITION OF INTERNAL DIVERSITY

As I begin writing this chapter, I have just returned from a ceremony celebrating the ordination to Unitarian Universalist (UU) ministry of a recent seminary graduate who grew up in a Muslim family and continues to identify herself theologically with that religious tradition. The very fact of such a person receiving UU ordination dramatizes a central commitment of the UU movement as followed in the United States of America – its self-proclaimed identity as a theologically open, non-creedal association of congregations in which membership affiliation entails no commitment to any particular set of religious beliefs.

Several features of this ordination ceremony illustrate the ways in which UU worship liturgies reflect theological diversity and multifaith inclusivity. The front cover of its order of service displayed a novel transformation of the flaming chalice, a symbol that has become very widely used in Unitarian and Universalist congregations

UU chalice:     UU chalice with
typical form     Muslim theme[1]

in recent decades. The figure shows, in the left image, one of the basic forms in which this protean symbol is typically represented and, in the right image, its adaptation for the ordination of this young Muslim woman. Her ceremony also included a telling of the ancient Muslim story of Hajar (Hebrew: Hagar) and the Holy Water of Zamzam, music from Roman Catholic and ecumenical Protestant sources, references to scriptures from Islamic, Hebrew, Jewish, and

---

1    Artwork created by Alex Kapitan in honor of the ordination of Ranwa Hammamy. Used with permission. Alex Kapitan is a lifelong Unitarian Universalist and, as of this writing (2017), the LGBTQ and Multicultural Programs Administrator for the Unitarian Universalist Association. I thank my ministerial colleague, the Rev. Mr. Barb Greve, for assistance with permission to use this image.

Christian traditions, and a reading of Mohja Kahf's poem, 'Hajar Writes a Letter to Sarah as a Cathartic Exercise Suggested by Her Therapist' (Kahf 2016).

This ordination ceremony, while a bit unusual, is not exceptional in UU practice. Liturgies that incorporate contrasting sources and images are quite common in Sunday morning UU worship. Our congregations are bonded with one another, not in affirming any detailed theological doctrine, but rather in covenantal faithfulness to a 450-year-old tradition that has been guided by broadly humanistic principles of mutual respect for individual integrity, personal ethical living, and communal activism for social justice. With our internal theological openness, the Unitarian Universalist approach to interfaith worship is thus grounded in quite a natural and long-standing way on the reality that every Sunday morning service of congregational worship in our churches is, to a greater or lesser degree, *already a multifaith event*. Indeed, in their collective bylaws, UU congregations express their gratitude 'for the religious pluralism which enriches and ennobles our faith' and explicitly cite the value of not only 'Jewish and Christian teachings' of love, but also 'humanist teachings' of reason and science and, more broadly, 'wisdom from the world's religions.'[2]

## SETTINGS AND PURPOSES OF INTERFAITH WORSHIP

With such appreciative interweaving of diverse sources in our own worship, American UU clergy and laity are especially open to participating in interfaith worship services. At the local level, one of the most common occasions for such observances falls on the Wednesday evening before the US Thanksgiving Day, when people from Jewish, Protestant, Roman Catholic, and increasingly Muslim and Eastern Orthodox congregations gather in many cities and towns across America.

But why such interfaith worship? What purposes does it serve and what values does it exemplify? The various religious communions participating in joint services of this kind would perhaps give distinctive answers to these questions. Most participants would agree, however, that interfaith worship offers an opportunity to affirm and raise awareness of shared social and community values across a spectrum of doctrinal and creedal differences. Unitarian Universalists often

---

2    Bylaws of the Unitarian Universalist Association, Art II, Sec. C-2.1 (see www.uua.org/sites/live-new.uua.org/files/uua_bylaws_2015.pdf).

express this attitude in the conviction that 'we need not think alike to love alike.'[3] Communal worship services can thus lay and reaffirm a shared foundation for cooperative work toward the common good in local communities. Moreover, to the extent that such interfaith worship is seen from outside by the wider public, perhaps through local media coverage, larger numbers of people may be educated and led to greater appreciation of the salutary possibilities of interfaith cooperation and the ways that religious differences need not prevent pursuit of common values and goals.

This broader value of interfaith worship becomes more sharply focused whenever it takes the form of outspoken advocacy against some current specific social or political evil. A dramatic example of such public witness occurred in the fall of 2016 when representatives of many faith traditions, including large numbers of UU clergy, gathered with native leaders in the US state of North Dakota at the site of an unfinished oil pipeline that threatened to pass through land sacred to local American Indians. Joint worship in collective song, prayer, and prophetic proclamation served to demonstrate interfaith solidarity on behalf of shared values for environmental protection and the rights of native peoples not to have their sacred lands violated by corporate profiteering.

A further value of interfaith worship is that the gathering of a multifaith body of clergy and laity into a shared sacred space of liturgy and proclamation may foster the educational and spiritual goals of mutual learning, understanding, appreciation, and good will among participants with differing beliefs. Although the purpose is not and never should be proselytizing, it can and does often happen that experiencing the words and rituals of another faith tradition will serve to give someone a new or perhaps deeper insight into his/her own faith. In interfaith prayer, I may help others say what they know not how to say for themselves, and they may likewise help me say what I know not how to say for myself.

---

3    This phrase, often falsely attributed to Transylvanian antitrinitarian leader Dávid Ferenc, actually paraphrases Methodist founder John Wesley: 'Though we cannot think alike, may we not love alike?' Wesley, 'Catholic Spirit,' Sermon 39, http://wesley.nnu.edu/john-wesley/the-sermons-of-john-wesley-1872-edition/sermon-39-catholic-spirit (8 September 1749, in Smith's chronology). See Smith 1982.

## A HISTORY OF MUTUAL LEARNING
## THROUGH DIALOGUE

From a UU perspective, this possibility of mutual learning through interfaith worship, and more broadly through dialogue, should not be underestimated. In the Unitarian tradition, beginning with the practice of dissenting dialogue among the proto-unitarian Polish Brethren in the 1560s, it has always been recognized that human beings, as finite and self-interested creatures, are fallible, and that religious convictions and institutions are always in need of being deepened, clarified, or even revised (*semper reformanda!*) through an epistemic process of dialogue between persons of differing views. In its internally 'interfaith' constituency, Unitarian tradition has diligently maintained a 'principle of mutability'[4] and a practice of free inquiry as essential conditions for ever advancing its vision of human meaning and possibility. Radical Reformation scholar George Hunston Williams described the commitment to multifaith engagement as 'mutually corrective pluralism' (1979, p.35) and identified it particularly with the pursuit of interconfessional dialogue by proto-unitarians in Poland, especially with their Roman Catholic interlocutors:

> Confident in the ultimate unity of the true Church of Christ, the sectarians, including *conspicuously* the Polish Brethren, long persisted in the hope that the colloquies with the magisterial divines would be eventually consummated by some *fresh illumination* leading to oneness of mind and heart [my emphasis].[5]

---

4    It was the openness of radical Puritans or Independents to new light, and especially the shifting confessional identity of John Smyth (c.1570–1612) over the later years of his life, that moved Presbyterian Robert Baylie in *Dissuasive from the Errours of the Time* (London, 1645, p.101) to disparage a 'principle of mutability' that he discerned in the refusal of these 'seekers' to be pinned down to any clear or final statement of their own doctrine. Turning from his native Anglicanism, Smyth had associated himself successively with Puritans, Separatists, Baptists, and finally Dutch Mennonites. The ascription of such 'mutability' to radical practices more than a century earlier was made in the 1960s by Franklin Littell, who found such a principle at work in the disputational practices of continental anabaptists in the 1520s–1530s, based on their belief 'that in the process of a full and fair discussion something could be learned which was apparent to none of the participants at the beginning' (Littell 1963, p.269).

5    Williams 1992, p.1256. See also Atkinson 2004.

This historical Unitarian commitment to dialogue, spanning theological diversity within congregations as well as across institutional divisions between separate religious communions, goes far to explain contemporary UU openness to interfaith worship. But simple openness or good will does little by itself to suggest what kinds of form and content are needed for worship that can be meaningful to a gathering of people accustomed to perhaps widely diverse liturgical patterns. Familiarity with those differences and sensitivity to them is essential, of course, but beyond that, in what specific ways do we meet the challenges of bridging theological and ecclesiastical diversity?

Fortunately, the need to address that same theological diversity *within* each UU congregation has given us many years of liturgical experience with much the same *de facto* interfaith sensibility that is required for, and can be translated into, the wider and more embracing interfaith settings which are our subject here. The crafting of liturgy entails the interweaving of a number of components – most prominently song, chant, silence, prayer, sermonic words – but prayer stands out as perhaps the most sensitive, and thus the most challenging, even the most vexed, of these elements. So, I turn now to consider what may be learned from approaches to prayer among Unitarian Universalists both individually and in the context of congregational worship.

## LITURGY AND PRAYER IN THE INTERFAITH CONTEXT

Consonant with our theological diversity, attitudes toward the meaning and value of prayer, in both its private and communal forms, vary widely among Unitarian Universalists. The very idea of prayer itself is entirely rejected or seen as problematic by some UUs, especially those self-identified as atheists. Nevertheless, after a period of reaction against prayer and other kinds of traditional liturgical language in the 1950s–1980s, many Unitarian Universalists are now appreciatively recovering such usages. It is fairly common in UU congregations for the worship leader to introduce a time of 'silence, centering, meditation, and prayer,' thus inviting each worshipper to name that segment of the liturgy in words that are most individually comfortable. Spoken prayers will then often begin with quasi-personal phrases of address: 'Spirit of Life,' 'Source of all Being,' or 'Infinite Fount of Love,' that offer worshippers a range of connotations that can appeal to different spiritual sensibilities and are less distractingly fraught with the anthropomorphic imagery so often associated with 'God.'

Understandings of the *meaning* of prayer among UUs are also varied, but there are two points on which most UUs would tend to agree. First is rejection of any petitionary interpretation of prayer, even if the spoken prayer is petitionary *in form*. Abstract and impersonal concepts or substitutions for 'God,' such as those just mentioned above and favored by many UUs, are helpful in undercutting the idea that our prayerful words are directed at some entity whose 'mind' we imagine we can change or whose 'plans' we can persuasively influence. Second is the view that the deepest effect or power of prayer is to bring about change or deeper awareness on the part of the one who is praying. Such change can of course come from private prayer but may often be enhanced in a communal setting. One prominent UU minister, the Rev Nancy McDonald Ladd, recently wrote: 'I truly do not care if a god...ever hears me when I pray, but...praying together with others is among the most transformative work that I do' (Ladd 2017, p.20). This understanding of prayer is evident in the view of another of my UU ministerial colleagues, the Rev Cheryl Walker. She writes of a friend, a self-identified atheist, who once told her, 'I don't pray, but there are times when I sit and pour out what is in my heart into the universe.' In response, my colleague muses:

> If there is a better definition of prayer than that, I am not sure what it is... Too often we get so stuck on the address that we are unable to get to the message. Prayer need not have an addressee, because it is the addresser that matters, for in prayer we know that, ultimately, we are the ones being changed. (Walker 2014, p.50)

These understandings of prayer may actually be much more common across a wide spectrum of traditional religious communions than is commonly supposed, at least among philosophers and clergy, if not at the popular level. Contemporary process theologian Bob Mesle calls attention to the 'very curious' way in which the petitionary form of prayer is at odds with what most Christians actually believe. A worship leader may pray, for example, 'Dear God, we ask your Spirit to be with us in this hour.' In response, asks Mesle (1993, p.110), 'Does any theistic Christian think that God's Spirit might not be present at any time or place?' Answering his own question, Mesle counters that what we are actually doing is 'inviting the *people* to open up to that spirit.' Such views have been long substantiated in the Western religious tradition as far back as Immanuel Kant in 1793, who dismissed prayer aimed at pleasing God as 'fetish faith' (Kant 1960, p.180). The late twentieth-century Unitarian theologian, Henry Nelson Wieman, made a related distinction between true prayer as 'an attempt to adjust [one's own] personality,' and magic, which attempts to 'exercise coercive power...through controlling a deity' (Wieman and Westcott-Wieman 1935, p.130).

All this suggests a way of appreciating and fashioning forms of prayer that can work effectively in broader interfaith contexts. What provides a shared starting point or assumption in any interfaith gathering is our common humanity, and that recognition can guide us in choosing the elements of worship. We may also presume that all present share some notion that we are gathered to render service to a larger reality or source of value and meaning, however diversely named and understood. It is with this common purpose in mind that my UU ministerial colleague, the Rev. Ginger Luke, writes that whenever she is called upon to offer a prayer in some public, and therefore mixed-faith context (city council meeting, local school board invocation, etc.), she typically begins, 'In the name of all that is sacred and holy...' (Luke 2017, p.22). Such an opening invites each worshipper to think of, or substitute, an image or word appropriate to her/his own religious tradition. Similar sensibility can be seen in these words of invocation, written by another UU ministerial colleague, Norm Naylor:

> Do not leave your cares at the door. Do not leave there your pain, your sorrow or your joys. Bring them with you into this place of acceptance and forgiveness. Place them on the common altar of life. Come then, and offer yourself to potential transformation by the creative process that flows through you and all life.[6]

## CONCLUSION

Interfaith worship, at its best, focuses in this way on shared human concerns and needs, human joys and sorrows, human hopes and cooperative work for the common good. This is not to say that theological matters are unimportant or that we should aim for some

---

6    Naylor 1997. I'm grateful to another of my ministerial colleagues, the Rev. Anne Hines, for calling these words to my attention.

bland lowest common theological denominator, but only to affirm the value of speaking in ways that leave worshippers free to undergird the articulation of a shared vision with particular doctrines and images from their own varied religious traditions.

In summary, then, I argue that Unitarian Universalist approaches to interfaith worship grow naturally out of our experience with religious diversity within our own tradition. Such worship seeks, through emphasis on the common humanity that binds us across diverse theologies, to promote good will and deeper mutual understanding between persons of different beliefs, to embody and proclaim the promise of interreligious cooperation to the wider world, and to celebrate the commitments that enable cooperative interfaith work for shared visions of justice and the common good.

## REFERENCES

Atkinson, J. (2004) 'Engaged dissent among the Polish Brethren.' In A.McNary Forsey (ed.) *The Role of the Dissenter in Western Christianity: From Jesus through the 16th Century*. Berkeley, CA: Starr King School for the Ministry.

Kahf, M. (2016) *Hagar Poems*. Fayetteville, AR: University of Arkansas Press.

Kant, I. (1960) *Religion within the Limits of Reason Alone*, trans. T.M. Greene and H.H. Hudson. New York: Harper & Row.

Ladd, N.M. (2017) 'The call to prayer.' *UU World 31*, 1, 20.

Littell, F.H. (1963) 'The radical reformation.' In S.C. Neill and H.-R. Weber (eds) *The Layman in Christian History*. London: SCM Press.

Luke, G. (2017) 'Love as the ethical basis.' *UU World 31*, 1, 22.

Mesle, C.R. (1993) *Process Theology: A Basic Introduction*. St Louis, MO: Chalice Press.

Naylor, N.V. (1997) 'UUMA worship materials collection.' Accessed on 7 December 2018 at www.uua.org/worship/words/opening/5211.shtml.

Smith, T. (1982) 'A chronological list of Wesley's sermons and doctrinal essays.' *Wesleyan Theological Journal 17*, 2, 88–110.

Walker, C.M. (2014) 'The outpouring of the heart.' In B.D. Carley and L. Hallman (eds) *Not for Ourselves Alone*. Boston, MA: Skinner House.

Wieman, H.N. and Westcott-Wieman, R. (1935) *Normative Psychology of Religion*. New York: Thomas Y. Crowell.

Williams, G.H. (1979) 'From freedom, reason, tolerance, right behavior, and salvation by character: Toward a liberal Christian concept of man and the world.' In Peter Iver Kaufman (ed.) *Collegium Proceedings. Collegium: Association for Liberal Religious Studies 1*, 9–59.

Williams, G.H. (1992) *The Radical Reformation*, 3rd edn. Sixteenth Century Essays and Studies, vol. 15. Kirksville, MO: Sixteenth Century Journal Publishers.

## FURTHER READING AND LISTENING

Greenebaum, S. (2014) *Practical Interfaith: How to Find Our Common Humanity as We Celebrate Diversity.* Woodstock, VT: Skylight Paths Publishing.

LeFevre, P. (1981) *Understandings of Prayer.* Philadelphia, PA: Westminster Press.

*Liturgy* (2011) 'Interreligious Prayer' special issue, *26*, 3.

Mesle, C.R. (1993) 'Prayer, Liberation, and Healing.' In *Process Theology: A Basic Introduction.* St Louis, MO: Chalice Press.

Prose, B. (2013) 'Why Pray?' A sermon delivered on Sunday 3 February 2013, during 'The Point', the humanist service at All Souls Unitarian Church, Tulsa, Oklahoma. Accessed on 16 November 2018 at www.youtube.com/watch?v=nfbjK6ec3bA.

# Reflection

## The Editors

As we have seen, some contributors to this volume have expressed concern about aspects of interfaith worship and prayer as compromising their own firmly held beliefs. In their view, there is the danger that religious principles and convictions might be compromised by certain types of interfaith worship. Such hesitations are not, however, shared by the Unitarian contributors. In his chapter Jay Atkinson stresses a central commitment of the Unitarian movement: its identity as a theologically open, non-creedal association of congregations in which membership affiliation entails no commitment to any particular set of religious beliefs. As Atkinson notes, Unitarian liturgies incorporate sources and images from a variety of traditions – in this respect they are inherently interfaith events. Religious pluralism is thus acknowledged and celebrated, and both clergy and laity are especially open to participating in interfaith worship services.

One of the most common occasions for such observances takes place before US Thanksgiving Day when Jews, Protestants, Roman Catholics and Muslims as well as Eastern Orthodox congregations gather together.

In answer to the question as to what purposes such interfaith worship serves, Atkinson explains that it offers an opportunity to affirm and raise awareness of shared values across a spectrum of doctrinal and other differences. A further value of interfaith worship is the fostering of educational and spiritual goals of mutual learning, understanding, appreciation and goodwill among participants of different traditions. The aim should never be proselytising; rather, the experience of the words and rituals of another faith can enable participants to gain a deeper understanding of their own traditions.

Atkinson stresses that, from a Unitarian perspective, the possibility of mutual learning through interfaith worship is of central importance. Since its beginnings, Unitarianism has always recognised that human beings are fallible, and hence that religious convictions and institutions are always in need of being renewed through the process of dialogue. Nevertheless, some broad patterns of belief may be discerned. According to Atkinson, petitionary understandings of prayer, for example, would be rejected by most Unitarian Universalists. As a result, abstract and impersonal concepts of the divine are favoured by many Unitarian congregations in order to counter the idea that prayerful words are directed at a Divine Reality to whom requests can be made. Unitarianism affirms (in line with many religions) that the most important effect of prayer is to bring about change or deeper awareness on the part of the person who is praying.

Atkinson maintains that a shared starting point in any interfaith gathering is our common humanity. This recognition can guide the faithful to choose the key elements of worship. Worshippers are gathered to render service to a larger reality or source of value and meaning, however understood. In this context, Atkinson cites the words of the Rev Ginger Luke who writes that whenever she is called upon to offer a prayer in an interfaith context, she begins with the words: 'In the name of all that is sacred and holy'. Such an utterance invites each worshipper to substitute an image or word that is appropriate in that person's tradition. For Atkinson, interfaith worship grows out of our experience of religious diversity within one's own tradition and seeks the common humanity that binds all human beings together.

Feargus O'Connor similarly extols interfaith worship and explains how worshipping with members of other faith traditions is a central feature of his ministry. Interfaith dialogue and worship are at the heart of his activity and he shares the same assumptions as Atkinson about its value. In his view, such interfaith activity is vital to counter religious bigotry and communal hatred. Yet, he points out that in some contexts interfaith worship can be problematic. He states that he has a peculiarly Unitarian difficulty: participating in worship in which Trinitarian language is used by those who seem insensitive to the fact that some may find it theologically objectionable. Here he raises a concern facing various religious traditions which gather together for prayer and worship.

Thus, both the content and the intention of prayer can be problematic for Unitarians. All religions need to be sensitive to the views of others in prayer and worship, which is why some prefer silence or a ritual. It should also be observed, of course, that one religion should not make assumptions about another without investigating the true significance, for example of prayer. So, a term such as 'petitionary prayer', in the view of many, may not imply a God who needs persuading to change his or her mind, but rather be a request for strength to, for example, work hard for mercy and peace.

In such a case, the onus is on the believers, having opened themselves to the wonder and mystery of the Divine.

Chapter 14

# BAHÁ'Í

## 1

## The Perspective of One Bahá'í

Wendi Momen

It is permitted that the peoples and kindreds of the world associate with one another with joy and radiance. O people! Consort with the followers of all religions in a spirit of friendliness and fellowship. (Bahá'u'lláh 1978: 22)

They that are endued with sincerity and faithfulness should associate with all the peoples and kindreds of the earth with joy and radiance, inasmuch as consorting with people hath promoted and will continue to promote unity and concord, which in turn are conducive to the maintenance of order in the world and to the regeneration of nations. Blessed are such as hold fast to the cord of kindliness and tender mercy and are free from animosity and hatred. (Bahá'u'lláh 1978: 36)

## THE PRINCIPLES

### Relationship to those of other faiths

With these few words above does the founder of the Bahá'í Faith (see Bahá'í Faith; Momen with Momen 2006), Bahá'u'lláh (1817–1892; see Momen 2007) describe the relationship which Bahá'ís are to have with the followers of other religions. Shoghi Effendi (1897–1957), the Guardian of the Bahá'í Faith, underscored this when he wrote in 1935: 'Bahá'u'lláh indeed, urges His followers to consort with all religions and nations with the utmost friendliness and love. This constitutes the very spirit of His Message to mankind' (cited in Hornby 1994, p.163). There are no prohibitions about Bahá'ís praying with people of other religions or in their places of worship.

## The nature of religion

This principle arises from the teachings of Bahá'u'lláh regarding the nature of religion. He describes the progressive and continuing nature of God's guidance to humanity through the founders of the religions of the world:

> It is clear and evident to thee that all the Prophets [founders of the world religions] are the Temples of the Cause of God, Who have appeared clothed in divers attire. If thou wilt observe with discriminating eyes, thou wilt behold Them all abiding in the same tabernacle, soaring in the same heaven, seated upon the same throne, uttering the same speech, and proclaiming the same Faith. Such is the unity of those Essences of Being, those Luminaries of infinite and immeasurable splendour! Wherefore, should one of these Manifestations of Holiness proclaim saying: 'I am the return of all the Prophets,' He, verily, speaketh the truth. In like manner, in every subsequent Revelation, the return of the former Revelation is a fact, the truth of which is firmly established... (Bahá'u'lláh 1976: 51)

Thus, for Bahá'ís, the attitude one is to have towards other religions is respect and appreciation, arising from a profound understanding that the followers of all religions are followers of God, believers in God, and that there is a familial relationship among them.

It is therefore not very difficult for Bahá'ís to worship with people of other faiths, which they often do. For Bahá'ís, prayer goes hand in hand with service to others and they are encouraged to work together with neighbours to better their communities: '[Worship] cannot afford lasting satisfaction and benefit to the worshipper himself, much less to humanity in general, unless and until translated and transfused into...dynamic and disinterested service to the cause of humanity' (Shoghi Effendi 1995, p.186).

## Prayer and worship

Prayer is described as 'the essential spiritual conversation of the soul with its Maker' (Universal House of Justice 2014). Bahá'ís pray both privately and with others. Bahá'u'lláh and His son 'Abdu'l-Bahá revealed many prayers (*dua*) for all occasions which are used in both private prayer and in collective worship. Bahá'ís may also pray using the scriptures of other religions or their own words.

Bahá'ís are to pray daily and must choose one of three obligatory prayers (*salat*) to say each day in addition to other prayers they may offer. Daily obligatory prayers are said privately. The obligatory prayer for the dead is the only obligatory prayer for collective worship and is said by one person at a funeral while others stand in silence.

In addition, Bahá'ís are encouraged to seek the Will of God and to pray for, inter alia, the health and wellbeing of others; their children; their parents; their own spiritual health; the progress of the Cause of God; the peace, prosperity and safety of the world and humanity; to offer thanksgiving and give praise to God; and in times of difficulty and decision-making.

Bahá'ís engage in collective worship on many occasions, for example at the beginning and end of meetings, at the Nineteen Day Feast (the gathering every Bahá'í month, comprising 19 days, at which Bahá'ís in a locality pray, consult and break bread together) and at holy day commemorations. Many Bahá'í meetings, particularly holy days, are open to people of all faiths and none.

## The House of Worship

The Bahá'í teachings call for the establishment, over time, of Houses of Worship (*Mashriqu'l-Adhkár*: 'the Dawning-place of the praise of God') in every hamlet and city. There are at present nine Houses of Worship, one each in Africa, Europe, Australia, India, Samoa and Cambodia, and in North, South and Central America. Several others are currently being built in Colombia, Vanuatu and elsewhere. The House of Worship is open to people of all religions and none, and services there often include readings from the holy scriptures of other faiths:

> Within the central edifice there shall be read, chanted or sung only the words of the Sacred Scriptures of the revealed religions, or hymns based upon those words. (Bahá'u'lláh 1973, p.61)

The nature of these gatherings is for prayer, meditation and the reading of Writings from the Sacred Scriptures of our Faith and other Faiths; there can be one or a number of readers; any Bahá'í chosen, or even non-Bahá'í, may read. The gatherings should be simple, dignified, and designed to uplift the soul and educate it through hearing the Creative Word. (Shoghi Effendi in Hornby 1994, p.607)

## THE PRACTICE

The principles explaining that 'we must pray together' are embedded in Bahá'í scripture and are clearly articulated. The way in which these principles are put into practice by individual Bahá'ís and by the Bahá'í community as a whole are, in my experience, very closely aligned to these teachings.

### Relationship to those of other faiths

Individual Bahá'ís and the Bahá'í community in general are positive about praying together with members of other religions. They like to participate in, and are supporters of, interfaith and multifaith organizations and services. They enjoy praying with people of other faiths and those who are of no faith, and they seem to revel in those occasions when people of many different faiths come together in worship. Many Bahá'í communities celebrate World Religion Day, the third Sunday in January, which the American Bahá'ís inaugurated in 1950 to promote interfaith understanding and which is characterized by prayers and readings from many faith traditions.

### The nature of religion

Bahá'ís see religion as one phenomenon, unfolding to humanity like successive chapters of a never-ending book. Bahá'ís recognize that there are differences in the ways in which religion is understood and practised but these are not considered to be of such great significance that they outweigh the commonalities, and thus Bahá'ís tend to focus on these similarities in their relationships with those of other faiths.

Bahá'ís are forbidden to proselytise but are urged to share their religion with others, the attitude being that of one offering a gift to a king.

## Prayer and worship

Bahá'ís may pray using the scriptures of other religions or their own words but they tend to read, recite, sing or chant the prayers revealed by Bahá'u'lláh and 'Abdu'l-Bahá on most occasions.

Bahá'ís are usually happy to pray in any space where others are praying, including churches, synagogues, mosques, temples or other religious places, as well as in their own homes and in the homes of others, outdoors, in schools or other places where people gather to pray. They often join others in prayer at times of crisis or thanksgiving, including public observations such as national commemorative services in the United Kingdom at Westminster Abbey and St Paul's Cathedral, where for many years Bahá'ís representing the national governing council, the National Spiritual Assembly of the Bahá'ís of the United Kingdom, have joined other religious leaders in prayer and reflection.

Because prayer and service are intimately linked together for Bahá'ís, they especially like to work alongside those of other faiths to improve their communities or to overcome local problems. This aspect of the Bahá'í Faith is widely practised at the level of the neighbourhood, where Bahá'ís and their friends study together and learn to offer moral education classes for children, and junior youth empowerment programmes for young people between the ages of 12 and 15, as well as developing the skills to address issues and difficulties facing the community, be it access to basic health care, agriculture or protecting the environment.

## The House of Worship

As there are only a few Houses of Worship across the world, at present Bahá'ís host devotional gatherings at the neighbourhood level, often in their own homes, with family, friends and neighbours. These may be weekly, monthly or at some other regular interval, depending on the resources and capacity of the local Bahá'ís and their neighbours. The purpose of these devotional gatherings is not only to bring people closer together and to celebrate their common spiritual heritage but primarily to enhance the devotional and spiritual character of a neighbourhood, awaken spiritual susceptibilities in individuals and to infuse them with the spiritual capacity to perform acts of service together for the benefit of their communities.

The programme for the devotional gathering is up to the host and those who attend. There is no fixed pattern. Some have formal programmes, with printed prayers and readings drawn from Bahá'í scripture and other holy books, which are read by different people in turn to the whole group or by one or two people while others listen. Other devotional gatherings are very informal, with those attending choosing prayers and readings from books that are supplied, or reading from apps on their phones which provide a large number of Bahá'í texts in over seventy languages. At other gatherings those attending may be asked to bring a prayer or verse of scripture to share. As those who attend come from many faith communities, the prayers and readings reflect this diversity. Many devotional gatherings include prayers and readings set to music and sung, or include instrumental music and poetry, as Bahá'u'lláh (1992: 38) has indicated that He has 'made music as a ladder for your souls, a means whereby they may be lifted up unto the realm on high'.

Where a devotional gathering is well established, the host might suggest to others that they might like to host them in their own homes. Thus, the number of devotional gatherings in a neighbourhood or town increases over time, with new people attending those most convenient for them. Where this has happened, those hosting the gatherings are often not themselves Bahá'ís and are likely to choose scriptures from their own faith traditions, but the spirit of reading from the holy books and prayers of other religions is usually maintained in practice.

For example, in 2003 my husband and I decided to host devotional gatherings in our home once a month and have done so ever since. We invite our neighbours and some friends from a nearby town. Over the years we have experimented with different formats, using readings and prayers from different holy scriptures on a particular theme, interspersed with music. We have chosen the overall theme for this year to be the divine attributes that we strive to reflect in our lives. Our recent devotional meeting was on the theme of compassion, with readings from Buddhist, Muslim, Jewish, Christian and Bahá'í scriptures. We prayed that we might develop compassion within ourselves and that the world be more compassionate, focusing particularly on refugees and other displaced people, especially children. Those attending on that evening included a Muslim Berber from Algeria, a Jamaican Methodist, a follower of White Eagle, a spiritual organisation based on teachings from a spirit in the higher realms named White Eagle, as well as Anglicans and

Bahá'ís. Our Methodist friend has been hosting her own devotional gatherings once a month for about a year, and a very elderly Anglican neighbour has just begun his own. After the devotional prayers, we generally study a prayer together.

Over the years we have bonded with our neighbours at a very deep level. We are true friends; we enrich each others' lives and have a spiritual connection. We share our ideas on life: points of view about religion and social affairs, and acts of service. We also laugh quite a lot, share stories and eat lots of good food.

## UNHELPFUL EXPERIENCES

My experience of occasions when people of different faiths pray together is largely positive. Occasionally there are difficulties, sometimes owing to misunderstandings or a miscommunication about the nature of an activity. Sometimes – infrequently – a member of one faith community will use the opportunity of sharing prayers to proselytise, to question the validity of another religion, make fun of it, make negative remarks about the religion and its followers or to denigrate the prayer or the person offering it. Sometimes people inadvertently fail to respect another religion, because they do not know the practices and traditions of that faith. I have occasionally seen people of one faith refuse to pray with people of another or refuse to go into their place of worship. In an effort to avoid difficulties, the interfaith group to which I belong begins its meetings with silence rather than prayers, which is acceptable but not wholly in the spirit of the idea that if we are truly to understand one another and build bonds of friendship, we should be able to pray with one another.

## SUMMARY

The Bahá'í teachings prescribe friendliness and fellowship as the characteristics of the relationship of Bahá'ís with people of other faiths. This arises from Bahá'u'lláh's description of the nature of religion as the progressive revelation over the millennia of God's guidance to humanity, that is, that there is one religion of God, progressively revealed over time.

Prayer is described in the Bahá'í teachings as the soul's conversation with God and both obligatory prayers and general worship are prescribed. Prayers are to be said both privately and collectively. Bahá'ís may pray using the scriptures of other religions or their own words but they tend to read, recite, sing or chant the revealed prayers, both when praying as an individual and when worshipping with others.

There are no prohibitions about Bahá'ís praying with others; rather, they are encouraged to do so. And in practice they do so often, both on public occasions and in their own homes.

> Gather ye together with the utmost joy and fellowship and recite the verses revealed by the merciful Lord. By so doing the doors to true knowledge will be opened to your inner beings, and ye will then feel your souls endowed with steadfastness and your hearts filled with radiant joy. (Bahá'u'lláh, no date)

## REFERENCES

The Bahá'í Faith. Accessed on 7 December 2108 at www.bahai.org.

Bahá'u'lláh (no date) *The Importance of Deepening Our Knowledge and Understanding of the Faith*. Haifa: Bahá'í World Centre.

Bahá'u'lláh (1973) *Synopsis and Codification of the Kitáb-i-Aqdas*. Haifa: Bahá'í World Centre.

Bahá'u'lláh (1976) *Gleanings from the Writings of Bahá'u'lláh*, 2nd edn. Wilmette, IL: Bahá'í Publishing Trust.

Bahá'u'lláh (1978) *Tablets of Bahá'u'lláh Revealed after the Kitáb-i-Aqdas*. Haifa: Bahá'í World Centre.

Bahá'u'lláh (1992) *The Kitáb-i-Aqdas*. Haifa: Bahá'í World Centre.

Hornby, H. (1994) *Lights of Guidance: A Bahá'í Reference File*, 3rd edn. New Delhi: Bahá'í Publishing Trust.

Momen, M. (2007) *Baha'u'llah*. Oxford: Oneworld.

Momen, W. with Momen, M. (2006) *Understanding the Bahá'í Faith*. Edinburgh: Dunedin Academic Press.

Shoghi Effendi (1995) *Bahá'í Administration*. Wilmette, IL: Bahá'í Publishing Trust.

Universal House of Justice (2014) Letter of December 18. Available at https://www.payamha-iran.org/node/160?language=en, accessed on 27 February 2019.

# 2

## 'Consort with All Religions with Amity and Concord'

## George Merchant Ballentyne

Ask Bahá'ís if we are in favour of people from different religions praying together and you will find yourself pushing at an open door. Bahá'ís would probably say that this doesn't happen often enough, that we should not wait for a special reason to do so, and that wherever and whenever it takes place, it should be more accessible and inclusive. Praying together is, of course, just one form of interreligious dialogue.[1] Bahá'ís contribute to all forms, whenever opportunities present themselves. But this form in particular is one for which we are well adapted, to which we believe we can make a positive contribution and in which that contribution can really stand out.

Of all religious groups, Bahá'ís are arguably the least likely to worry about compromising our principles, conceding ground as a distinct faith community or putting our beliefs at risk by taking part in such activities. This is a very 'Bahá'í' thing to do. Bahá'u'lláh (1993, 144, p.72) instructs his followers to 'Consort with all religions with amity and concord, that they may inhale from you the sweet fragrance of God.'[2] We are convinced that the more people see us engaged in this way, the more familiar they become with Bahá'í teachings, the more they hear of Bahá'í readings and prayers, the greater will be the recognition of the authenticity of the Bahá'í Faith, the more widespread the acknowledgment of the station and mission of Bahá'u'lláh – and the stronger our impact on one of the most pressing issues of our time:

> Gird up the loins of your endeavour, O people of Bahá, that
> haply the tumult of religious dissension and strife that agitateth

---

1    Seena Fazel discusses six forms of dialogue (after Eck) and their relevance to the Bahá'í community: 'parliamentary dialogue', 'institutional dialogue', 'theological dialogue', 'dialogue in community', 'spiritual dialogue' and 'inner dialogue'. See Fazel 1997, pp.137–157.

2    Bahá'u'lláh (1817–1892) 'Prophet-Founder' of the Bahá'í Faith, after whom the religion is named. He is one of the three 'central figures' of the Bahá'í Faith, along with the Báb (1819–1850) and 'Abdu'l-Bahá (1844–1921). For a brief introduction to the life and mission of Bahá'u'lláh see Braybrooke 2017.

the peoples of the earth may be stilled, that every trace of it may be completely obliterated... Religious fanaticism and hatred are a world-devouring fire, whose violence none can quench. The Hand of Divine power can, alone, deliver mankind from this desolating affliction. (Bahá'u'lláh 2005, 132.2, pp.325–326)

Passages such as this set the direction for our dialogue with different religions. It also describes a clear outcome for our engagement: one which is of obvious benefit to all, not just something that would profit Bahá'ís.

If anyone knows the first thing about the Bahá'í Faith, they will surely know that it 'upholds the unity of God, recognizes the unity of His Prophets, and inculcates the principle of the oneness and wholeness of the entire human race' (Shoghi Effendi Rabbani 1980, p.v). According to the Bahá'í worldview, it is impossible for anyone to claim monopoly on the truth – especially when it comes to matters of religion or belief. Bahá'u'lláh's teachings on continuity and universality of revelation underpin our active commitment to good relations between faiths.[3]

The fundamental principle enunciated by Bahá'u'lláh...is that religious truth is not absolute but relative, that Divine Revelation is a continuous and progressive process, that all the great religions of the world are divine in origin, that their basic principles are in complete harmony, that their aims and purposes are one and the same, that their teachings are but facets of one truth, that their functions are complementary, that they differ only in the nonessential aspects of their doctrines, and that their missions represent successive stages in the spiritual evolution of human society. (Shoghi Effendi Rabbani 1980, p.v)

Praying together and visiting different places of worship as a way of building good relations has a notable pedigree in the Bahá'í Faith. 'Abdu'l-Bahá refers to his experience in the West shortly before the First World War:

All must abandon prejudices and must even go to each other's churches and mosques, for, in all of these worshipping places, the Name of God is mentioned. Since all gather to

3   For a fuller discussion see Fazel 2007.

worship God, what difference is there? None of them worship Satan... They hold aloof from one another merely because of unfounded prejudices and dogmas. In America I went to the Jewish Synagogues, which are similar to the Christian Churches, and I saw them worshipping God everywhere.

In many of these places I spoke about the original foundations of the divine religions, and I explained to them the proofs of the validity of the divine prophets and of the Holy Manifestations. I encouraged them to do away with blind imitations. All of the leaders must, likewise, go to each other's Churches and speak of the foundation and of the fundamental principles of the divine religions. In the utmost unity and harmony they must worship God, in the worshipping places of one another, and must abandon fanaticism. ('Abdu'l-Bahá, quoted in Esslemont 2006, pp.133–134)

Rather than being a nice idea, this is a 'must' and has been a fundamental part of the Bahá'í programme for a century and more.

I accepted the Bahá'í Faith in 1979, at the age of 19, in my native city of Glasgow. For many years now I have lived and worked in Leicester, which has been described as 'the most multicultural city on the planet' (Popham 2013). Given Leicester's public image, there are surprisingly few opportunities for people of different religions to pray together here. I will briefly mention four ways in which I have prayed, worshipped or meditated with people of different backgrounds, heritage and traditions – in public or in private.

## VIGILS

These are usually held in response to conflict, disaster or terrorist acts, expressing common determination that nothing will be allowed to threaten good community relations, that our diverse communities stand together on the side of good. In the past, these were normally styled 'prayer vigils' and took place out of the public eye. Now they are more mainstream, to the extent of being covered on TV and radio. Local authorities, police, schools, colleges and universities, mass media and other secular agencies are normally involved as a matter of course, which helps in planning, publicising and delivery. Facebook, Twitter, Instagram, Snapchat can all enhance or intrude on the experience, connecting diverse people and places, uniting in observance or dividing by argument. Conventional or cultural aspects make the experience more accessible to people who would not identify with any of the faith communities: lighting, bearing and placing candles; signing books of condolence (physical and virtual); laying of flower tributes; writing messages in coloured chalk on pavements and walls; holding hands in public. A moment of silence can make a strong impression, especially in the midst of a normally bustling city centre. Aguilar writes about experiencing 'loud dialogue in silence' (2017, p.81).

Easing community tensions is a laudable outcome and no one is going to protest against such joint testimony and common witness. I do regret, however, that the vigil has become one of the few ways in which we seem able to display in public our harmony and diversity. Even so, there's now less devotional content, with more attention focused on the soundbite. These events present an opportunity to sermonise or speechify but, when given the chance, we prefer to use the time to share some relevant passage from the Bahá'í writings. In doing so, we would hope to keep the gathering centred on a point of principle, around which most of those present could agree – and to do so in a thoughtful, reflective way. Bahá'ís share a belief in the special potency of revealed scripture, that it has a transformative power which no human utterance, no matter how eloquent and moving, can match. To quote Bahá'u'lláh (2005, 74.1, p.160), 'every single letter proceeding out of the mouth of God is indeed a mother letter, and every word uttered by Him Who is the Well Spring of Divine Revelation is a mother word'. When the opportunity arises to take part in this kind of event, a Bahá'í would rarely, if ever, pass up the chance to share the 'creative word'. Our individual contribution may be no more than to set the context for the sake of the audience and convey the expected social graces.

My most memorable experience of stepping out of the way so that the message can speak for itself was at a multifaith vigil in Leicester's Cathedral Gardens, autumn 2015. We came together one sunny Sunday afternoon in sympathy and shame over treatment of Syrian refugees in Europe, following publication of the haunting photos of the body of three-year-old Alan Kurdî, washed up on a Turkish beach. I am usually full of confidence at such events. That day, however, I felt thoroughly shaken and didn't know how to respond. At the last moment, I decided to read a chapter from *Paris Talks*, a compilation of short public addresses given in that city by 'Abdu'l-Bahá in 1911. This particular talk, entitled 'The Duty of Kindness and Sympathy Toward Strangers and Foreigners' ('Abdu'l-

Bahá 2011), took three minutes to read aloud. At the end of the programme, an Anglican priest told me she wasn't used to Bahá'ís speaking like that. 'Well, I don't know which Bahá'ís you've been listening to!' I said, then asked her to expand. She replied, 'I'm used to Bahá'ís being...' at which she made an exaggerated motion of her body and arms, like a tree swaying. 'I'm used to Bahá'ís just going this way or that, whichever way the wind's blowing. But what you just read – that was *strong*!' I used the same passage in a multifaith service at the Church of the Resurrection, before what is arguably the most multicultural and variegated Christian congregation in Leicester. A woman there told me that she had been moved to tears by 'Abdu'l-Baha's words. 'Abdu'l-Bahá's exemplary status as 'the embodiment of every Bahá'í ideal, the incarnation of every Bahá'í virtue' (Shoghi Effendi Rabbani 1991, p.134) is perhaps our greatest source of strength. For those who do not know his life and work, his words help convey that strength. Much of what 'Abdu'l-Bahá wrote or said was to audiences or enquirers approaching him in what we'd consider an interfaith context. Extracts from his writings and talks often feature in compilations of readings suitable for use in such occasions, available for anyone to use.[4] We make no secret of the fact that there is no copyright on the Bahá'í writings and we are not proprietorial about them.[5]

## REGULAR DATES IN THE INTERFAITH CALENDAR

I have shared Bahá'í prayers at a variety of occasions that come round on an annual basis and welcome devotional input from different sources. These have included Holocaust Memorial Day, World Interfaith Harmony Week, Racial Justice Sunday, Inter Faith Week, Armistice Day (most recently, at one held in a gurdwara) and World Religion Day – founded in 1950 by Bahá'ís in the USA, since taken up across the globe by other faith communities (the 2017 celebration in Leicester was hosted by the Sant Nirankari Mission). I have also had the privilege of standing in for other faith communities unable

---

4    The 'Unity Prayer' of 'Abdu'l-Bahá, included in Brownstein 2014, is one of the most commonly used devotional passages for Bahá'ís when contributing to interreligious worship.

5    The Bahá'í Reference Library (www.bahai.org/library) is the authoritative online source of Bahá'í writings. It contains selected works of Bahá'u'lláh, the Báb, 'Abdu'l-Bahá, Shoghi Effendi and the Universal House of Justice, as well as other Bahá'í texts.

to provide a representative to these events for one reason or another – as I have also done at public vigils. Whenever that has happened, I have read from their scripture, without thinking it necessary to state in public my own affiliation.

## DEVOTIONAL MEETINGS ARRANGED BY PEOPLE OF VARIOUS FAITHS

Mentioning here just one memorable instance, I read from Bahá'í scripture in the intimate settings of a small church in Oakham, at a meeting of the Fellowship of Contemplative Prayer. Bahá'u'lláh's 'Hidden Words' (2006) sit well with this quietist form of devotional practice, which allows participants to dwell on a chosen sacred text in a short but intense period of reflection: 'O son of spirit! My first counsel is this: Possess a pure, kindly and radiant heart, that thine may be a sovereignty ancient, imperishable and everlasting' (Bahá'u'lláh 2006, no.1). It would be safe to say that a small number of Bahá'ís had heard of the Fellowship of Contemplative Prayer. Even fewer ever had the chance to practise it. I was able to introduce it to a group of them, some of whom were attracted by it, found themselves temperamentally suited to it and used it to reveal deeper meaning in Bahá'í scripture as well other inspirational texts. Bahá'ís can benefit by adopting or adapting practices developed by others, while steering clear of the pitfalls of cultural appropriation: 'Bahá'u'lláh has specified no procedures to be followed in meditation, and individual believers are free to do as they wish in this area, provided that they remain in harmony with the Teachings' (Universal House of Justice 1983).

## DEVOTIONAL MEETINGS ARRANGED BY BAHÁ'ÍS

It is common for Bahá'ís – as individuals, families or small groups – to host informal devotional meetings in their homes or neutral venues, normally with friends and close contacts, who are welcome to bring favourite passages, religious or secular, from a variety of sources. These are not unlike the house groups in Christian congregations. They are, by nature, small-scale and low-key, but none the less impactful. 'Immerse yourselves in the ocean of My words, that ye may unravel its secrets, and discover all the pearls of wisdom that lie hid in its depths', wrote Bahá'u'lláh (1993, 182, p.86). Knowing the value of these pearls, it is understandable that we would want

264    Interfaith Worship and Prayer

to share them, in this informal atmosphere of mutual respect and spiritual communality, which is now done in thousands of locations around the world.

Bahá'ís are forbidden to proselytise, so we must not take part in interfaith worship (or any other form of dialogue) with the intention of 'converting' anyone or proving a point. We must be ever mindful that we should be going about this work with purity of motive. Whenever a legitimate opening presents itself, however, we are obliged to present Bahá'u'lláh's message 'like a gift to a king'.[6]

> Consort with all men, O people of Bahá, in a spirit of friendliness and fellowship. If ye be aware of a certain truth, if ye possess a jewel, of which others are deprived, share it with them in a language of utmost kindliness and goodwill. If it be accepted, if it fulfil its purpose, your object is attained. If anyone should refuse it, leave him unto himself, and beseech God to guide him. Beware lest ye deal unkindly with him. A kindly tongue is the lodestone of the hearts of men. It is the bread of the spirit, it clotheth the words with meaning, it is the fountain of the light of wisdom and understanding. (Bahá'u'lláh 2005, 132.5, pp.326–327)

For many navigating the maze of interfaith relations, often encountering discouragement or opposition within their communities, such a statement may seem an elusive hope. For we Bahá'ís, it is an ever-present reality, no matter how effectively it may be obscured. When we pray with people of other affiliations, we hope that they can take inspiration from the texts that mean so much to us.

We would rather people from different religions pray together as part of regular, friendly, normal engagement, rather than in response to crises and calamities. Yet even this is in keeping with Bahá'í teachings – that if we do not overcome division and work together for the common weal, circumstances will force our hand. Bahá'u'lláh wrote that 'The well-being of mankind, its peace and security, are unattainable unless and until its unity is firmly established' (2005, 131.2, p.324). Praying together will not, by itself, bring about the unity that will transform the fortunes of humanity. But it will help establish that unity on a genuine foundation, and give it direction, life and meaning.

---

6    Briggite Hasselblatt, quoted in National Spiritual Assembly of the Bahá'ís of the United States 1956.

# REFERENCES

'Abdu'l-Bahá (2011) *Paris Talks: Addresses Given by 'Abdu'l-Bahá in 1911.* Wilmette, IL: Bahá'í Publishing.

Aguilar, M.I. (2017) *The Way of the Hermit: Interfaith Encounters in Silence and Prayer.* London: Jessica Kingsley Publishers.

Bahá'u'lláh (1993) *Kitáb-i-Aqdas: The Most Holy Book,* trans. Shoghi Effendi *et al.* Wilmette, IL: Bahá'í Publishing.

Bahá'u'lláh (2005) *Gleanings from the Writings of Bahá'u'lláh,* trans. Shoghi Effendi *et al.* Wilmette, IL: Bahá'í Publishing.

Bahá'u'lláh (2006) *The Hidden Words,* trans. Shoghi Effendi. Wilmette, IL: Bahá'í Publishing.

Braybrooke, M. (2017) 'A vision of global peace: Bahá'u'lláh – founder of the Bahá'í Faith.' *The Interfaith Observer,* 15 April. Accessed on 17 November 2018 at www.theinterfaithobserver.org/journal-articles/2017/3/23/bahullh-founder-of-the-bah-faith.

Brownstein, T. (ed.) (2014) *The Interfaith Prayerbook.* Lake Worth, FL: Lake Worth Interfaith Group.

Esslemont, J.E. (2006) *Bahá'u'lláh and the New Era: An Introduction to the Bahá'í Faith.* Wilmette, IL: Bahá'í Publishing.

Fazel, S. (1997) 'Interreligious dialogue and the Bahá'í Faith: Some preliminary observations.' In J.A. McLean (ed.) *Revisioning the Sacred: New Perspectives on a Bahá'í Theology,* Studies in the Babi and Bahá'í Religions vol. 8. Los Angeles, CA: Kalimát Press. Accessed on 17 November 2018 at https://bahai-library.com/fazel_interreligious_dialogue.

Fazel, S. (2007) 'Bahá'í approaches to Christianity and Islam: Further thoughts on developing an inter-religious dialogue.' *Bahá'í Studies Review,* 14. Accessed on 17 November 2018 at https://bahai-library.com/fazel_christian_islam_dialogue.

National Spiritual Assembly of the Bahá'ís of the United States (1956) *Bahá'í News,* Jan.

Popham, P. (2013) 'We're all in this together: How Leicester became a model of multiculturalism (even if that was never the plan...)' *Independent on Sunday,* 27 July. Accessed on 17 November 2018 at www.independent.co.uk/news/uk/this-britain/were-all-in-this-together-how-leicester-became-a-model-of-multiculturalism-even-if-that-was-never-8732691.html.

Shoghi Effendi Rabbani (1980) *The Promised Day Is Come.* Wilmette, IL: Bahá'í Publishing Trust.

Shoghi Effendi Rabbani (1991) *The World Order of Bahá'u'lláh*. Wilmette, IL: Bahá'í Publishing.

Universal House of Justice, Department of the Secretariat (1983) Letter to the National Spiritual Assembly of the Bahá'ís of Norway, 1 September. Accessed on 17 November 2018 at https://www.bahai. org/library/authoritative-texts/the-universal-house-of-justice/ messages/19830901_001/1#062765015.

# Reflection

## The Editors

Throughout this volume various contributors – while endorsing interfaith prayer and worship – have been concerned that participants might in some way compromise their religious beliefs. George Merchant Ballentyne, however, is adamant that this should not be an issue. He states that, of all faith communities, Bahá'í is arguably the least likely to be worried about sacrificing principles and putting faith at risk. Rather, he writes that participating in interfaith worship is completely consonant with the highest ideals of the Bahá'í Faith. Bahá'u'lláh, he points out, instructed his followers to consort with the adherents of all religions. This serves as a means of informing outsiders of Bahá'í teachings – the more they learn about Bahá'í readings and prayers, the more they will be able to understand the mission of Bahá'u'lláh.

He goes on to explain the nature of Bahá'í belief. Bahá'ís uphold the unity of God, the unity of his prophets, and inculcate the principle of the oneness and wholeness of the entire human race. According to the Bahá'í worldview, it is impossible for anyone to claim monopoly on the truth, particularly in matters of religion. The central principle enunciated by Baha'u'llah is that religious truth is not absolute but relative and that divine revelation is a continuous and progressive process. Further Baha'u'llah held that all the great religions of the world are divine in origin, that their basic principles are in completely harmony, that their aims and purposes are one and the same, that their teachings are but facets of one truth, that their functions are complementary, and that their missions represent successive stages in the spiritual evolution of humankind. In her contribution Wendi Momen similarly stresses that interfaith prayer is a key element of Bahá'í activity. The principles underlying the imperative of worshipping with members of other traditions are embedded and clearly indicated in Bahá'í scripture. Bahá'ís, she emphasises, enjoy participating in and are supporters of interfaith services. They see religion as a single phenomenon, unfolding to humanity like successive chapters of a book.

These two contributions highlight the importance of interfaith encounter in the Bahá'í Faith. It is of central significance and is interwoven into the fabric of Bahá'í belief. As we have seen throughout this book, other religions have in different ways accommodated themselves to interfaith worship and prayer while attempting to retain their overarching religious beliefs. Even nontheists have found ways to accommodate themselves to communal worship with those who believe in a creator God. For Bahá'ís interfaith prayer poses no such difficulties. Instead, they rejoice in such activity, believing that it is entirely consistent with their theological assumptions.

The Bahá'í Faith is a religion which teaches the essential worth of all religions and the unity and equality of all people. Even though Bahá'ís believe that God is single and all powerful, Bahá'u'lláh taught that religion is progressively revealed by one God through manifestations of God who are the founders of world religions throughout history. Hence, Buddha, Moses, Jesus and Muhammad should be perceived as teachers of divine truth. As a consequence, Bahá'ís regard the major religions as fundamentally unified in purpose. Bahá'ís reject all notions of racism and nationalism, believing in the goal of a unified world order that ensures the prosperity of all.

This is the context in which interfaith prayer and worship is celebrated. Believing in the unity of God, the unity of religion, and the unity of humanity. Bahá'ís are committed to working with all peoples. In this quest, worshipping with Jews, Christians, Muslims, Buddhists, Hindus, Shintos and others is a critical step in the development of humanity. Such rituals fulfil the vision of Shoghi Effendi, the Guardian of the Bahá'í religion in the early part of the twentieth century, of the distinguishing principles extolled by Baha'u'llah:

> The independent search after truth, unfettered by superstition or tradition; the oneness of the entire human race, the pivotal principle and fundamental doctrine of the Faith; the basic unity of all religions, the condemnation of all forms of prejudice, whether religious, racial, class or national...and universal peace as the supreme goal of all mankind. (Shoghi Effendi 1979 [1944], pp.281–282)

## REFERENCE

Shoghi Effendi (1979 [1944]) *God Passes By*. Wilmette, IL: Bahá'í Publishing Trust.

Chapter 15

# CONCLUDING REFLECTION

## Alan Race

The clamour for dialogue and cooperation between faith communities has been increasing around the world for at least the last fifty years. Motivations for this have been various, ranging from the desire of individuals to expand their spiritual horizons to the need to overcome suspicions between religions for the sake of increasing prospects for peace in the world. A lesser-known dimension of these encounters has been the practice of interfaith prayer and worship. But this too is now gathering pace and all of the chapters in this book tell of occasions when people of different traditions come together, under many conditions and circumstances, for the purpose of raising hearts and minds in prayerful ways.

It is right that this book takes a global view, for not only has the world become a global village but it also reminds us of the fundamental desire of the human heart and mind everywhere to place itself in the context of what can be called the universal sense of the sacred. Religious ritual is a vehicle for expressing our dearest hopes and dreams, our deepest hurts and angers, our greatest joys and celebrations – in short, the full gamut of emotions in the search for what it is to be fully human. When we place different traditions side by side we see how human needs, frailties, desires and aspirations are often similar the world over. Yet religious rituals are not only expressive of our search for human meaning, they are also means for activating that search and they do that using the means familiar in worship settings – for example, through the scriptural rehearsal of foundational stories and experiences, or the repetition of familiar beliefs which may even be acted out in symbolic gestures.

The recognition of the human search for meaning and the activation of that meaning through the ritual actions of separated traditions sets up a tension when it comes to reflecting on prayer and worship in an interfaith setting. The chapters in this book all acknowledge both sides of this tension. We share familiar human needs and aspirations as one human family yet placing those needs and aspirations in the presence of the sacred highlights our separated, even fractured, humanness. Another way of putting this tension is to say that religious ritual both draws boundaries between groups whilst the very prayer that is enacted within those boundaries points the human heart beyond those restrictions to that sacred reality which runs through and hovers over all of us.

This dual effect of prayer accounts for the strangeness and the resonance between faith communities when we join together in prayer and worship. Those who value the peace of silence in meditation will be disturbed by the noisy exuberance found in some other forms of worship; those who concentrate on a perceived transcendence without seeing the need for worldly mediation will be shaken by those who revel in the smells of incense, the sensations of images or dance with scriptures as gateways to holiness. Yet the strangenesses that strike us in interfaith worship can be equally resonant with what we have learned through nurture in one tradition alone. We human beings are wonderfully different, within and between cultures, within and between individuals, and this too must be taken into account when we come together to pray. In interfaith worship the variety of ritual forms may be present for all to experience. There is no reason why the worship boundaries drawn by any single tradition ought not to be transgressed for the sake of a greater sense of the sacred.

The contributions in this book speak of safeguarding particular shapes and forms of prayer and worship, especially the more liturgical forms. This is to be respected for it is here that the core experiences which define a tradition are maintained. However, this is not to say that these forms cannot be revised in the light of new knowledge or changed cultural perceptions, but revision is likely to be cautious. On the other hand, the contributions welcome the opportunities for coming together, whether this be in response to disaster; a national emergency; a celebration of local cultural and ethnic diversity; an international event such as the Olympic Games; an affirmation built around, say, themes of human rights or justice. The occasions are becoming more numerous and varied. The twin pulls of the strong in-group reliance on a tradition's particular focus on foundational experiences, and the summons to join the out-groups for the purposes of greater solidarity are becoming more and more complementary for all of us.

That said, interfaith prayer and worship is not without problems. Some of these have been outlined by the contributors to this collection which therefore contains varying degrees of enthusiasm for the interfaith enterprise, though none are wholly resistant to the prospect. Sometimes suspicion might arise because of history, especially the political and religious negatives associated with colonial history; sometimes because of fears over the loss of identity and anxiety about being swallowed up in a common religious soup; sometimes because of unresolved disputes over religious doctrines. That said, there is general agreement that shared prayer and worship is not only permissible but necessary in certain circumstances, especially those associated with response to tragedy or emergency.

Does interfaith worship involve us in compromise, encouraging a smoothed-out or watered-down expression of the sacred? Any such fear may partly be the result of lack of familiarity with other customs or partly an inherited prejudice about what prayer intends in other traditions. Theologically, interfaith worship could represent a muddle by well-meaning people or a refusal to face fully the fact of definite differences arising from multiple traditions being put together. The interfaith elephant in the room is the question residing at the centre of the worship occasion: 'Whose God? Which God?' It is a question that is generally most acute when the design of interfaith worship is built around a theme (e.g. international peace and justice, civic cohesion) rather than one which invites contributions to a format based mainly within one tradition.

The theological tension over 'Whose God? Which God?' might have to be lived with rather than expecting it to be resolved neatly. Still, there are a number of points which can be made which may help to alleviate the worst impact of the tension or at least indicate a wider interfaith context for consideration. Let me pick up on three such points, and in doing so I will draw upon discussions within interfaith relations debates that need to be borne in mind when it comes to interfaith prayer and worship.

My first point recalls some words from the early-twentieth-century pioneer of the classic psychological study of religious experience, William James. He writes, in the prose style of the period, in his celebrated book, *The Varieties of Religious Experience* (1901, p.327):

> Ought all men to have the same religion? Ought they to approve the same fruits and follow the same leadings? Are they so like in their inner needs, that, for hard and soft, for proud and humble, for strenuous and lazy, for healthy-minded and despairing, exactly the same religious incentives are required? Or are different functions in the organism of humanity allotted to different types of man, so that some may really be the better for a religion of consolation and reassurance, whilst others are better for one of terror and reproof?

James's study of religious experience across traditions led him to see that no one religion could answer all of the psychological needs of human beings, which are complex and varied. If that is the case, then might it be that differences between religions should be celebrated and not be fearful of being placed in conjunction with one another? It is as though human beings are bound to want to express themselves in a variety of styles and forms. In this sense the religions serve purposes which resonate with different psychological types: the religions have need of each other if they are to serve humanity as a whole! Interfaith worship could well be necessary because human beings as such are made differently and not simply because there is a need to come together as communities, say, in the face of adversity, important as that is.

My second observation stems from the experience of interfaith encounter in a monastic setting. In 1984 one of the founders of the Centering Prayer movement in the United States, Fr Thomas Keating, a Cistercian monk, invited spiritual teachers from Christian, Muslim, Jewish, Buddhist, Hindu and Native American backgrounds to gather at St Benedict's Monastery, Snowmass, Colorado, for silent meditation and the sharing of spiritual journeys. The encounter revealed a remarkable result. They compared their experiences based on religious practices and discovered much overlap in terms of the shape of their religious assumptions, purposes and journeys. This discovery was not expected and so became more significant. Of the eight points of overlap between them, it is worth mentioning the following three as being relevant to the issues at the heart of interfaith prayer:

1. Faith as an open, personal, and accepting response to Ultimate Reality operates at the heart of every system of religious belief.

2. Every human person has the potential within them for transformation, or salvation, or blessedness, however different traditions describe this.

3. The realization of oneness with Ultimate Reality is not generated by self-effort but is the result of experience and it leads to disciplined practice. (Keating 1993)

These points of agreement do not demonstrate that the religious experiences of the varying traditions were at their core levels substantially the same. But it does indicate a high functional similarity in relation to key religious orientations and expectations. As time went on, Keating admitted that it was the points of disagreement which came to dominate discussion but also that, paradoxically, along with disagreement came an increase in solidarity between traditions, as differences were received by the whole group as a gift.

If, indeed, faith does precede belief systems then the door is opened for interfaith solidarity in worship to be experienced as a time of 'gift', where the potential for human wholeness can be welcomed precisely because of, and not in spite of, different orientations alive in different traditions.

My third reflection for helping us to negotiate religious difference in an interfaith setting picks up on one meaning of interfaith dialogue. Normally we think of interfaith dialogue as being a cerebral exercise only, an exchange designed to increase understanding between traditions, to find points of contact and alienation and to ask questions about why such radical differences of beliefs exist in the world and what that means for our several traditions. However, dialogue is a broad category that includes 'spiritual dialogue', which has been explored most fruitfully in monastic settings. This raises the possibility that interfaith worship can be thought of as one form of 'spiritual dialogue', one form among others of interfaith encounter and exchange.

In dialogue we learn 'about' one another, we learn 'with' one another and we learn 'through' one another. There is a movement which draws us closer to one another at levels which go beyond the comparison of beliefs at the level of the mind only. Whether we are working actively for social justice, seeking peace and reconciliation, responding to the challenges of ecological destruction, developing the mind through science and education or deepening our human capacities through the arts, religious people instinctively place all of these endeavours in the context of prayer so as to connect them with the sacred. They are also reasons for mutual learning between traditions and we do this through dialogue. If that is the case, then dialogue leads us to interfaith prayer as the rightful context in which the dialogue can fully bear fruit. In the conclusion to their insightful book, *Prayer in World Religions* (1990, p.150), Denise and John Carmody make a similar point, as follows:

> The fully adequate foundation of interreligious dialogue probably has to be not just discussion of prayer (taken as the most distinctively religious act) but also common practice of prayer. Only when the partners to dialogue experience something of the prayer life of their fellow partners will the dialogue be fully grounded.

This represents a stunning invitation to interfaith prayer and worship as deserving of a place at the heart of the developing dialogue movement between traditions. The chapters in this book do not on the whole approach shared worship with this in mind, but their hospitable tone suggests that they might well be open to the possibility.

I have suggested that there are broader concerns being addressed through discussions of interfaith relations that could have a positive bearing on interfaith prayer and worship. These do not resolve the essential tension between prayer's rootedness in particular traditions, with their accompanying theological habits of mind on the one hand, and on the other, the pull towards cooperation between faith communities, a pull which shows every sign of becoming more and more significant as time passes. In most respects it is outside cultural forces – forces which welcome faith contributions for the building up of social cohesion or international peace and justice – that drag the faiths into common cause. This entails that if the faiths are to make an impact in wider society, they would be strengthened in these endeavours by also seeking ways of cooperation at their deepest levels, which is the level of prayer and worship.

A great part of what has kept faiths from cooperating with one another has been not only theological but also political. It is not just that traditions other than one's own are different, but they have been labelled as dangerously different. It is a short step from there to imagining that others require defeat – and in battle, if preaching isn't forceful enough. Ultimately, undoing the deep-seated political mistrust between traditions is a theological matter. If our prayer is focused theologically on a certain perception of the sacred then can that theological focus be opened up in ways that draw traditions away from past antagonisms into more generous, fruitful and mutually beneficial relationships? If so, what kind of theology could help in this crucial matter?

The second chapter in this book supports what has been called a pluralist theology of religions, in other words, a position that counts the major world religions as communities of authentic transcendent vision and human transformation. The religions reflect an experience of the sacred that has endured over time, offer the world a vision of being human that leads to a fulfilled life, and therefore reflect something of that ineffable mystery which connects us all with one another. It is not necessary to be a pluralist in order to engage in interfaith prayer, and not all of the chapters in this book explicitly support a pluralist position. Still, provided pluralists are clear that this does not mean that all religions are 'the same underneath' their outward expressions, it is hard not to draw the conclusion that such an outlook has a greater chance of being hospitable to interfaith prayer and worship than other stances in the theology of religions.

This book could not have been conceived fifty years ago. At that time the dialogue movement had not gained the momentum it now has, the study of religious traditions had not become established in schools and universities, the experience of immigration and therefore of meeting people of different faiths was still minimal compared to the present day, and theological exploration was fairly confined to separate enclaves. All of this has now changed and, even if we wanted to, there is no going back. The advantage of this book over others dealing with interfaith prayer and worship is that it consists of the views of representatives of many world religions. Some of these voices are rarely heard. Moreover, the contributions are full of surprising and unexpected insights. One remarkable feature, for example, is that both theists and nontheists are able to find ways in which they can come together and engage with each other in the heart of what each stands for.

Such spiritual openness to the strange and unfamiliar, championed by interfaith prayer and worship, represents a new moment in a developing interfaith story. If we can learn openness through trusting of difference the faiths will contribute much to a society and world that needs such openness and trust for its future sustainability. Support therefore for interfaith prayer and worship is part of a wider global cultural shift and if it is embraced stands to contribute significantly to the emerging and unstoppable reality of interfaith awareness and hope.

## REFERENCES

Carmody, D. and Carmody, J. (1990) *Prayer in World Religions*. Maryknoll, NY: Orbis.

James, W. (1974) 'The value of saintliness.' Lectures XIV and XV in *The Varieties of Religious Experience*. London: Fontana.

Keating, T. (1993) 'Theological issues in meditative technologies.' *The Way Supplement 78*, Autumn, 54–63.

# Biographical Notes on Contributors

## CHAPTER 1: INTRODUCTION

**Dan Cohn-Sherbok** studied philosophy at Williams College in the USA, was ordained a Reform rabbi at the Hebrew Union College–Jewish Institute of Religion and received a PhD in theology at Cambridge University. He taught theology at the University of Kent, UK and was Professor of Judaism at the University of Wales where he is currently emeritus professor. He is the author and editor of numerous books dealing with Judaism and interfaith dialogue and edited *Sensible Religion* with Christopher Lewis (Routledge, 2014).

## CHAPTER 2: THE ARGUMENT FOR INTERFAITH PRAYER AND WORSHIP

**Christopher Lewis** is a Christian priest who has taught doctrine and ethics in an Anglican seminary in the UK, has worked in parishes and three cathedrals and has been the head of an Oxford University college, Christ Church. His doctorate is from Cambridge University. He has collaborated with Dan Cohn-Sherbok on a number of projects including an interfaith book on life after death: *Beyond Death* (Macmillan, 1995).

## CHAPTER 3: HINDUISM

**Anantanand Rambachan** is Professor of Religion at St Olaf College, Minnesota. Dr Rambachan is also visiting professor at the Academy for the Study of World Religions at the University of Hamburg in

Germany. His major books include: *Accomplishing the Accomplished: The Vedas as a Source of Valid Knowledge in Shankara* (University of Hawaii Press, 1991), *The Limits of Scripture: Vivekananda's Reinterpretation of the Authority of the Vedas* (University of Hawaii Press, 1994), *The Advaita Worldview: God, World and Humanity* (State University of New York Press, 2006) and *A Hindu Theology of Liberation: Not-Two is Not One* (State University of New York Press, 2015).

**Shaunaka Rishi Das** is Director of the Oxford Centre for Hindu Studies. He is a Hindu cleric, and Hindu chaplain to Oxford University. Shaunaka served as Chair of the Northern Ireland Interfaith Forum, and as a trustee of the Interfaith Network UK. He edited the ISKCON Communications Journal and founded and led the ISKCON Interfaith Commission. He was a member of the Commission on Religion and Belief in British Public Life, convened by the Woolf Institute, Cambridge. The Indian government appointed him to the International Advisory Council of the Auroville Foundation.

## CHAPTER 4: AFRICAN TRADITIONAL RELIGION

**Nokuzola Mndende** holds a PhD in Religious Studies from the University of Cape Town. She is a research associate at the University of Free State (UFS) and is also a director of Icamagu Heritage Institute for African Traditional Religion. She has been a lecturer of religion at the University of Cape Town and University of South Africa (UNISA). She has published several books and papers on African Traditional Religion. She has served in two government commissions and policy-making bodies on religious affairs.

**Hebron L. Ndlovu** is presently associate professor in theology and religious studies, and Dean of the Faculty of Humanities at the University of Swaziland. He received his training in theological and religious studies at the University of Botswana and Swaziland, McCormick Theological Seminary, and McMaster University. At UNISWA he teaches African Religion, Introducing the Study of Religion and Religions of the World. His research interests are African sacred monarchies, traditional healing and modernity, interaction of African Religion and Christianity and multireligious education. His most recent publications are in the areas of indigenous African Religion, African Christianity and religious education.

## CHAPTER 5: JUDAISM

**Aaron Rosen** is Professor of Religious Thought at Rocky Mountain College and Visiting Professor at King's College London (KCL). He taught previously at KCL, Yale, Oxford and Columbia, and received his PhD from Cambridge. He has curated various exhibitions and written widely for scholarly and popular publications. He is the author of *Art and Religion in the 21st Century* (Thames and Hudson, 2015), *Imagining Jewish Art* (Routledge, 2009) and *Brushes with Faith* (Cascade, 2019), as well as various edited books, including *Encounters: The Art of Interfaith Dialogue* (Brepols N.V., 2018). He regularly curates exhibitions and is the co-founder of the international public arts project Stations of the Cross.

**Alan Brill** is the Cooperman/Ross Endowed Chair for Jewish–Christian Studies at Seton Hall University, USA and is the author of *Thinking God: The Mysticism of Rabbi Zadok of Lublin* (KTAV Publishing House, 2002), *Judaism and Other Religions: Models of Understanding* (Palgrave Macmillan, 2010) and *Judaism and World Religions* (Palgrave Macmillan, 2012). Brill received his rabbinical ordination from Yeshiva University and his PhD from Fordham University. He was a Fulbright Senior Scholar awardee to teach at Banares Hindu University in Varanasi, India. Brill has completed a forthcoming book entitled *Rabbi on the Ganges: A Jewish Hindu Encounter*.

## CHAPTER 6: JAINISM

**Vinod Kapashi** has written 16 books on Jain and non-Jain topics. His PhD thesis on 'Nine Sacred Recitations of Jainism' was widely acclaimed by the critics. He takes a keen interest in interfaith activities in the UK and is an executive committee member of the World Congress of Faiths. He also served as president of the Harrow Interfaith Council in the past. He is president of Mahavir Foundation, a religious charity, which has provided a temple for the local community. He has travelled widely and has lectured on different topics related to the Jain faith.

**Natubhai Shah**, a retired medical doctor and Jain scholar, is Chair/CEO of the Jain Network. Dr Shah's main works include the creation of the beautiful Jain Temple in Leicester, the establishment of Jain studies in universities, authoring *Jainism: The World of Conquerors* (two volumes; Academy Press, 1998), and interfaith and community work. He represents Jains at the highest level in the UK and is involved in developing an exciting Jain Centre in London. Notable honours include 'Man of the Year' by American Biographic Institute; 'Jain Ratna' by the Prime Minister of India in 2001; MBE in 2012; Barnet Civic award in 2014.

## CHAPTER 7: BUDDHISM

**Bogoda Seelawimala** is head of the London Buddhist Vihara and the Chief Sangha Nayaka of Great Britain. Venerable Seelawimala was born in Sri Lanka and ordained in the Theravada Buddhist Tradition Higher Ordination in 1973. His BA and MA are from Peradeniya University, Sri Lanka. He has taught at Dharmaraja College and been an executive member of the Interfaith Network, Buddhist chaplain for the London Olympic Village (2012), a representative at the Commonwealth Day Observance, a hospital chaplain, on the Board of Reference Heathrow Multi-Faith Chaplaincy and President of Sri Lankan Sangha Sabha, UK.

**Vishvapani Blomfield**, who lives in Cardiff, Wales, was born Simon Blomfield in a Reform Jewish family in London – his father was a Kindertransport refugee – and received ordination into the Triratna Buddhist Order and the name Vishvapani in 1992. His writing includes the book *Gautama Buddha: The Life and Teachings of the Awakened One* (Quercus, 2011) nd he is the Buddhist contributor to Radio 4's *Thought for the Day*. As well as teaching in Buddhist settings, he teaches mindfulness in secular settings including schools, workplaces and prisons.

## CHAPTER 8: ZOROASTRIANISM

**Jehangir Sarosh** OBE is married with three children, five grandchildren and a beautiful wife. For the past forty years he has served on various national and international organisations. He is co-president of The World Council of Religions for Peace and co-founder of the European Council of Religious Leaders (ECRL), has served ECRL as its co-moderator and secretary general and currently is the executive director of Religions for Peace. His passion is to help religions cooperate for the renovation of the world (the purpose of life according to Zoroastrianism).

**Behram Deboo** (co-author with Maneck Bhujwala) comes from Gujarat, India, and has a BSc and BS. He studied Avesta and Pahlavi for three years and received medals in Avesta and mathematics. He was active for eight years on the Interfaith Council of Washington. Besides being the founder of the Zoroastrian Society of Washington State, he served as president and secretary. He has spoken at North American Zoroastrian congresses and also at World Zoroastrian congresses: in Bombay, 1985 and in Tehran, 1996. He was ordained as an assistant priest. He is a senior editor of *The Zoroastrian Journal* published by the California Zoroastrian Center, Westminster, CA.

**Maneck Bhujwala** (co-author with Behram Deboo) was born in India, has a MSEE, MBA, and MA Interfaith Action, co-founded Zoroastrian Associations in Southern and Northern California; represented the Zoroastrian community at interfaith events; and served on Stanford University Associated Religions board. He is past president, Greater Huntington Beach Interfaith Council; board member, South Coast Interfaith Council; board member, North American Interfaith Network; Director, World Zoroastrian Organization; Co-Chair, Interfaith Activities and Research/Preservation Committees of the Federation of Zoroastrian Associations of North America; writes articles in news media; gives talks at interfaith and Zoroastrian conferences; and serves as a Zoroastrian priest.

## CHAPTER 9: SHINTOISM

**Yoshinobu Miyake** was born in 1958 in Osaka, Japan. Rev Miyake studied at Doshisha University in Kyoto and at Harvard University, and publishes frequently. He is the Superior General of Konko Church of Izuo. For the past 35 years he has been active worldwide in the interfaith field. In 1997 he established the RELNET Corporation, whose website publishes widely on religion-related matters in Japanese. He served as general secretary of the G8 Religious Leaders Summit, 2008. Most recently, he was appointed as Chair of the International Shinto Studies Association (ISSA).

**Yasuhiro Tanaka** is the 204th chief priest of the Kamo-wake-ikazuchi-jinja Shrine, which is the oldest shrine in Kyoto. The Very Rev Yasuhiro Tanaka was formerly deputy chief priest of Meiji-Jingu, which is the biggest shrine in Tokyo.

## CHAPTER 10: CHRISTIANITY

**Hugh Ellis** has been a priest in the Church of England since 1991; he has served as the rector of Bradfield & Stanford Dingley, Berkshire; team rector of the Langport Area Team Ministry, Somerset and currently as team rector of the High Wycombe Team Ministry. He has chaired the Council of Christian & Jews in Berkshire and the South Somerset Multifaith Forum. Currently, he leads a local Jewish, Christian, Muslim group and is vice-chair of the High Wycombe's Council of Christian–Muslim Relations. In addition, he chairs the Wycombe Refugee Partnership.

**Sheryl A. Kujawa-Holbrook** holds posts of vice president, academic affairs; faculty dean; professor of practical theology: Claremont School of Theology, USA; professor of Anglican Studies: Bloy House Episcopal Theological School, Claremont. An Episcopal priest, she is author of 17 books/training manuals and numerous journal articles. She is a board member of the *Journal of Interreligious Studies* and the Kaleidoscope Institute. Recent books include *Pilgrimage – The Sacred Art: Journey to the Center of the Heart* (Skylight Paths, 2013) and *God Beyond Borders: Congregations Building Interreligious Community* (Pickwick Wipf & Stock, 2014). From 2010 to 2011 she was a fellow in the Christian Leadership Initiative, sponsored by the American Jewish Committee and the Shalom Hartman Institute in Jerusalem.

**Marcus Braybrooke**, after studying in India, joined the World Congress of Faiths in 1964 and is now joint president. He has been a vicar, director of the Council of Christians and Jews and co-founder of the the Faith&Belief Forum. He has arranged many interfaith services, some at Parliaments of World Religions, and with his wife Mary attended the Assisi Day of Prayer for Peace. He has edited reports on interfaith worship. His books include *1,000 World Prayers* (O Books, 2009), *Meditations for a Peaceful Heart and Peaceful World* (Godsfield, 2004) and *Beacons of Light* (O Books, 2003).

## CHAPTER 11: ISLAM

**Ibrahim Mogra** is a community imam and a visiting imam, University of Leicester and De Montfort University. Shaykh Ibrahim trains imams, clergy and RE teachers. He is trained in classical theology and traditional sciences of Islam, holds religious credentials from Dar al-'Ulum, Holcombe, UK and advanced theological qualifications from Al-Azhar University, Cairo and an MA from the School of Oriental and African Studies, London. He is co-chair of the Christian–Muslim Forum and member of Religions for Peace UK and the European Council of Religious Leaders. He is founder and principal, Khazinat al-'Ilm, Madaris of Arabic and Muslim Life Studies, Leicester.

**Monawar Hussain** is the Muslim tutor at Eton College, Windsor, Muslim chaplain to the Oxford University Hospitals NHS Foundation Trust and the founder of The Oxford Foundation. Imam Monawar read Theology at the University of Oxford, has an MA in Abrahamic Religions from the University of London and trained as an imam under the tutelage of the late Sheikh Dr Zaki Badawi KBE at the Muslim College, Ealing, UK. His dissertation, entitled *Spiritual Journeying: An Exploration in the Light of Spenser's The Faerie Queene and Attār's Conference of the Birds*, was published in 2016.

**Usama Hasan** is head of Islamic studies at Quilliam, the world's first counter-extremism organisation. Before joining Quilliam, Imam Sheikh Dr Usama Hasan was a senior lecturer in engineering at Middlesex University (2003–2012), visiting associate professor at the National University of Science and Technology (NUST) in Pakistan (2002–2003) and a consultant in artificial intelligence in UK industry (1997–2003). He holds a PhD, MSc and MA in physics and artificial intelligence from the universities of Cambridge and London and is a fellow of the Royal Astronomical Society and of the Muslim Institute.

## CHAPTER 12: SIKHISM

**Pashaura Singh** is professor and Dr Jasbir Singh Saini Endowed Chair in Sikh and Punjabi studies at the University of California, Riverside. He is the author of three Oxford monographs (Oxford University Press): *The Guru Granth Sahib: Canon, Meaning, and Authority* (2000), *The Bhagats of the Guru Granth Sahib: Sikh Self-Definition and the Bhagat Bani* (2003) and *Life and Work of Guru Arjan: History, Memory, and Biography in the Sikh Tradition* (2006). He has also edited seven volumes, including *Sikhism in Global Context* (2011) and *The Oxford Handbook of Sikh Studies* (2014), both published by Oxford University Press.

**Nikky-Guninder Kaur Singh** (co-author with Lucy Soucek) is the head of the Department of Religious Studies at Colby College, and holds the Crawford Family Professor Chair. Dr Singh has published extensively in Sikh studies. Her books include *Of Sacred and Secular Desire* (I.B. Taurus, 2012), *Sikhism* (I.B. Taurus, 2011), *Cosmic Symphony* (Sahitya Akademi, 2008), *Birth of the Khalsa* (SUNY, 2005), *The Name of My Beloved* (Penguin, 2001) and *The Feminine Principle* (CUP, 1993). She has served on the editorial board of several journals including *History of Religions*, *Journal of the American Academy of Religion* and *Sikh Formations*.

**Lucy Soucek** (co-author with Nikky-Guninder Kaur Singh) is a 2018 graduate from Colby College who majored in religious studies and theatre and dance. She published in *Change Magazine* on the importance of interfaith understanding at educational institutions such as Colby. Lucy conducted research projects on the Sikh diaspora in Vancouver, British Columbia, and the vibrant interfaith community of Fresno, California. She interned with the Pluralism Project at Harvard University and interned with the podcast Ministry of Ideas, an initiative of the Religious Literacy Project at Harvard Divinity School.

## CHAPTER 13: UNITARIANISM

**Feargus O'Connor** has since 2006 been the honorary secretary of the World Congress of Faiths (the fourth Unitarian minister in this office since its foundation in 1936) and is founding chair of the Animal Interfaith Alliance, which witnesses for interfaith action for animals. He is the founder of the Gandhi Schweitzer Universal Kinship Appeal of the Dr Hadwen Trust for Humane Research and of the Clara Barton Disasters Emergency Appeal of the British Red Cross, a Unitarian initiative. A member of the Gandhi Foundation and Amnesty International, he is minister of St Albans Unitarians and of Golders Green Unitarians, London.

**Jay Atkinson** grew up in the American Midwest in a mixed Quaker–Methodist family, left the church as a young adult, and discovered Unitarian Universalism at age 29, while pursuing a PhD in nuclear physics. This led him to a renewed journey in personal theology and a new career path. After earning a BA in religious studies, an AM in divinity and a doctorate in ministry, he served 32 years in Unitarian Universalist parish ministry and is now a research scholar at Starr King School for the Ministry in Berkeley, California.

## CHAPTER 14: BAHÁ'Í

**Dr Wendi Momen** MBE, JP, founder trustee of the Multi-Faith Centre at the University of Derby, is now honorary vice president; trustee of Bedford Council of Faiths; governor, London School of Economics; retired deputy chaplain (multifaith) at Hinchingbrooke Hospital, Huntingdon; founder and currently president of ebbf (Ethical Business Building the Future); and member of the National Spiritual Assembly of the Bahá'ís of the UK.

**George Merchant Ballentyne** became a Bahá'í in 1979, in his native Glasgow, aged 19. He has worked in the publishing industry and adult education, where he specialised in teaching adults with mental health issues. He was employed by Leicester Council of Faiths as equality and diversity officer, 2006–2013. He currently works at Leicester City Council as voluntary and community sector engagement manager. His first degree is from the Open University, in English literature and religious studies. His MA, in modern literature (theory and practice), is from the University of Leicester.

## CHAPTER 15: CONCLUDING REFLECTION

**Alan Race** has written widely in the fields of the Christian theology of religions and interfaith dialogue. The Rev Dr Alan Race is executive chair of the World Congress of Faiths and editor of its journal *Interreligious Insight*. His book *Christians and Religious Pluralism* (SCM Press, 1983, revised and enlarged 1993) is a classic in interfaith literature. He was ordained in the Church of England in 1976 and has combined ministry with theological teaching, lecturing and publishing. He was presented with the Interfaith Gold Medallion by Sir Sigmund Sternberg in 2007.

# Index